The Battle of Britain
on Screen

Titles available and forthcoming in the *Societies at War* series

War Damage in Western Europe
Nicola Lambourne

War Aims in the Second World War
Victor Rothwell

The Battle of Britain on Screen:
'The Few' in British Film and Television Drama
S. P. MacKenzie

British Children's Fiction in the Second World War
Owen Dudley Edwards

The Second World War and Forced Migration Movements in Europe
Rainer Schulze

Britain, Ireland and the Second World War
Ian S. Wood

Sweden, the Swastika and Stalin:
The Swedish Experience in the Second World War
John Gilmour

Prisoners of War in the Far East, 1942–45
Kent Fedorowich

Propaganda and War, 1939–45
Robert Cole

The Battle of Britain on Screen

'The Few' in British Film and Television Drama

S. P. MacKenzie

Edinburgh University Press

For Lori

S. P. MacKenzie, 2007

Edinburgh University Press Ltd
22 George Square, Edinburgh

Typeset in Melior by
Iolaire Typesetting, Newtonmore, and
printed and bound in Great Britain by
Antony Rowe Ltd, Chippenham, Wilts

A CIP record for this book is available from the British Library

ISBN 978 0 7486 2389 1 (hardback)
ISBN 978 0 7486 2390 7 (paperback)

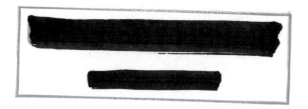

Contents

Figures

Acknowledgements

I would like to thank the staff of the following libraries and archives, without whose assistance the research for this book could not have been carried out: the BBC Written Archive; the British Film Institute National Library and special collections department; the British Library; the British Newspaper Library; the Churchill Archive Centre; the Imperial War Museum department of documents and department of sound; the Liddell Hart Centre, Archives, King's College London; the Mass-Observation Archive; the National Archives, Kew; the National Film and Television Archive; the National Sound Archive; the Royal Air Force Museum department of Research and Information Services; and the inter-library loans department of Thomas Cooper Library, University of South Carolina. Thanks are also due to Canal + Image UK, ITV, MGM and London Features International for permission to reproduce images to which they hold the copyright.

In addition I wish to acknowledge the patient assistance of Roda Morrison, Esmé Watson, and other members of the editorial and production team at Edinburgh University Press, as well as the useful comments made by readers on the original proposal and by Paul Addison and Jeremy Crang on the completed typescript. Points on which other readers may take issue are, of course, entirely my responsibility.

Introduction

More than half a century after the firing stopped, the Second World War continues to resonate in the public imagination. For many decades now, whole shelves have been devoted to it in bookshops great and small, as specialist and general publishers have fed an apparently insatiable appetite for works devoted to the battles, figures, and events of the war. In the 1950s dramatic accounts of various operations that had occurred between 1939 and 1945 were a money-spinning staple of the British cinema industry. And ever since watching the small screen supplanted visiting the big screen as a common social habit, these films have continued to be major draws on television and, from the 1980s, in video outlets as well. The arrival of satellite broadcasting and the consequent expansion in the number of available channels in Britain over the last decade have seen a concomitant growth in the number of documentary and other television programmes devoted to the events and personalities of the war years. 'English culture', as Richard Cockett once observed, 'is saturated by images of the Second World War'.[1]

Within this barrage of words and images, some subjects have tended to resonate more persistently than others, not least anything dealing with events that have long been popularly regarded as among Britain's finest hours: Dunkirk and the Blitz, for example, or, of course, the Battle of Britain. The last, in fact, which was fought out in the skies between the middle of June and the latter part of September 1940 and resulted in the defeat of the *Luftwaffe* and any prospective enemy invasion by RAF Fighter Command, has ranked among the most often represented events of the war both on the page and on the screen. As a perusal of the British Library catalogue indicates, there have been over 230 books – new or republished versions of existing works – with 'Battle of Britain' in the title or subtitle, a number which by no means exhausts what has been written on the subject. And, as the following chapters will show, even before it actually occurred as well as long afterwards, the battle was of recurring interest to film-makers interested in dramatising the exploits of The Few.[2]

No length of film, of course, whether raw footage, out-takes, finished documentaries, or – least of all – dramas in which fictional characters are situated in the known past, can be regarded as historical truth. Post-modernist claims concerning the essential equality of all forms of representation aside, it must be recognised that film-makers' biases – whether in relation to the script, narration, or what is and is not committed to film or videotape – along with external constraints ranging from censorship and cinematic conventions to time limits, budgets, and the availability of period props – mean that what one sees is merely a version of what happened, not some panoptical photographic reproduction. 'It is a truism', as Tony Aldgate has written, '. . . that film is not some unadulterated reflection of historical truth captured faithfully by the camera.'[3]

Yet, for several reasons, it would be a mistake just to write off films as having no connection with history. First, the simple, if sometimes unpalatable, fact is that average people spend far more time in front of a screen than they do reading a book (assuming that they read books at all, which many do not); which means that, for the majority of the population, it is not the printed page but the screen that gives them whatever sense they may have of the past. Furthermore, what is said to be entertainment tends to trump what is presented as educationally valuable (i.e. documentaries) in terms of the choices made about what to watch. As Arthur Marwick has admitted: 'more and more of the population learn smatterings of history from film and television' and thereby 'the distinction between fact and fiction' is not always appreciated. History on screen, in short, needs to be taken into account because, however flawed the results in terms of accuracy and nuance, to those not reading into the subject it is the dominant means of communicating what happened in the past.[4]

In at least a few instances, furthermore, the reactions of audiences to what they see can influence subsequent behaviour. After it was released the racist messages contained in D. W. Griffith's 1915 film *Birth of a Nation*, for example, appear to have helped to fuel the resurgence of the Ku Klux Klan in the American South. The hugely sympathetic public reaction to the airing of the NBC melodrama mini-series *Holocaust* in West Germany in 1978, to take another case, is thought to have had a direct impact on the government's decision to suspend the statute of limitations in the case of Nazi crimes.[5]

What is more, some optimists have claimed, while there may well be factual and other errors present in any screen account of a past event or person, there are also likely to be some more basic historical truths being presented. In short, viewers may be misled on specific details but, in many cases, will still gain some elementary knowledge of a period with which they were probably unfamiliar before sitting down in front of the screen. 'Even problematic films frequently offer insights', Robert Brent Toplin has argued.[6]

A fourth reason screen representations should be taken seriously by historians, and the one most pertinent to this study, is that they can tell us things about the time in which they were made and shown. The information being conveyed, the questions being posed, and the way in which events and persons are treated can, and usually do, change over time; each 'take' on a particular subject and how it is received being a reflection of the conventions, expectations, fears, and hopes of society during the period in which it appears. As K. R. M. Short succinctly put it a quarter of a century ago, 'historians can use film as evidence in their study of political, economic or social history'.[7]

This monograph is an attempt to understand how the representation of the Battle of Britain has evolved over time on screen in relation to changing attitudes and circumstances. Though documentaries and pieces in which the battle plays an incidental role will be mentioned – ranging from a Ministry of Information-sponsored short, *Fighter Pilot*, made at the end of the battle, to relevant episodes of the contemporary historical crime drama series *Foyle's War* – the main focus here will be on feature-length films and multi-part television dramas in which the Battle of Britain clearly permeates the plot. Each of the major fictional representations will be examined in turn, starting with *The Lion Has Wings* and ending with *A Perfect Hero*, the intent being to explain both the making of each piece and how audiences reacted can be interpreted in the context not only of external constraints but also in terms of evolving attitudes towards the war in general and the Battle of Britain in particular. How the events of that summer in 1940 have been recreated as drama, both on the big screen and the small screen, reflects and illustrates the way in which people conceived of the Battle of Britain at a particular time.

Such screen representations can, in short, help us to understand how the battle has evolved in the popular consciousness within Britain from the period before it took place to beyond the fiftieth anniversary of the actual event.[8]

There are, of course, potential pitfalls for the historian when grappling with period drama on the big or small screen. One is to judge a particular piece mainly in terms of the period accuracy – or, more commonly, lack thereof – of everything from dialogue, costumes and props to plot developments and the mannerisms of the actors. This ignores the fact that film-makers always lack time, money, and sometimes other resources, and are at root seeking to create something that – while they hope it is as 'real' as they can make it – can last only a matter of hours on screen and must appeal to a contemporary audience. Another related danger involves the historian judging a piece in his or her own aesthetic terms: that is to say, allowing how one reacts at an emotional level to, say, a particular cast or a particular script to influence what one writes about the piece. What may be acceptable coming from a film critic is not something in which the historian should indulge. What matters is not how the historian reacts to a particular piece but how people reacted at the time it appeared and afterwards. I like some of the pieces on the Battle of Britain more than others but that is a matter of personal taste, and taste, of course, can vary radically from one viewer to another. While I tend to feel that *Battle of Britain* (see Chapter 5) is rather good, for example, a recent biographer of Michael Caine has dismissed it as simply a 'rabble-rousing . . . sub-pornographic' display of military hardware.[9] What interests me as an historian, as opposed to an individual film enthusiast, is what film-makers, critics, and audiences made of these representations, even – indeed, perhaps especially – if the results run counter to my own preferences. How well I have succeeded in this will, of course, be for the reader to judge.[10]

Notes

1. R. Cockett in *Times Higher Education Supplement*, 25 April 1997, p. 18; see e.g. Michael Paris, *Warrior Nation: Images of War in British Popular Culture* (London: Reaktion, 2000), ch. 7; Mark Connelly, *We Can Take It! Britain and the Memory of the Second World War* (Harlow: Longman, 2004); see also Richard Weight, *Patriots: National Identity in Britain, 1940–2000* (London: Macmillan, 2002), pp. 340–7. On the British war film genre see e.g. Robert Murphy, *British Cinema and the Second World War* (London: Continuum, 2000).

2. There are, for example, titles such as Richard Overy's *The Battle* (London: Penguin, 2000) that do not include the phrase but are nevertheless books devoted to the subject. There have been more than half-a-dozen video documentaries on the battle, and British-made television documentary series on World War II, from *War in the Air* in the mid 1950s to *The World at War* in the early 1970s and beyond, have tended to highlight the battle. At least a quarter of the exhibit space at the Royal Air Force Museum is devoted to the battle in the form of a Battle of Britain Hall. On the origins of this phenomenon see also Weight, *Patriots*, pp. 67–8.

3. Tony Aldgate, 'The Battle of Britain on Film', in Paul Addison and Jeremy A. Crang (eds), *The Burning Blue: A New History of the Battle of Britain* (London: Pimlico, 2000), pp. 207–8; see also Jeremy Black, *Rethinking Military History* (London: Routledge, 2004), p. 34. For a slightly post-modernist view see e.g. Robert A. Rosenstone, *Visions of the Past: The Challenge of Film to Our Idea of History* (Cambridge, MA: Harvard University Press, 1995), p. 127 et al.; Tony Barta (ed.), *Screening the Past: Film and the Representation of History* (Westport, CT: Praeger, 1998), pp. ix–x. On the story conventions of big-screen drama see Robert Brent Toplin, *Reel History: In Defense of Hollywood* (Lawrence, KS: University Press of Kansas, 2002), ch. 1.

4. Arthur Marwick, *The New Nature of History: Knowledge, Evidence, Language* (Chicago: Lyceum, 2001), pp. 238–9; see Black, *Rethinking*, p. 35; Toplin, *Reel History*, ch. 6.

5. Toplin, *Reel History*, pp. 184–94.

6. Ibid., p. 62; ibid., p. 114. Toplin does, however, concede that there are cases where the larger historical truths are also lost. Ibid., p. 69.

7. K. R. M. Short (ed.), *Feature Films as History* (Knoxville, TN: University of Tennessee Press, 1981), p. 16; see also Toplin, *Reel History*, p. 42.

8. It should be noted that this study does not seek to investigate how these representations were received in other countries such as the United States or West Germany. Though potentially fruitful in terms of revealing how other nations have understood the Battle of Britain, such efforts would have involved significant detours from the main task of explaining how the British themselves have viewed the event, and were therefore reluctantly left aside.

9. Christopher Bray, *Michael Caine: A Class Act* (London: Faber and Faber, 2005), p. 116.

10. See e.g. in reference to the sometimes difficult relationship between documentary film-makers and historical advisers, Michael Nelson, 'It May be History, But is it True?', *Historical Journal of Film, Radio and Television* 25 (2005), pp. 141–6. On the essential difference between screen historical drama and history on the page see e.g. Mark C. Carnes (ed.), *Past Imperfect: History According to the Movies* (New York: Henry Holt, 1995), pp. 9–10; see also *The Economist*, 26 January 2002, p. 74; and also, in reference to documentary, the comments by Neal Acherson in *Making the Series: 30th Anniversary Retrospective* (Freemantle Media, 2004) attached to the thirtieth-anniversary DVD edition of *The World at War*.

FIGURE 1 Situation under control: Ralph Richardson in *The Lion Has Wings* (London Films, 1939).

BFI Stills, courtesy of London Features International plc.

1

The Battle Foretold:
The Lion Has Wings (1939)

There was one excellent sequence – the sequence of the preparation against, and the waiting for the arrival of, the German bombers over England.

Foreign Office assessment, November 1939[1]

As well as being a central feature of the popular mythology that grew up around the war, the Battle of Britain must rank among the most widely anticipated events of the twentieth century. For at least a decade prior to the war, people from all walks of life had been thinking, talking, and writing about a future conflict in which aerial armadas would play a decisive role. Rather paradoxically, in light of the pride subsequently taken in the actual battle, this anticipation was heavily tinged with dread.

In the interval between the world wars there had developed a widespread belief that, if another general conflict were to erupt in Europe, it would feature mass bombing raids on towns and cities of unendurable intensity and general frightfulness. Gas as well as high explosive and incendiary devices would be used on a massive scale from the first air raid onwards, laying waste to vast areas of the capital in particular and killing huge numbers of people. Ground and air defences would be brushed aside and essential public services, such as hospitals and fire brigades, rapidly swamped by the sheer scale of the destruction.

This was a common vision both inside and outside government circles. As early as 1925 an inter-service committee, extrapolating from the limited data generated by the small air raids mounted in World War I, presented a hypothetical scenario in which London would collapse after suffering three days of aerial bombardment in which almost four thousand people would be killed and over seven thousand others seriously injured. Photographs and reports of the destruction wrought by Japanese bombers on Shanghai in 1931 were accompanied by the apocalyptic images of cities in ruins contained in lurid novels such as *The Gas War of 1940*. In famously explaining to the House of Commons later that year that the 'bomber will always get through', Stanley Baldwin was merely expressing the widespread consensus – supported by the Air Ministry as a means of procuring funding for the build-up of an RAF deterrent bomber force – that, as the writer Beverley Nichols put it in 1933, '*no great city can be defended against air attack*'.[2]

FIGURE 2 'Everytown' after the first air raid, *Things to Come* (London Films, 1935).

BFI Stills, courtesy of London Features International plc.

Anyone who, by some mischance, remained unaware of what aerial warfare was thought to mean would have been rapidly educated if they had seen *Things to Come*, the large-scale futuristic epic brought to the screen by London Films mogul Alexander Korda in early 1936. Written by H. G. Wells on the basis of an earlier novel, *Things to Come* postulates a war beginning in December 1940 in which fleets of hostile bombers devastate 'Everytown' in a matter of minutes. A few lines from the Wells treatment give an indication of what he saw happening in his mind's eye:

Sirens, whistles and hooters. Panic working up in Square. Quick flashes of military working anti-aircraft guns. Again, to crowded Square, terrified faces looking up. Increased panic. Aeroplanes overhead. Anti-aircraft firing rather helplessly . . . A tramcar runs down the street, it lurches and falls sideways across the street. The façade of a gigantic general store falls into the street. The merchandise is scattered and on fire. Window dummies and wounded civilians lie on the pavement . . . Bomb bursting in crowded Square. Cinema crashing in ruins . . . A bomb bursts a gas main, a jet of flame, the fire spreads . . . Officials distributing gas masks, the crowd in a panic. Fight for masks. Official swept off his feet.

When translated on to film by director William Cameron Menzies and set-designer Vincent Korda, who built the square to resemble central London, an even greater level of destruction was arranged. 'The opening passages of the film are realistic (and, consequently, unnerving)', Elizabeth Bowen admitted in *Sight and Sound*. As Campbell Dixon explained for the benefit of *Daily Telegraph* readers: 'Through the Christmas rejoicings come rumours of war, and then out of the sky the first shattering blow – an air raid, marvellously produced, that leaves the city, like other cities, in ruins.' Other critics were equally awestruck. 'Shown on the wide screen,' Paul Holt wrote in a review for the *Daily Express*, 'this is as imposing a display of destruction as Hollywood can provide in its most lavishly destructive moments.' The *Times* critic found this part of the film so true to life as to be 'really appalling', while the *Manchester Guardian* reviewer could only 'admit and deplore' what seemed the likely future for the capital and other cities.[3]

The way in which the general public shied away from attending the film as a consequence of its graphic depiction of the horrors of aerial warfare served only to underline the extent to which people thought such a scenario too likely by half to be considered entertainment. Air Commodore L. E. O. Charlton, in his book *War Over England*, which also appeared in 1936 (joining a growing list of similarly doom-laden titles), postulated that the capital and other cities would be crippled in a matter of days if a surprise attack took place. 'Adequate local defence against air attack, even without the use of the element of surprise,' was impossible, 'because the enemy could always be in full strength over the desired spot, whereas the defending forces must of necessity be widely distributed.' Newsreels chronicling the destruction of Guernica in April 1937 by German bombers operating in Spain did little to ease the gloom; by this point the Air Ministry was estimating that a massive assault by the *Luftwaffe* would kill or maim 150,000 Londoners within a week.[4]

As it happened, official policy was now shifting away from the premise that nothing could be done to stop aerial Armageddon, other than creating a deterrent bomber force, and towards the notion that an effective air defence system could be created.

RAF Fighter Command, founded in 1936, could look forward to more resources being funnelled its way in the form of personnel for new squadrons that would eventually be equipped with swift monoplane interceptors capable of overhauling and shooting down fast monoplane bombers. With the progressive development of an advanced command and control network – in which ground observers, anti-aircraft defences and, ultimately, the first radar early warning chain all played a role alongside the fighter squadrons – the RAF and the supporting services were to prove with resounding clarity in 1940 that the bomber would *not* always get through.[5]

The public, however, possessed only a partial and incomplete picture of what was being done to improve the country's ability to defend itself and, by and large, still expected war to begin much as depicted in *Things to Come*: hence the overwhelming sense of relief that accompanied news of the Munich Agreement in September 1938 that staved off an apparently imminent war with Hitler's Germany and its supposedly massive *Luftwaffe*. The authorities at home may even have inadvertently reinforced popular perceptions as to the nature of aerial bombing with a couple of short films meant to drum up recruiting for active and passive ground defence services.

In the spring of 1937 *The Gap*, a thirty-eight minute Gaumont-British Instructional film made with the co-operation of the Air Ministry and at the instigation of the War Office, appeared in various cinemas as part of their daily programmes. Designed to drum up recruiting for the anti-aircraft units of the Territorial Army (TA), the storyline of the film involved a surprise aerial attack on the capital that succeeds with devastating effect because of a gap in the ground defences that could have been plugged if the TA had possessed enough volunteers. Donald Carter, the director of *The Gap*, was able to draw on thousands of troops and tons of equipment along with dozens of RAF bombers and fighters. As a result, the attack was, as Graham Greene put it for *Spectator* readers, 'impressively conveyed'. Such realism, though, only reinforced the sense among some viewers that the bomber would indeed always get through: 'the film does nothing to allay this fear which must be in the mind of everyone who sees it', argued William Farr in his negative review for *Sight and Sound*.[6]

The same problem doubtless existed when *The Warning*, a thirty-minute British National film supported by the defence services, appeared in early 1939. *The Warning* aimed to draw in recruits for the Air Raid Precautions (ARP) organisation through showing what the ARP would do in case of an emergency. Once again a major air raid – this one staged in Nottingham – is central to the plot and, while the civil defence services are not shown here as being over-whelmed in the manner of *Things to Come*, there is still plenty of death and destruction. 'Much of the photography is extremely realistic and the ruination caused by bombing raids is vividly portrayed', explained the reviewer for the *Monthly Film Bulletin*. The sight of RAF biplane fighters in action but unable to stop the raid also probably did little to raise the spirits of those who sat through *The Warning*.[7]

Hence, when war finally came in September 1939, there existed widespread public concern that the *Luftwaffe* would sooner or later launch a massive blow against London against which the RAF and other defences would prove inadequate. *An Englishman's Home*, an Aldwych feature film developed before the war but released about a month after the war began, was a spy story that, among other things, showed an enemy air raid that meets with little opposition. 'Twice the "air raid" caused a good deal of laughter and jibes [because of crude production values],' Len England discovered on the basis of what Mass-Observation participants saw at five London cinema showings, 'twice it was received in complete silence, and once an observer reported signs of hysteria'.[8]

Alexander Korda, meanwhile, perhaps uneasily aware that one of his own products had done much to reinforce the fear of bombing, had been negotiating with the Air Ministry before the outbreak of war about making a film in which the strength of the RAF resulting from various recent expansion schemes would be showcased. By the time an agreement was reached on 1 September 1939, war with Germany was a virtual certainty. The head of London Films immediately set about creating what would soon be titled *The Lion Has Wings*, a feature film that would contain a message diametrically opposite to that of *Things to Come*.[9]

Gathering together various directors, writers, and technicians then at work on other London Films projects at Denham Studios, such as *The Thief of Baghdad*, the larger-than-life Hungarian émigré and patriot-by-adoption told the assembled group 'that we were to make a film to reassure the public of the power of the Royal Air Force', as Ian Dalrymple, the man Korda placed in charge of the project, later recalled. Such a project could work only if it could be completed and exhibited in a timely manner. That in turn depended on the government reversing the decision it made on the outbreak of war to close the cinemas because of the danger posed by bombing – something that came to pass within a few weeks. It was also dependent on support from the new wartime propaganda arm, the innocuous-sounding Ministry of Information; and, of course, on the backing of the RAF itself. Having proved himself a past master of managing to get the Prudential to back his endeavours, and knowing he had the support of no less a personage than the new First Lord of the Admiralty, his friend Winston Churchill, Korda was able to convince the Ministry of Information and the Air Ministry that it would be a good idea to make a feature film. It would aim, as Dalrymple later put it, 'to reassure the British public that they weren't all going to get blown to pieces in five minutes' because the RAF was quite capable of handling the *Luftwaffe*.[10]

The Lion Has Wings was made in great haste over the course of a few weeks in September and early October, with no less than three directors involved – Michael Powell, Brian Desmond Hurst, Adrian Brunel – and a host of players working at Denham – Ralph Richardson, Merle Oberon, June Duprez, Anthony Bushell, and Ronald Adam, to name but a few – all working under the overall supervision of Dalrymple. Multiple directors were necessary both because of the speed with which it was expected that the project could be completed and because of the multiple subjects Dalrymple intended to cover. *The Lion Has Wings* employed a mixture of documentary footage and staged sequences held together by the familiar voice of the Gaumont-British newsreel commentator E. V. H. Emmett. It sought to explain Hitler's responsibility for the war, the war-readiness of British industry, the effectiveness of RAF bombers and, above all, show audiences why the destruction of any enemy bomber fleet was assured. Explaining why Londoners and other urban folk could rest easy in their beds remained a central preoccupation of the production: hence the defeat of a *Luftwaffe* raid would form the climax of the film.[11]

As with other sections of the film, the sequences dealing with the raid could be based in part on old newsreel and other footage; including, as it turned out, extracts from *The Gap*. But, even with such film to hand, it was clear that some work would have to be done on location as well as sound stages in order to gain some necessary verisimilitude.

Dalrymple assigned Michael Powell to take care of this and, with assistance from the Air Ministry in the form of a liaison officer, Squadron Leader H. M. S. Wright, he was able to direct his camera at the pilots, ground staff, and Spitfires of 74 Squadron, located at RAF Hornchurch. Pilot Officer D. 'Sammy' Hoare later recalled what this was like for those air force personnel directly involved:

> The whole business was looked down upon somewhat by 'A' Flight who weren't involved at all; it was only 'B' Flight who were doing the flying for *The Lion Has Wings*. For about a week we had the film crew on the airfield who were taking lots and lots of shots of the tents we lived in, the aircraft pens, and a few take-offs and landings. We were still wearing our smart white flying suits at the time, and it was a very entertaining week. We had lots of beer flowing and we joined in with the film crew. It was all rather amusing, but it was all rather frowned upon by 'A' Flight who were seriously concentrating on their training at the time, while we were just flying around for the fun of it.[12]

Authentic-looking control rooms, based on technical advice from the Air Ministry, were constructed at Denham. The RAF liaison officer also proved helpful in the construction of a vital mock-up for close-up cockpit shots, as Powell explained in his memoirs:

> Squadron Leader Wright managed to give me the fuselage of a crashed Spitfire, plus two odd wings from some other station, and we brought the lot back to Denham and set it up on one of the big stages with lots of room around it. I surrounded it with wind machines and arranged with the engineering department so that the whole thing was on a platform that could be tipped and turned and made to do all sorts of things, including dips and swings against a night background.

Using a variety of effects, including back projection, recording battle noise, and even firecrackers, Powell was seeking to give the impression that the RAF could 'blow the Luftwaffe out of the sky'.[13]

Hurriedly shot, assembled and edited at a cost of about £30,000, the completed version of *The Lion Has Wings* ran for a mere seventy-five minutes on screen, almost twenty minutes of which, cut by Henry Cornelius, were devoted to air defence and the outcome of any attempt by the *Luftwaffe* at a knock-out blow. 'What is of constant interest is how we can protect our country from undesirable visitors,' intones Emmett. 'What is the organization that exists to counter, and eventually conquer, German bombing attacks?' The answer, illustrated with available footage, was 'fast machines, fighters, interceptors, and of course personnel'. Planes and pilots, though, were only part of Britain's defences against air attack. In addition there existed:

> A new form of defence never before tried in warfare: the balloon barrage. A chain of blimps that trail invisible steel wires: death to the invader. The object of the balloon barrage is to force enemy planes to a height at which they can become a better target for anti-aircraft fire, or an easier victim for defending fighters. Not only that – accurate bombing becomes impossible.

The specifications of the newest anti-aircraft guns were classified but, as Emmett explained, using typically over-the-top newsreel-style prose, 'it is sufficient to know that they fling upward a hail of metal that changes the sky into an inferno'. No enemy plane would be safe even at night. 'Searchlights pierce the darkest corners of the heavens' and ground observers were 'always on the lookout'.[14]

Having established the general picture, the film then moves through a staged scenario into the specifics of how an enemy attack on the capital would be defeated. Stereotypically authoritarian Nazis are shown preparing to launch a series of night raids, news of which reaches the Air Ministry through a spy ring. (According to his memoirs Powell had planned to hint at the existence of radio direction-finding (RDF), better known as radar, but there is no evidence of this in the finished film, which is hardly surprising in light of how secret this technology still was at this point.)[15] Robert Rendel, playing the Chief of Air Staff, is then shown ordering the raising of the balloon barrage, after which the scene shifts to a Denham sound stage where a huge plotting room is shown in which RAF personnel are seen busily at work under the watchful eye of the C.-in-C. (played by Archibald Batty). 'Somewhere in Britain,' Emmett confidently intones, 'its existence and communications completely protected from the enemy, is an organization known as Fighter Command.'

> It is in direct communication with the Air Ministry and all defence units. In supreme control is the Air Officer Commanding in Chief. He is the brain. The whole of the rest of the organization are his nerves, his limbs, his fingers. A large staff of telegraphists remains on duty night and day to receive reports as they come in from every

part of the country: observer posts, and all other sources of information.

Warned by phone of the expected raid, the C.-in-C. in turn alerts the Observer Corps, ARP, anti-aircraft and searchlight units, and three regional fighter groups. 'Britain, soldier and civilian, stands on guard', Emmett asserts.

Presumably because the amount of contemporary footage would not suffice for a feature-length film, there follows a rather odd two-minute interlude in which scenes from the 1937 Korda epic *Fire Over England* appear as the narrator uses the destruction of the Spanish Armada as a simile for the imminent defeat of the *Luftwaffe*. Then it is back to Fighter Command HQ, where three enemy raids are shown being plotted as they head for London. The C.-in-C. alerts 'Southern Command' HQ by phone, where the controller (played by John Longden) in turn telephones 'RAF Brackstead' and orders the station commander (played by Ralph Richardson with great panache) to use '299' Squadron to intercept the first raid. There follow action sequences in which pilots of 'A Flight' scramble, Spitfires take off, orders are given over the radio by the station commander concerning height, speed and direction. The sequences culminate in a dogfight in which two German bombers – utilising fleeting footage of various types of older German planes and even British types as well as models – are downed before the rest turn for home without having reached their target. A similar fate befalls the second raiding force as a result of ack-ack fire and the intervention of Spitfires from 'B Flight'. As 'A Flight' is shown landing to rearm and refuel, Emmett assures viewers that 'ground staff are waiting, and they race out to the machines that have come back for a second breath. In the ghostly shrouded blackness of the aerodrome, every-thing goes with clockwork smoothness, as if they were working in broad daylight [which, in fact, they were, since Powell could only film during the day].' Finally, it is the turn of the third raiding force. This time it is the balloon barrage, about which much fuss had been made earlier in the film, that is shown deterring the enemy from pressing on to central London. 'They climb and climb,' the narrator relates, 'they dare not face the entanglement of those awful strands of steel.' Forced up too high for accurate bombing, raid number three also turns back towards the North Sea. The enemy's ordeal, however, is not over. Brackstead is contacted once again and ordered to send '301 Squadron' in pursuit. Just over the English coastline the bombers are overhauled and four more machines plunge down burning and out of control as a result of deadly Spitfire attacks. The bomber, if *The Lion Has Wings* was to be believed, would not only not always get through, but also most probably would never get through at all.[16]

This was, to say the least, a highly optimistic scenario. All things considered, the depiction of a smooth and effective chain of command at work in *The Lion Has Wings* was not that far off the mark. But, while the following year Fighter Command would demonstrate its effectiveness during the day (albeit not without loss and not without many raids getting through to their targets), night interception proved a much more difficult proposition. Only with the introduction of a fast and heavily armed twin-engine fighter, the Bristol Beaufighter, the advent of an effective Airborne Interception (AI) radar set, and the spread of inland ground control stations in 1941 would the RAF begin to find and shoot down night raiders with anything approaching regularity. Even then, no night raid would ever be entirely turned back.[17] From a contemporary standpoint, furthermore, the newsreel-style presentation of, and stiff-upper-lip acting in, *The Lion Has Wings* come across as old-fashioned to an almost comical degree. What, though, did those who went to see the film think when it appeared at the end of October and on into November 1939?

There was no doubt that the speed with which *The Lion Has Wings* had been put together was not an asset in the eyes of some of the more discriminating among those who watched it. 'From a technical point of view it is remarkable that any full-length film could have been produced in less than two months', a Foreign Office official noted, 'but all through the film shows signs of hurry. Technically it is extremely indifferent and uneven, with dull cutting, mixed photography, and complete lack of any internal rhythm.' The reviewer for the *New Statesman* opined that, among other problems with the film, 'it does seem questionable whether the balloons will cause such surprise and consternation as the film suggests'. Graham Greene, writing for *The Spectator*, noted that using footage from *The Gap* tended to remind those who had seen it what happened to London in that film, adding that the Nazis might have a point when they questioned the reality of aerial combat in which 'all the deaths are German and all the heroics English'. On a related theme, other critical viewers found the contrast between good-looking, mostly white-clad RAF officers and villainous-looking *Luftwaffe* types dressed in dark flying kit an all-too-obvious metaphor. 'We know it is propaganda,' a member of the Royal Air Force wrote in a letter to the magazine *Picturegoer*, 'but why do all the British pilots and crews appear as strong, healthy young men and the Germans as bearded, tough-looking brutes?' Just as bad, from the perspective of *The Aeroplane*'s man, was the indiscriminate way in which footage of different and unlikely types of British and German aircraft had been jumbled together to create the raiding force. There were also continuity lapses 'such as Spitfire pilots [in close up] dramatically banging shut their cockpit covers in sequence after leaping up and then [in long shot] taking-off with all of them open'. According to a member of Mass-Observation, a claim made by the RAF commander, played by Ralph Richardson, early in *The Lion Has Wings* – 'we've never been better prepared' – provoked audible derision among members of one audience. In the eyes of a famous documentary film-maker not involved in the Korda project, this and other failings made it 'a ghastly bloody film'. Michael Powell himself later admitted that 'some stagy episodes were rather embarrassing' and that *The Lion Has Wings* had been a 'hodgepodge' and 'an outrageous piece of propaganda'.[18]

Yet, in the last months of 1939, it is important to note that *The Lion Has Wings* received more positive than negative attention from the trade press, film magazines, and many newspaper critics, not least with respect to its depiction of the country's defences. Campbell Dixon wrote a review for the *Daily Telegraph* in which he singled out, among other things, the apparent restrained realism of the actors playing RAF fighter pilots alongside their real-life counterparts. The *Manchester Guardian* critic found the raid sequences 'enthrallingly produced', while his counterpart for the *Yorkshire Post* thought the depiction of the RAF was 'most impressive'. *The Times* found the way in which the raid was handled both dramatic and exciting. 'I found this film of absorbing interest', Paul Holt explained to readers of the *Daily Express*, stressing among other things the 'big thrill' provided by seeing how well organised the RAF was to repel real invaders. In his opinion *The Lion Has Wings* was 'first-rate', a sentiment echoed by A. T. Borthwick in the *News Chronicle* ('singularly impressive') and Joyce Jeffreys in the *Sunday Pictorial* ('comforting and inspiring'). The fan magazines were equally enthusiastic, *Picturegoer* ('inspires confidence') and *Picture Show* ('an absorbing record') both also singling out the RAF sequences for special praise. For more discerning film-goers, the reviewer writing for the British Film Institute's *Monthly Film Bulletin* reported that the film 'admirably fulfils its object – to inspire quiet confidence in the hearts of those who see it.'[19]

On the whole, the public seemed to agree with the critics when, in

November, the film was shown in no less than two hundred cinemas around the country. A Mass-Observation survey of over a hundred people who had seen it revealed that almost 73 per cent had liked or strongly liked it. Many recognised its propagandistic quality; but, whatever its faults (and there were many) The Lion Has Wings successfully met a need for reassurance among audiences. Though the war had not opened as anticipated with a knock-out blow aimed at London, there was still a good deal of anxiety through the winter of the Phoney War. That The Lion Has Wings could serve to relieve that anxiety, however temporarily, was illustrated by a remark made by a twenty-five year-old women after she saw the film: 'It makes you feel much safer.'[20]

The robustness of its message evidently contrasted favourably in people's minds with the subsequent effort by London Films to recycle a troubled docudrama feature film from the latter 1930s, entitled Conquest of the Air, by adding a new ending showing the introduction of the Spitfire and Hurricane into RAF service. The new ending, however, was far less assertive than that projected by The Lion Has Wings. The declaration that 'England is ready for the time when action will follow mere words' simply could not compare with a staged demonstration of what this would mean in practice. Re-released in the spring of 1940, Conquest of the Air was judged to be 'rather heavy and uninspiring' by the Monthly Film Bulletin and made no impression at the box-office. In marked contrast, enough people saw The Lion Has Wings to make the film the number one cinema attraction of November 1939 and the second highest grossing film of the year, a year in which approximately nineteen million cinema tickets were sold each week.[21]

That public anxiety about bombing was partly assuaged – but only partly – by The Lion Has Wings was evident in the way audiences reacted when Things to Come was re-released in March 1940. Len England of Mass-Observation recorded that 'shots of thousands of planes [sic] crossing the coast caused some laughter, but the actual shots of air raid panic, of gas-masks being issued, of people running for shelter, and so on, were received in silence and with interest'.[22]

Overall The Lion Has Wings had succeeded in counteracting the earlier sense that a Battle of Britain would be catastrophic in nature. The chaps of Fighter Command were ready, and the raiders would not get through the nation's defences. A year after it was made, however, the message of The Lion Has Wings was rendered moot by the experience of the actual Battle of Britain and then the Blitz. In

reality events turned out to be worse than *The Lion Has Wings* had
projected but not as apocalyptic as *Things to Come* had suggested.
From now on the question would no longer be 'what will it be like?'
but instead 'how shall we remember it?'[23]

Notes

1. National Archives [hereafter NA], FO 371/22841, file A9056/7052/45, f. 116,
   13 November 1939.
2. Beverley Nichols, *Cry Havoc!* (London: Cape, 1933, p. 65; 270 HC Deb. 5s., col.
   622; 'Miles' [Stephen Southwold], *The Gas War of 1940* (London: Eric Partridge,
   1931); see Keith Middlemass and John Barnes, *Baldwin: A Biography* (London:
   Weidenfeld and Nicolson, 1969), pp. 732–3. On the 1925 figures see Charles
   Webster and Noble Frankland, *The Strategic Air Offensive Against Germany
   1939–1945*, Vol. 1 (London: HMSO, 1961), pp. 62–3.
3. *Manchester Guardian*, 22 February 1936, p. 10; *The Times*, 21 February 1936,
   p. 12; *Daily Express*, 21 February 1936, p. 19; *Daily Telegraph*, 21 February 1936,
   p. 10; *Sight and Sound*, spring 1936, p. 10; H. G. Wells, *Things to Come* (London:
   Crescent Press, 1935), p. 34. This treatment was a heavily reworked version of
   H. G. Wells, *The Shape of Things to Come* (London: Macmillan, 1933). The
   review in *Flight* magazine was among the relatively rare cases of unalloyed
   praise for the film ('a superb production'), but this was doubtless in part simply
   because of the way in which it showcased aviation. See *Flight*, 27 February 1936,
   p. 219. On the making and reception of the film see Christopher Frayling, *Things
   to Come* (London: BFI, 1995).
4. L. E. O. Clarke, *War Over England* (London: Longman, Green, 1936), p. 196. This
   book was timely and successful enough to be reissued in 1938. On the projected
   casualty figures see Uri Bailer, *The Shadow of the Bomber: The Fear of Air
   Attack and British Politics, 1932–1939* (London: Royal Historical Society, 1980),
   p. 130. On novels projecting an aerial Armageddon see I. F. Clarke, *Voices
   Prophesying War: Future Wars, 1763–3749* (Oxford: Oxford University Press,
   1992), pp. 142, 153–4. On the film *Things to Come* cutting too close to the bone
   for many cinema-goers, see Frayling, *Things to Come*, p. 76; see also e.g. Boyd
   Cable, 'When War Does Come: Terrifying Effects of Gas Attacks' in John
   Hammerton (ed.), *War in the Air: Aerial Wonders of Our Time*, Vol. I (London:
   Amalgamated, 1936), pp. 272–4.
5. On the development of Fighter Command see e.g. Peter Flint, *Dowding and
   Headquarters Fighter Command* (Shrewsbury: Airlife, 1996); Richard Hough
   and Denis Richards, *The Battle of Britain: The Jubilee History* (London: Hodder
   and Stoughton, 1989). On the development of radar see David Zimmerman,
   Britain's Shield: Radar and the Defeat of the Luftwaffe (Stroud: Sutton, 2001).
6. *Sight and Sound*, Summer 1937, p. 89; David Parkinson (ed.), *Mornings in the
   Dark: The Graham Greene Film Reader* (Manchester: Carcanet, 1993), p. 198; see
   also, however, W. Bannister in Jeffrey Richards and Dorothy Sheridan (eds),
   Mass-Observation at the Movies (London: Routledge and Kegan Paul, 1987),
   p. 48. On the making of *The Gap* see NA, WO 32/2689; see also *Glasgow Herald*,
   8 April 1937, p. 12. Though the file on the matter no longer exists, the Foreign
   Office index indicates that the propaganda ministry in the Third Reich condemned *The Gap* through the press as being anti-German. See Foreign Office,

Index to the Correspondence of the Foreign Office, 1937 (London: HMSO, 1970), vol. 1, p. 506.

7. *Monthly Film Bulletin*, 31 January 1939, p. 63. On the making of *The Warning* see NA, INF 5/59. See also Michael Paris, *From the Wright Brothers to* Top Gun: *Aviation, Nationalism and Popular Culture* (Manchester: Manchester University Press, 1995), p. 107.

8. Tom Harrisson Mass-Observation Archive [hereafter M-O], FR 57, p. 14. On *An Englishman's Home*, a rather poor-quality rendition of a Guy du Maurier story, see *Monthly Film Bulletin*, 31 October 1939, p. 185.

9. On the circumstances surrounding the genesis of *The Lion Has Wings* see John Ware, *The Lion Has Wings* (London: Collins, 1940), p. 168. On Korda's clandestine activity on behalf of HMG and his eagerness to make a propaganda film in case of war see Charles Drazin, *Korda: Britain's Only Movie Mogul* (London: Sidgwick and Jackson, 2002), pp. 212–19. See also National Film and Television Archive, 'Filming for Victory: British Cinema, 1939–1945' (BBC, 1989), Michael Powell comments.

10. I. Dalrymple quoted in Elizabeth Sussex, *The Rise and Fall of British Documentary: The Story of the Film Movement Founded by John Grierson* (Berkeley: University of California Press, 1975), p. 124; Dalrymple, Ian, 'The Crown Film Unit, 1940–43' in N. Pronay and D. W. Spring (eds), *Propaganda, Politics and Film, 1918–45* (London: Macmillan, 1982), p. 209. On the Korda meeting see Michael Powell, *A Life in Movies: An Autobiography* (London: Heinemann, 1986), p. 329. On dealings with the MoI see Drazin, *Korda*, p. 221. On the closing and re-opening of cinemas see Guy Morgan, *Red Roses Every Night* (London: Quality, 1948), p. 23. In the film's credits Korda is listed as producer and Dalrymple as associate producer. It was Dalrymple, however, who appears to have done most of the basic production chores.

11. On *The Lion Has Wings* see also Robert Murphy, *British Cinema and the Second World War* (London: Continuum, 2000), pp. 16–18; James Chapman, *The British at War: Cinema, State and Propaganda, 1939–1945* (London: I. B. Tauris, 1998), pp. 59–64.

12. D. S. Hoare quoted in Richard C. Smith, *Hornchurch Scramble: The Definitive Account of the RAF Fighter Airfield, its Pilots, Groundcrew, and Staff*, Volume One, *1915 to the End of the Battle of Britain* (London: Grub Street, 2000), pp. 55–6. On Powell being assigned to cover the RAF see Powell, *Life in Movies*, p. 331; Ian Christie (ed.), *Powell, Pressburger and Others* (London: BFI, 1978), p. 26.

13. Powell, *Life in Movies*, p. 335. On the control rooms see K. R. M. Short, *Screening the Propaganda of British Air Power: From R.A.F. (1935) to* The Lion Has Wings *(1939)* (Trowbridge: Flicks Books, 1997), p. 23.

14. All quotations here and after are from the completed film. On production costs see Paul Tabori, *Alexander Korda* (London: Oldbourne, 1959), pp. 216, 218. Though he had in fact received help from official sources (see e.g. NA, FO 371/22840, file A7720/7052/45, minute 1) and United Artists, Korda did nothing to stop stories that he had financed *The Lion Has Wings* out of his own pocket. See Michael Korda, *Charmed Lives: A Family Romance* (New York: Random House, 1979), p. 137; Drazin, *Korda*, pp. 221–2, 228.

15. Powell, *Life in Movies*, pp. 334–5.

16. For further details of the making and content of *The Lion Has Wings* see Short, *Screening Propaganda*.

17. See e.g. Roderick Chisolm, *Cover of Darkness* (London: Chatto and Windus, 1953); C. F. Rawnsley and Robert Wright, *Night Fighter* (London: Collins, 1957); Peter Townsend, *Duel in the Dark* (London: Harrap, 1986).

18. Powell interview in *The South Bank Show: Michael Powell* (ITV, 26 October 1986); Powell, *Life in Movies*, p. 330; Harry Watt in Sussex, *Rise and Fall*, p. 120; M-O FR 24, 'The Cinema in the First Three Months of the War', in Richards and Sheridan, *Mass-Observation*, pp. 167–8; *The Aeroplane*, 9 November 1939, p. 563; *Picturegoer*, 13 January 1940, p. 18; *The Spectator*, 3 November 1939, p. 619; *New Statesman*, 4 November 1939, p. 644; NA, FO 371/22840, A9056/7052/457, 13 November 1939; see also M-O, FR 57, p. 11. On the casting of RAF and *Luftwaffe* pilots in *The Lion Has Wings* see Powell, *Life in Movies*, p. 335. Despite the doubters, *The Lion Has Wings* was a mild success in the United States: see Nicholas John Cull, *Selling War: The British Propaganda Campaign Against American "Neutrality" in World War II* (New York: Oxford University Press, 1995), p. 49. On the reaction in Germany – supposedly either hilarity or rage – see C. A. Oakley, *Where We Came In: Seventy Years of the British Film Industry* (London: Allen and Unwin, 1964), p. 155; Tabori, *Korda*, pp. 217–18.

19. *Monthly Film Bulletin*, 30 November 1939, p. 201; *Picture Show*, 2 December 1939, p. 10; *Picturegoer*, 18 November 1939, p. 20; *Sunday Pictorial*, 5 November 1939, p. 16; *News Chronicle*, 31 October 1939, p. 7; *Daily Express*, 31 October 1939, p. 11; *The Times*, 31 October 1939, p. 4; *Yorkshire Post*, 28 November 1939, p. 3; *Manchester Guardian*, 31 October 1939, p. 7; *Daily Telegraph*, 31 October 1939, p. 8; see also *To-day's Cinema*, 31 October 1939, p. 10; *Picturegoer*, 16 December 1939, p. 14; Short, *Screening Propaganda*, pp. 158–9; NA, FO 371/22841, file A9056/7052/45, f. 116.

20. Mass-Observation material reproduced in Short, *Screening Propaganda*, pp. 153, 149. The number of cinemas where *The Lion Has Wings* played comes from Tabori, *Korda*, p. 217.

21. *Monthly Film Bulletin*, 30 June 1940, p. 87. On ticket sales see Antony Aldgate and Jeffrey Richards, *Britain Can Take It: The British Cinema in the Second World War* second edition (Edinburgh: Edinburgh University Press, 1994), p. 3. On box-office performance of *The Lion Has Wings* see *Kinematograph Weekly*, 11 January 1940, p. 7; see also Julian Poole, 'British Cinema Attendance in Wartime: Audience Preference at the Majestic, Macclesfield, 1939–1946', *Historical Journal of Film, Radio and Television* 7 (1987), p. 20. On *Conquest of the Air* see Paris, *Wright Brothers*, p. 104; see also (in relation to lack of impact) *Kinematograph Weekly*, 9 January 1941, p. 26. Churchill had first got to know Korda while assisting with the scenario for *Conquest of the Air*. See Churchill College Cambridge, Churchill Papers, CHAR 8/514, ff. 67, 84–91.

22. M-O, FR 57, p. 15. On continuing worries about bombing see e.g. NA, INF 1/250, Home Morale Emergency Committee, interim reports, 22–3 May 1940.

23. It was only after the Battle of Britain was over that a sense of its significance began to develop. See e.g. Elias Canetti, *Party in the Blitz: The English Years* (New York: New Directions, 2005), p. 142. The way in which current events trumped screen aerial combat once the Phoney War ended was illustrated by the reaction to *Squadron 922*, a short film dealing in slightly fictionalised form with the defeat of a German bombing raid on the Firth of Forth in 1939. As the reviewer for the *Manchester Guardian* put it when *Squadron 922* was released in July 1940, if the film had been distributed when it was finished at the end of April 'it would almost certainly have outranked "The Lion Has Wings" as a propaganda picture', but was now irrelevant. *Manchester Guardian*, 2 July 1940, p. 6. On the making of *Squadron 922* see Harry Watt, *Don't Look at the Camera!* (London: Elek, 1974), pp. 130–4.

FIGURE 3 Leslie Howard as Reg Mitchell oversees the assembly of the first Spitfire in *The First of the Few* (British Aviation Pictures, 1942).

2

Spitfire of Dreams:
The First of the Few (1942)

I think we've got something here.
Leslie Howard, November 1941[1]

As soon as it was clear that the *Luftwaffe* had been comprehensively defeated in the daylight battles over England in August and September 1940, and the threat of invasion thereby averted, film companies began thinking about celebrating this singular victory on celluloid. For a number of reasons, though, it would take almost a year for a British feature film in which the Battle of Britain played a significant role to reach the screen; and almost two until audiences were able to judge the major effort by Leslie Howard to interpret the outcome of the battle with reference to the career of R. J. Mitchell, designer of the Spitfire.

Associated Talking Pictures, better known as Ealing Studios, was first off the mark with a script entitled *Battle for Britain*, a melodramatic story set in the south-east at the time of Dunkirk that climaxes in the destruction of a major enemy air raid at night. The company decided before proceeding with production to query the social reporting organisation, Mass-Observation, as to the likely success or failure of a film based on their script. The resulting report, delivered in November 1940, was not at all encouraging. According to Len England and Tom Harrisson, the majority of audiences currently went to the cinema to get away from the war and not to relive it on screen. There were, furthermore, a number of problems in the script itself, the most important of them related to the way in which the air raid was handled. On the basis of people's experiences of the air war during the hours of darkness – when, in marked contrast to the daylight hours, the RAF was patently unable to engage enemy raiders – the way in which the story posited enemy aircraft being shot down in large numbers by searchlight-led anti-aircraft fire and fighter planes at night was bound to be seen by audiences as contrary to the known facts. 'However uncritical they are of films in general,' Len England stressed in the cover letter accompanying the report, 'they know from bitter experience what night raids are like, and the film will seem merely a travesty'. Though other Ealing melodramas in which wartime events played a role proved successful at the box office both before and after this point, it was decided not to proceed with this production and consequently *Battle for Britain* disappeared without trace.[2]

The British arm of Twentieth Century–Fox was next into the lists with a plan for a feature film about the battle, the ambitious size and scope of which were outlined in an announcement that appeared in *Kine Weekly* on 9 January 1941:

'Spitfire', the ambitious Twentieth Century picture to be directed at Sheppard's Bush by Carol Reed, will be produced on a spectacular scale. Topical interest in aerial warfare, the progress of the mighty Empire Air Force, and the gallantry of the R.A.F., are features of 'Spitfire' which will make it one of the outstanding productions of 1941. The story centres round the activities of a typical defence squadron of the R.A.F., the members of which have been drawn from all parts of the British Empire. A star of international repute will head the brilliant cast, and close co-operation between the Air Force and the Air Ministry has already been given in the preparation of the film.

John Mills was subsequently mentioned as a possible lead, and there was talk of the film being made in Technicolor; but, in the end, Reed took on *Young Mr. Pitt* instead and nothing came of the project. Apart from anything else *Spitfire* might have seemed too similar in basic subject matter to a Hollywood production then in development by Twentieth Century–Fox that would emerge in October 1941 as *A Yank in the RAF*.[3]

Meanwhile, neither the failure of such projects nor the insistence by the Air Ministry that RAF operations and security concerns take absolute precedence over the needs of film production companies dampened the spirits of those who thought films in which the Battle of Britain featured would be successful. One only had to look at bookstalls in the first months of 1941 to find evidence that people were very interested in what had happened in the skies over south-east England the previous year. In March an Air Ministry pamphlet had been published under the title *The Battle of Britain*. Written by a former assistant librarian of the House of Commons, Hilary St John Saunders, the pamphlet did not contain illustrations, an author credit, or the names of any of those pilots and commanders who took part. The Ministry of Information expected about 50,000 copies of the threepenny [three old pence] pamphlet would be sold within the United Kingdom. Instead over a million were snapped up within a matter of weeks. In all, 2,099,900 plain copies were sold, along with 2,250,000 of an illustrated version published in April. The 'official account' contained in *The Battle of Britain*, as the reviewer for the *Times Literary Supplement* put it, gave the 'full story [it did not] of the terrific air fighting over south-east England last summer and autumn'. A more wide-ranging look at events entitled *The Battle of Britain, 1940*, penned by J. M. Spaight, a former principal assistant secretary at the Air Ministry, that contained a foreword by the father of the RAF, Lord Trenchard, went through three reprints in the course of May and June 1941. People obviously knew that a victory had been won, but they were still anxious to know what form it had taken and to learn the details. The BBC, meanwhile, had great success with feature radio programmes that combined airfield re-cordings and dramatised speech to chronicle what had happened. The battle, in short, remained topical, and thus a suitable backdrop for drama in the eyes of film-makers. The Spitfire, what was more, had captured the popular imagination: hence, for example, the lovingly rendered footage of one such new machine being put through its paces in the Crown Film Unit half-hour documentary *Ferry Pilot*, made the same year.[4]

Next to take up the challenge of employing the Battle of Britain as a plot setting after Twentieth Century–Fox had bowed out was the British arm of another Hollywood studio, RKO Radio Pictures. Under the overall supervision of producer William Sistrom, director Brian Desmond Hurst – who had worked on *The Lion Has Wings* – translated an original story by Terence Young on to the screen in the spring and summer of 1941 under the title *Dangerous Moonlight*. The abridged synopsis provided in the pressbook gives a good idea of the melodramatic nature of the film:

Stefan Radetsky [played by Anton Walbrook], a famous Polish pianist serving with his country's air force, meets Carole Hughes [played by Sally Gray], an American newspaperwoman, during a vicious air attack on Warsaw. After the fall of Poland, Stefan and his friend, Mike Carroll [played by Derrick De Marney, who had acted as a navigator in *The Lion Has Wings*], an intrepid Irish flyer, go to New York, where the musician is to start a concert tour in aid of Polish relief.

Stefan and Carole meet again and after a short romance are married. The tour proves successful, but Mike comes to England to join the Polish forces in this country. When France falls, Stefan feels an irresistible urge to follow Mike. Despite Carole's entreaties that he is better serving his country through his music, Stefan leaves America. Mike is killed in aerial combat and later, Stefan is seriously injured, losing his memory. Carole comes to Britain and aids Stefan's recovery. The grand finale comes with a re-union between the couple.[5]

For the sequences set during the Battle of Britain – which in all take up eleven minutes of screen time in a film that lasts only ninety-eight minutes – as well as those that take place on a Polish airfield, Sistrom and Hurst relied on the co-operation of the Air Ministry and RAF. To supplement the Spitfire cockpit constructed for *The Lion Has Wings*, a complete Spitfire was made available for taxiing shots as well as close-ups and longer shots of Walbrook and De Marney climbing into, as well as walking to and from, their aircraft. Shooting took place on two Royal Air Force aerodromes near London, while a number of Polish pilots serving with the RAF were drafted in for non-speaking parts. In addition, a good deal of official footage, including gun-camera shots, was provided to add verisimilitude to the dogfight scenes and thereby highlight, as the pressbook put it, 'Walbrook's thrilling exploits in the "Battle of Britain"'.[6]

As a serious feature, *Dangerous Moonlight* has not stood the test of time very well but, when it was first shown in mid-August 1941, the critics generally reacted positively, a number focusing in particular on the thrilling combat sequences. According to *The Times* reviewer, these scenes quickened the pulse and were no less impressive because they were 'mostly made up of photographed fact': the imaginary hero 'loses nothing in our estimation when he is credited with deeds which have actually been done'. The *Daily Telegraph* critic, while finding the love story dragged even more slowly than his counterpart at *The Times* suggested, concurred in arguing that watching the battle scenes, 'Junkers and Heinkels – real Junkers and Heinkels – swaying uncertainly in the reflector-sight for a second or two and then coming to pieces before your eyes', made 'a brilliant climax' and were worth the price of admission. Whether drawn by fighting or romance, audiences seemed to agree that

Dangerous Moonlight was worth seeing: when the film was placed on general release in September 1941, it did reasonably well at the box-office.[7]

Meanwhile the studios based in California, always on the look-out for new settings for tried-and-true plot devices, had turned their attention to the events surrounding the battle and generated no less than three variations on the same basic story. Reactions within Britain to these made-in-the-USA pictures would vary a great deal.

The first to appear in British cinemas towards the end of 1941 was *International Squadron*. This was a Warner Brothers picture starring Ronald Reagan as Jimmy Grant, a devil-may-care American test pilot who joins the RAF after ferrying a plane to England and enduring an air raid on London. His selfishness, though, causes two other pilots to die unnecessarily before Grant atones by making the ultimate sacrifice in a raid on the French coast. Using a mixture of stock footage and 'Spitfires' that looked nothing like the real thing, the cheaply made *International Squadron* was a version of an earlier picture, *Ceiling Zero*, directed by Howard Hawks in 1936. It was hastily put together in order to cash in on public interest in the formation of the first RAF 'Eagle Squadron', manned by United States volunteers, just as the Battle of Britain was winding down.[8]

Some who saw *International Squadron* were admittedly impressed. 'R.A.F. background and atmosphere are astounding', enthused a fan magazine: 'Flying sequences are the best of the film'. At least one other reviewer was also content to bathe in the warm glow of Hollywood regard for Fighter Command. 'It quickly becomes clear that the machinations of our American cousin are merely the peg on which to hang a vivid tribute to the men of our Air Force,' wrote the reviewer for the *Manchester Guardian*, 'and one is left with the feeling that this is one of the best pieces of British propaganda that the Americans have ever done for us.' Others were not so sure that a typically maverick Hollywood sky hero really belonged among The Few. 'The "hero" in this melodrama is such a thoroughgoing rotter that it is difficult to see anything to commend in the character', the reviewer for *Picture Show* admitted. 'This is an incredible story, only conceivable in Hollywood,' sniffed the *Monthly Film Bulletin*, 'and if the breaches of discipline perpetrated in the film were really part and parcel of the R.A.F. then the Battle of Britain could never have been won.' The industry paper, *To-day's Cinema*, meanwhile, warned prospective exhibitors that the film was utterly grotesque: 'Indifferent direction, unconvincing general portrayal, burlesque R.A.F. atmosphere'. *International Squadron* made little impression at the British box-office while turning a healthy profit in the United States and overseas markets as a whole.[9]

Hard on the heels of *International Squadron* came *A Yank in the RAF*, an effort by Darryl F. Zanuck of Twentieth Century–Fox to repeat the success of 1938's *A Yank at Oxford*. This time, with the co-operation of the Air Ministry, footage of Spitfires from 602 Squadron was taken in England; but in the hands of director Henry King relatively little of it was used in comparison to model work and footage of aircraft available in California. The plot of *A Yank in the RAF* bore similarities to *International Squadron* as well as to *A Yank at Oxford*. Tim Baker, a self-centred and bumptious ferry pilot played by Tyrone Power, joins the RAF in London but proves himself boorishly inconsiderate in love and war. Only after witnessing the death of a British pilot does Baker begin to shape up, redeeming himself in the aerial fighting over Dunkirk and being wounded (but not killed) in the process.[10]

It would have been clear to any British viewer at the time that Zanuck had got some of the details wrong; the uniforms and flying kit, for instance, did not match what was actually used by the RAF as seen on newsreels. And some observers found the love triangle centring on Betty Grable, among other aspects, too Hollywood by half. 'Curses,' grumbled J. E. Sewell in the *Daily Telegraph*, 'not loud but deep', in relation to its 'blondes-in-the-bombrack' approach. 'Hollywood doubtless meant well in making this film and is generous in its praise of the R.A.F.', *The Times* reviewer concluded, 'but unfortunately it falsifies the history in its reconstruction of the Dunkirk scenes, and its interpretation of the spirit of the men who fought there is crude and over-coloured.'[11]

The critic for the *Monthly Film Bulletin*, on the other hand, liked *A Yank in the RAF* very much, praising every aspect of the film from acting to aerial scenes: 'A most satisfactory production from every point of view'. *To-Day's Cinema*, significantly, suggested a profitable future for exhibitors: 'First-class general entertainment with out-standing star and subject appeal making it obvious box-office money spinner'. Cinema-goers, habitually attracted to Hollywood products and drawn by the star status of Tyrone Power and Betty Grable, bore out this prediction. *A Yank in the RAF* became the second most attended film in Britain in the course of February 1942.[12]

The third and final Hollywood contribution to the RAF fighter pilot mystique arrived in Britain at the beginning of August 1942. This was *Eagle Squadron*, a Universal picture produced by Walter Wagner that had begun life as a documentary project in 1940–41 but which, for a variety of reasons, had developed into a more conventional Hollywood product shot entirely in the United States with the exception of some opening shots of real-life Eagle Squadron pilots and pieces of footage supplied by the Ministry of Information. Once again the plot centred on a hot-shot American pilot, Chuck Brewer (played by a very young Robert Stack), who joins the RAF, flies a Spitfire as an individualist rather than as a member of the team, gets involved in a love triangle, and finally sees the light after another pilot gives his life in order to save him. It was, as the *Monthly Film Bulletin* put it, 'The mixture as before'.[13]

Like the other Hollywood productions, *Eagle Squadron* was not strong in terms of verisimilitude; so much so that, when the real Eagle Squadron pilots were shown the film they hated it so much that several walked out. British critics, however, were on the whole indulgent: 'if the hero's final feat of arms is somewhat steep,' *The Times* reviewer argued, 'the film is, after all, a romance, and not a documentary'. Campbell Dixon, writing for the *Daily Telegraph*, noted that it was 'not without its faults' but went on to add that 'its idealism is too lofty and its generosity to the R.A.F. and the British generally so touching that it would be churlish to dwell on them'. *To-Day's Cinema* predicted a rosy box-office future: 'Top-notch entertainment that cannot fail to gross heavily in every type of hall'. *Eagle Squadron* went on to earn the equivalent of over half a million dollars in the United Kingdom.[14]

A number of film critics had wondered why it was the Americans who were making all the recent films about the RAF. As it happened, even as the three Hollywood films were being made, work was underway on a British feature film in which the Battle of Britain assumed a more central position in the plot than had hitherto been the case. Though long in gestation, *The First of the Few* would eclipse its contemporaries when it reached the screen in Britain a few weeks after *Eagle Squadron*.[15]

Though it was the sturdy, hump-backed Hurricane that formed the backbone of RAF air defence in the summer and autumn of 1940, equipping no less than twenty-eight squadrons, it was the newer and more graceful Spitfire, with its clean lines and elliptical wings, which had immediately captured the public imagination, even though only nineteen Fighter Command squadrons then flew them. Symptomatic of most people's infatuation with the Spitfire was the way in which very few towns and associations chose to direct their monetary donations towards the theoretical purchase of any other type of aircraft: so much so that such sponsorship-style contributions were universally known as Spitfire Funds. Fame also extended to the plane's designer, R. J. Mitchell, the Spitfire being described by the staff of The Aeroplane, for example, as 'Mitchell's Masterpiece'; and, within a month or two of the end of the battle, Australian writer Henry C. James had begun work on a story of his life that was optioned by film producer George King.[16]

At the start of December 1940 he and his partner, John Stafford, were proudly announcing the shape of their projected film to the trade press. 'Two Englishmen together, with twenty-five years' experience of film production,' readers of Kine Weekly were breathlessly informed, 'will make the epic story of a great Englishman, the man who spent twenty-five years in pursuit of an ideal, the Englishman who flogged his brain and his energy to achieve the ultimate in fighter aircraft production, and died with his dream accomplished.' Hyperbole then took over:

He died that England might live, and England lives because he died.

Reginald Mitchell, inventor of the Spitfire, Englishman, visionary, and patriot, whose genius rides the skies of England, and whose winged avengers tear down the Goering gangsters from the blue, and send them crashing to the earth of mother England, which he loved.

So his story will be filmed; a story of devotion to an ideal, of suffering and courage, of unflinching endeavour, and unprecedented achievement; of a magnificent heart fighting a magnificent fight against the enemy of life. The first of the Few . . . he died, but the few fight on, the miracle men of the R.A.F. in the miracle machines of R. J. Mitchell.

Mitchell himself had died in 1936 but, with the support of his widow, who had helped James write his story, King and Stafford were 'determined to make the film of his life into his greatest monument, and to the immortal glory of the BOYS who meet their "finest hour" in the children of his dreams . . . the Squadrons of the Spitfire.'[17]

Turning the dream into a reality, however, would take some time. King got in touch with the multi-talented character actor, dramatist, and screenwriter Miles Malleson in the new year, asking him to produce in collaboration with the original author a film scenario based on the James story. The two partners also continued to bang the drum loudly, as the following item from Kine Weekly published at the end of March 1941 illustrates:

The production of 'The First of the Few', by British Aviation Pictures ... will mark a new milestone in the history of the kinema, because there is no greater real-life romance of this convulsed century of war, armistice and war, than that of 'R. J.' Mitchell, the English genius who created the Spitfires.

Spitfire is a name that has re-echoed its glory across the seven seas, and from the far corners of the five continents the glory of an achievement without precedent or parallel in the ancient or modern history of battle; a name that has been the watchword of the English-speaking peoples ever since that sunny September afternoon when the mite [sic] of the R.A.F. was flung into the arena of the air against the might of the Luftwaffe, and won the Battle of Britain, the greatest battle for survival ever known, and beyond comparison with any of the decisive battles in history.

'The First of the Few' is claimed to be the most inspiring film yet conceived by any producer, and the production of such a film at this time cannot be measured in mere terms of commercial enterprise. Rather, and as well, it is it is a work of the greatest possible value to the national effort. Because of its inspiring theme, and the inspiration and encouragement it will afford to every man and woman engaged in the war effort.[18]

King and Stafford were, however, small-time players in Wardour Street, and British Aviation Pictures essentially a holding company set up for the rights to the Mitchell story. For a film actually to be made, major backing would be needed.

At first it looked as if Metro-Goldwyn-Mayer would take on the job. Miles Malleson had mentioned the project to actor Robert Donat, who lived nearby, and he in turn became enthusiastic about playing R. J. Mitchell. Donat was under contract to MGM, who expressed interest as long as they could buy the full rights to the story. King, however, was not interested in having no further say in the project, and MGM backed away. Stafford then turned to another handsome English leading man, Leslie Howard, and talked to him about the possibility of him playing R. J. Mitchell in an American-financed production. Howard, then filming *Pimpernel Smith* at Denham studios, liked the story; but, in the wake of working on *Gone With the Wind* – which he had hated – did not want to work for Hollywood: 'I wanted to keep my independence.' Some months later he was approached again, this time apparently by King and without any Hollywood strings attached, and announced that he would not only star in the film but would act as producer and director. Presumably in return for some form of remuneration, King and Stafford accepted his offer to buy the rights. Thanks in part to the participation of his production manager, Phil Samuel, Howard was quickly able to convince J. Arthur Rank, head of General Film Distributors, to provide full financial backing for *The First of the Few* which began production in August 1941.[19]

The title was derived from a phrase the Prime Minister had used during a long speech on the war situation in the House of Commons on the afternoon of 20 August 1940 as the air battle over the English Channel began to heat up. 'The gratitude of every home in our Island, in our Empire, and indeed throughout the world, except in the abodes of the guilty', Churchill had argued, 'goes out to the British airmen who, undaunted by odds, unwearied in their constant challenge and mortal danger, are turning the tide of world war by their prowess and by their devotion.' The Prime Minister then added: 'Never in the field of human conflict was so much owed by so many to so few.' At the time, neither the speech nor this particular phrase caused much of a stir but, as the piece in *Kine Weekly* quoted above suggests, 'The Few' soon started to become a standard reference to the pilots of Fighter Command. Approached by King and Stafford through the Air Ministry, Churchill had given permission for his words to be adapted for the film's title at the start of 1941.[20]

A feature about the development of the Spitfire would necessarily require the co-operation of the Air Ministry and help from the company for whom Mitchell had worked, the Supermarine subsidiary of Vickers-Armstrong Ltd. Knowing that his words would be associated with the picture, the Prime Minister was happy to provide the film-makers with a note on Downing Street letterhead requesting all possible assistance, and even phoned up the chief of Fighter Command to make sure that all necessary access was granted. Tangible results included the loan of a Supermarine S6 seaplane to be used in the big tank at Denham for the Schneider Cup scenes, a Spitfire fuselage for close-up work, and Air Ministry permission for Howard to visit RAF Biggin Hill on multiple occasions to soak up the atmosphere of a Battle of Britain fighter station. A film crew under Howard's direction was also allowed to set up shop at RAF Ibsley and RAF Warmwell during the spring of 1941 in order to direct personnel from 118 Squadron and the Spitfires of 501 Squadron. The loan of a Blenheim bomber as camera ship as well as use of a captured Heinkel was agreed to for certain aerial sequences. Occasionally the war intruded: 'They would appear in a scene,' Howard related to a film critic of the pilots he was trying to direct, 'then suddenly dash off on a "scramble" or a "sweep"' but, on the whole, the production team received every possible consideration from all concerned.[21]

The combination of high-powered backers and the producer/ director's own influence as a major star of stage and screen meant that Howard could also draw together a highly talented cast and crew. David Niven, for instance, who would play the important supporting role of test pilot Geoffrey Crisp, was seconded from the army for nearly five months' work, while Howard was able to spend time testing a number of actresses to play Mrs Mitchell before settling on a very naturalistic Rosamund John. The screenwriter Anatole de Grunwald, with whom Howard had worked on his previous film, had helped Malleson produce a usable scenario by mid-September 1941. William Walton, who was working for the Ministry of Information, was then brought in to compose the musical score in May 1942. Talented crew-members included camera operator Jack Hilyard and lighting cameraman Georges Perinal; and when the strain of producing and directing in combination with giving regular talks for the BBC grew too much for Howard, he brought in his old friend Adrian Brunel to cover for him as 'Production Consultant'.[22]

The basic plot of *The First of the Few* was sketched out in the press booklet distributed to critics before the premiere of the film in August 1942:

It is September 1940. At a fighter station a group of young pilots await the order to 'scramble,' and pass the time discussing their aircraft, and wondering who designed the Spitfire. Wing Commander Geoffrey Crisp, flying veteran of the first World War, quietly remarks that the designer was R. J. Mitchell, and that he knew him well.

As Crisp unfolds his story, the Battle of Britain gives way to events in 1922, when R. J. Mitchell and his wife, a youngish couple, are picnicking on a cliff top. Mitchell is an aircraft designer and is fascinated by the action of a gliding gull. Dreamily, he foresees the time when he will create a stream-lined aeroplane based on the gull's graceful outline and flight.

Early in his career as an aircraft designer, Mitchell is joined by Crisp, an unemployed ex-R.A.F. Officer, who is only too glad to become a test pilot. Though still producing amphibian bi-planes Mitchell clings to his idea of a stream-lined monoplane capable of attaining speeds regarded by his associates as impossible.

Eventful happenings in the sphere of aviation depict Schneider Cup disappointments and successes, and Mitchell's final triumph with the Supermarine S.6, which won the trophy for Britain outright.

Mitchell, accompanied by his wife and Crisp, takes a well-earned holiday in Germany. He takes a keen professional interest in the German Glider Clubs and Gliders, but when he is the guest of a prominent flying club, he learns from an arrogant young German that the Glider movement is merely a cover for the development of a German Air Force in defiance of the Versailles Treaty. Cutting his holiday short, he returns hastily to England.

For some time Mitchell has secretly toyed with the idea of adapting the design of his Supermarine to give Britain the fastest and most formidable fighter in the world. Feverishly he goes to work, battling with technical prejudice and the limited budget imposed upon him by the industrial slump that is handicapping the country. Then comes the greatest blow of all. He falls ill, and thinking he is suffering from overwork, goes to see a specialist, who diagnoses an incurable malady. Mitchell is given one year to live unless he takes a complete rest, but he unhesitatingly decides to sacrifice himself, and produces the prototype of the Spitfire, and sees all production difficulties swept away a month or two before he dies.

Crisp's narrative finishes as the fighter pilots are recalled to realities by the 'scramble' signal, and the film finishes with the roar and rattle of the Battle of Britain on September 15th, 1940, when 185 Luftwaffe aircraft met their doom in the summer skies.[23]

A strong thematic message was offered to audiences in *The First of the Few* concerning the nature of the country and the best and brightest it could produce. Having established his credentials as the quintessentially English sensitively-artistic-but-morally-strong intellectual hero in previous films, most recently *49th Parallel* and *Pimpernel Smith*, Leslie Howard wanted to portray Mitchell in a similar vein. Despite the fact that it was about an aircraft designer, and therefore by implication about technology and industry, *The First of the Few* – like many other wartime films – depicted Britain in idyllic 'Deep England' rural-rather-than-industrial terms. Mitchell was portrayed as an oft-misunderstood artistic genius rather than a simple technological wizard, his designs as works of art instead of merely the products of cumulative aeronautical experience. Very early on in the film, for instance, several pilots looking up into the sky at another squadron's aircraft agree that the Spitfire 'is an artistic job'. 'That's not surprising,' comments Crisp, 'it was designed by an artist.' Almost immediately thereafter, as Crisp begins his tale, inspiration for a new design philosophy is shown arising from Mitchell dreamily gazing at gulls in flight. At the end of the film, after the station commander has finished his story of Mitchell's career, the pilots, with Crisp in tow, scramble once again to engage an enemy formation. Dogfights ensue and, though there are losses, 'Hunter' squadron triumphs and the *Luftwaffe* raid is turned back. Victorious, Crisp pulls back the hood of his aircraft, looks heavenward, and delivers the last lines of the film: 'Mitch! They can't take the Spit, Mitch! They can't take 'em!' This is followed by a model shot of multiple Spitfires streaking upwards towards a setting sun. The iconic status of the Spitfire is thereby confirmed: it becomes a work of genius, the beautiful-but-deadly fighter that won the Battle of Britain for England.[24]

The opening five-minute section of the film, in which Howard, using a montage of maps and German footage and a voice-over approach, chronicles Hitler's path of conquest down to the summer of 1940. Howard then impersonates Lord Haw Haw delivering the latest statements of impending doom for England from various Nazi leaders. All this was clearly designed to be rather like a newsreel in both look and sound. (The quotes attributed to Hitler, Goebbels and Goering, even if true in spirit, were in fact made up.) The aerial and airfield sequences which follow and which, after the extended flashback covering Mitchell's career, serve to book-end the film, were also intended to impart a sense of documentary realism to the story. These scenes, which lettering on the screen indicates are taking place on 15 September 1940 (identified in the best-selling official pamphlet as 'The Greatest Day'), consist in large part of footage showing the pilots and aircraft of 118 Squadron engaging in staged-but-realistic-sounding conversation at RAF Ibsley. When an intelligence officer says to a pilot 'Hello, Bunny, how'd you get on?' and that pilot (Wing Commander C. F. 'Bunny' Currant) replies 'Got an 88. Had a crack at a Dornier' – to which the intelligence officer responds 'Good show, old chap, that's grand' – the tendency today is to view this exchange as slightly ridiculous. Yet as another of the 118 pilots shown chatting away, Squadron Leader P. I. 'Bill' Howard-Williams, noted many decades later, 'in our defence, it was the language of the day'. What was more, these scenes included a lot of exciting footage of real 118 Squadron Spitfires (renumbered as 501 Squadron planes) landing, taking off, and – mixed in with models and stock footage – engaging in mock but realistic-looking dogfights with enemy aircraft. The main part of *The First of the Few* that such scenes bracket, however, is much more conventional screen drama, almost all of it shot on sound stages. It is indeed during Crisp's recounting of Mitchell's career that serious dramatic licence was taken.[25]

To achieve what he was aiming for, the producer/director took liberties with the facts. To prevent the audience from becoming confused by a march-past of faces it was necessary to amalgamate the various test pilots with whom Mitchell had worked into the single character of Geoff Crisp. (Phonetically similar, if in few other ways, to one of the Spitfire's first real test pilots, Geoffrey Quill.) Similarly, in an age where such things were not spoken of in public, the fact that Mitchell had died of rectal cancer was, understandably, glossed over. His illness is never clearly defined on screen, mention of it being confined to phrases such as 'something's wrong' and, more prominently, dialogue implying that work-related fatigue was at the heart of the matter. It might also be argued that to ignore the role of the Hurricane was quite understandable in a picture about the designer of the Spitfire, a plane that the public had already fallen in love with in any case. Other changes, designed to help project the underlying theme that Howard was seeking to convey, were perhaps more at variance with reality. Howard could do nothing about the fact that he neither looked nor sounded much like Mitchell, despite claims made to the exhibitors that 'the likeness is astounding'; but it was his choice to play the designer of the Spitfire as something of a dreamer, despite the fact that those who knew Mitchell described him as an eminently practical man. 'In my opinion,' as Geoffrey Quill put it to Gordon Mitchell, the designer's son, in reference to the scene in which Mitch takes inspiration from watching birds in flight, 'the last thing your father would have done, if he had had any problem with his designs, would have been to hang around watching bloody seagulls.' The section of the film in which Mitchell and Crisp visit Germany and discover plans for an expansionist air force was also a complete fabrication designed to emphasise how significant work on the Spitfire would be. To meet the same goal, the process whereby the Air Ministry came to approve the design of the Spitfire was modified, leaving out completely Mitchell's first attempt to produce a fighter (the Type 224, a resounding failure) and wrongly suggesting that it was only the persistence of a visionary that got the Spitfire into production just in time to save the country. The relevant scenes, as Gordon Mitchell put it, are 'pure fiction'.[26]

The critics and public, however, knew nothing about any distortions or omissions. What principally interested those who went to the cinema – it would soon be ascertained that around 70 per cent of the population went to the pictures regularly or occasionally and 1,494,000,000 cinema tickets were sold in 1942 alone[27] – was whether or not *The First of the Few* was worth the price of admission.

Though a number of them did wonder how accurate Leslie Howard had been in portraying R. J. Mitchell, most reviewers assumed that the story was true. More importantly, virtually every section of the popular and trade press was bowled over by *First of the Few*.

The quality newspapers and periodicals were unusually effusive. 'The story of Mitchell's part in the Schneider Trophy series, with the victory at Venice an exciting climax,' Campbell Dixon, writing for the *Daily Telegraph*, enthused, 'is alone worth half a dozen ordinary flying pictures; and the dazzling triumph of the bird-like Spitfire, conceived by the sea as the gulls wheeled overhead, is still to come.' According to the *Manchester Guardian* it was 'sensitive, broad in scope and implication, and governed by a regard for perspective'. Writing for *The Spectator*, Edgar Anstey took note of the way in which Mitchell's masterpiece was handled. 'The hero of *The First of the Few* is the Spitfire,' he explained, 'and the film contrives to invest this shining creature with all the historical monumentalism of H.M.S. "Victory".'[28]

The critics working for metropolitan mass-circulation papers were equally impressed with *The First of the Few*. 'It's absorbing stuff,' the *News of the World* opined, 'well dialogued, spectacular, and brilliantly produced.' In the *Daily Express*, meanwhile, Howard's effort was hailed as 'a tremendous story' in which 'officers and men of the R.A.F. pep up the cast to actuality, and the result is a superb picture, inspiring and real'. A. T. Borthwick of the *News Chronicle* agreed that the 'flying sequences are brilliant and thrilling', but added that 'it is the human aspect that enchains one's interest throughout'. A few days earlier Jympson Harman had already advised readers of the *Evening News* that Howard's epic was 'not just another war picture, but an inspiring, exciting human story of British endeavour that catches your throat'. It simply was, according to the *Evening Standard*, 'a really fine film'.[29]

'Excellent' was also the verdict of *Picture Show* which ran a short story based on the plot of *The First of the Few*. 'It is quietly dramatic, never sensational, and holds you throughout by its strong sense of conviction and realistic characterisation,' agreed *Picturegoer*. The whole thing was indeed 'brilliantly conceived, superbly produced and directed' according to the *Monthly Film Bulletin*, the rather more staid organ of the British Film Institute. Even *Documentary News Letter*, which tended to look down on feature film drama and thought too much had been made of Mitchell the man at the expense of the Spitfire as a machine, admired the 'superb flying sequences covering the Battle of Britain'.[30]

Probably adding to the highly positive attitude to the film, albeit indirectly and coincidentally, was a decision within the Air Ministry to start officially commemorating the Battle of Britain. Though there was some opposition to the idea on the grounds that the war was still going on and that it might not be wise to praise a single command, the decision was taken in the summer of 1942 to commemorate the battle by declaring 15 September Battle of Britain Day. This meant, among other things, extensive press coverage of an arranged reunion between the former C.-in-C. Fighter Command and some of the pilots who had fought under him, various retrospective articles on the battle, and a five-minute film courtesy of the Crown Film Unit entitled *The Day That Saved the World*. Thanks to production delays, *The First of the Few* was going out on general distribution at just about the same time and, as already noted, it too drew people's attention to the date 15 September 1940.[31]

To-Day's Cinema had argued from the start that the film was 'assuredly destined for terrific box office triumph'. So too had Maurice Cowen in the pages of *Picturegoer* – 'I will stake my reputation as a picker of winners that *The First of the Few* will be one of the finest films ever made in our studios' – after a visit to Denham the previous November. Such predictions turned out to be fully justified as people flocked to see the film through the late summer and autumn of 1942. A survey of contributors to Mass-Observation conducted in November 1943, asking those involved to discuss their favourite films of the past year, indicated the positive response to *The First of the Few*. A fair number of the two hundred-odd respondents listed the film as the first-, second-, or third-best film they had seen in the previous twelve months. Indeed, its performance at the box office was sufficiently strong to make *The First of the Few* the overall top attraction of September and the number-one British attraction of 1942.[32]

Through its great success, *The First of the Few*, along with the best-selling Air Ministry pamphlet and subsequent short films and press articles commemorating the anniversary, helped form and define the nature of the Battle of Britain in the public mind. It was thought of as an epic contest, stretching from July to October but a distinct battle nonetheless, which reached its climax on 15 September 1940, and in which an inferior number of British pilots had defeated a numerically superior German aerial armada. This victory had been achieved by young devil-may-care RAF pilots, Churchill's 'Few', all flying, at least in the popular imagination, the Spitfire, already an icon.

This was a position that can only have been reinforced among those who, the following year, saw how the United States War Department treated the battle in the fourth documentary of the *Why We Fight* series developed by Frank Capra. *The Battle of Britain*, which ran for almost an hour, consisted of documentary footage, most of which was courtesy of the Ministry of Information, animated maps developed under contract by Walt Disney, a vivid narration – written principally by Eric Knight and delivered on screen mostly by Walter Houston – and a melodramatic musical score courtesy of Demitri Tiomkin. As the series title implied, the *Why We Fight* films – there were seven in all – were designed to give US military personnel an idea of the world situation and how it had come about. *The Battle of Britain* episode was meant to show American troops the nature and the significance of what had been achieved by the British three years earlier: that is, the way in which Britain had stopped Hitler from achieving 'world domination'. The various phases of the battle were reworked in comparison with the official account contained in the Air Ministry pamphlet but here, too, the climax of the aerial day fighting was fixed as 15 September 1940 ('an historic three-dimensional battle took place'). This was a day on which the machine that had defeated the *Luftwaffe* ('the British Spitfire had proved to be one of the deadliest weapons ever put in the hands of man') showed its full worth. *The Battle of Britain* not only dealt with the summer and autumn of 1940. It also dwelt at length on the way in which the people of Britain had taken everything that Hitler could throw at them right through the winter of 1940–41, ending with an actor repeating the now famous phrase 'Never has so much been owed by so many to so few'.[33]

Not surprisingly the Prime Minister, whom the narrator claims was 'chosen' by the British people to lead them, liked what he saw when shown the film. Though it was designed to be compulsory viewing for United States Army personnel, the Prime Minister decided that *The Battle of Britain* should also be shown in British cinemas. The British version would come complete with a specially filmed introduction in which Churchill himself would praise the film and its accuracy, adding: 'Things are said about what we have done and how we behaved, which we could never have said about ourselves'.[34]

This was true enough; even if a lot of the footage came from earlier British newsreels, documentaries – everything from *London Can Take It* to *Target for To-night* – and even *The Lion Has Wings*, the narration was most definitely Made in America. Film critics seemed to agree with the Prime Minister. *The Battle of Britain* 'put the whole heroic picture into its proper perspective', according to *The Times*. Various parts of the film 'blow Britain's trumpet in ways that would make the Ministry of Information blush' (*Daily Express*) and were 'almost embarrassing to an Englishman who never knew that his race had such sterling qualities' (*Monthly Film Bulletin*). Yet the *Daily Express* critic thought it no bad thing to have others tell the people of Britain just how much they had endured – 'If you didn't feel like a hero then, maybe you'll feel like one now'. The *Monthly Film Bulletin* added that *The Battle of Britain* 'is the best film tribute Britain has ever received from America and its makers are to be congratulated'. Campbell Dixon in the *Daily Telegraph* took note of the fact that the actual footage 'has practically all been used before', but 'so warm-hearted is the commentary, that one cannot help being gripped again, and moved, and grateful'. The general public, however, possibly because of limited distribution, was apparently less enthusiastic. *The Battle of Britain* did not figure among the successful films at the British box office in the last months of 1943 or the first months of 1944.[35]

As for full-length dramatic representations, it turned out that the spectacularly successful *The First of the Few* was also the last wartime feature dealing with the battle. Partly, of course, this may have been the result of the enormous success of the Leslie Howard feature, which ran for months. *The First of the Few* had, after all, given the public a dramatised version of events in which it clearly took great pride, combining as it did elements of 'Deep England' fantasy with documentary-style realism in showing how the iconic Spitfire had triumphed over the enemy. It might well have been difficult to imagine a film dealing with the Battle of Britain that would not have been compared and found wanting. There was, however, a further compelling reason not to make the attempt.

The press and public were willing to join with the RAF in celebrating the Battle of Britain down to the end of the war – especially on 15 September 1945 when the first great flypast over London took place in the wake of final victory over the Axis powers. From the middle war years onwards, however, cinema industry executives increasingly felt, as the conflict went on, that cinema-goers wanted something other than combat pictures. 'One special point that you want to get your audiences to realise', exhibitors were warned even in 1942, 'is that "The First of the Few" is NOT A WAR FILM.'[36] That was debatable but, in subsequent years, the anti-war film trend meant that, among other things, no further attempt was made to focus on the Battle of Britain until near the end. Even then, the coverage was rather limited and oblique at best. There was the brilliant but extremely brief sequence in Powell and Pressburger's mystical *A Canterbury Tale* of 1944 in which the image of a fluttering hawk *circa* 1344 changes into a diving 1940-vintage Spitfire. *The Way To the Stars*, a Two Cities film which appeared in the spring of 1945, did allude to a neglected aspect of the Battle of Britain: the costly efforts by RAF bombers to strike at the invasion barges being assembled in French ports. It also included a brief and somewhat misleading scene in which Hurricanes are shown to be operating from bomber fields for local defence in the summer of 1940. But in this film, the plot of which spanned the entire war, the battle was incidental to a story that, at its core, was about Anglo-American relations. What was more, the war itself was being treated, in elegiac fashion, as a part of history. *The First of the Few* remained, therefore, the definitive wartime feature dealing with the Battle of Britain. How the subject would be treated in the post-war era, under more relaxed censorship conditions, would only begin to be come clear ten years after *The First of the Few* had been made.[37]

Notes

1. Leslie Howard comment to reporter on the set of *The First of the Few*, *Picturegoer*, 29 November 1941, p. 5.
2. Mass-Observation, FR 491, England to Nolbandov, 13 November 1940, enclosing Memo from Mass Observation on the suggested A.T.P. Film *Battle for Britain* with probable reaction of cinema audiences, 13 November 1940. On ATP/Ealing see Charles Barr, *Ealing Studios*, third edition (Berkeley: University of California Press, 1989). Mass-Observation, which was left-wing-realist in orientation, may have been biased against the sort of war melodrama that the public sometimes found rather appealing. On successful Ealing war melodramas, such as *Convoy* (1940) and *Ships With Wings* (1941) see James Chapman, *The British at War: Cinema, State and Propaganda, 1939–1945* (London: I. B. Tauris, 1998), pp. 181–4; Jeffrey Richards, 'Wartime Cinema Audiences and the Class System: The case of *Ships With Wings* (1941)', *Historical Journal of Film, Radio and Television* 7 (1987), pp. 129–41. On Mass-Observation see Penelope Summerfield, 'Mass Observation: Social Research or Social Movement?', *Journal of Contemporary History* 20 (1985), pp. 439–51.

3. *Kinematograph Weekly*, 9 January 1941, p. 86; see Nicholas Wapshott, *The Man Between: A Biography of Carol Reed* (London: Chatto and Windus, 1990), p. 135; *Kinematograph Weekly*, 7 July 1941, p. 2; see also the Air Ministry's reluctance to allow the Ministry of Information to make a film about the Battle of Britain without Air Ministry oversight in National Archives [hereafter NA], AIR 2/5322, encl. 9A, note by ACAS(G), n/d. On *A Yank in the RAF* see Mark Glancy, *When Hollywood Loved Britain: The Hollywood 'British' Film 1939–45* (Manchester: Manchester University Press, 1999), pp. 117–21.
4. *Times Literary Supplement*, 5 April 1941, p. 158; see J. M. Spaight, *The Battle of Britain, 1940* (London: Geoffrey Bles, 1941), p. 4; see also *Times Literary Supplement*, 31 May 1941, p. 264. For a more jaundiced reaction to the pamphlet see Orwell diary, 8 April 1941, in Peter Davidson (ed.), *The Complete Works of George Orwell*, Volume Twelve (London: Secker and Warburg, 1998), pp. 467–8. On the success of the Battle of Britain pamphlet by Hilary St John Saunders, *The Battle of Britain, August – October 1940* (London: HMSO, 1941), see NA, AIR 41/9, Propaganda and Publicity, f. 43; NA, AIR 19/258, encl. 5B, 7A. On Air Ministry policy towards requests from film companies for RAF help see NA, AIR 41/9, ff. 26–9; H. Chevalier, 'Film Policy of the R.A.F.: Support for the British Producer', *Kinematograph Weekly*, 28 November 1940, p. 33; see also M. Balcon letter, *Kinematograph Weekly*, 7 November 1940, p. 1. On BBC feature programmes see Siân Nicolas, *The Echo of War: Home Front Propaganda and the Wartime BBC* (Manchester: Manchester University Press, 1996), p. 201. On the singularly powerful Spitfire sequence in *Ferry Pilot* see e.g. Clive Coultass, *Images for Battle: British Film and the Second World War, 1939–1945* (London: Associated University Presses, 1989), p. 60; *The Times*, 16 January 1942, p. 6. It was also no accident that a British Movietone News short presented by the Ministry of Information and entitled *Fighter Pilot* – for which the Air Ministry had given help – that came out in December 1940 and which up to a point can be considered the first retrospective on the battle, dealt with Spitfires rather than Hurricanes. See 'Fighter Pilot' on DVD *Spitfire: Frontline Fighter* (Imperial War Museum/DD Video, 2004); NA, AIR 20/2950, Directorate of Public Relations, Progress Report for the nine months ended 30 September, 1941, p. 4. On public pride in the Battle of Britain see e.g. NA, CAB 102/848, A People at War: Thought and Mood on the Home Front, p. 5. See also Jonathan Glancey, *Spitfire* (London: Atlantic, 2006), pp. 191–4. Children's war literature also celebrated the Spitfire: see John Edward Kuykendall, '"The Unknown War": Popular War Fiction for Juveniles and the Anglo-German Conflict, 1939–1945' (PhD Thesis: University of South Carolina, 2002), pp. 156–7.
5. British Film Institute library [hereafter BFI], *Dangerous Moonlight* pressbook.
6. BFI, *Dangerous Moonlight* pressbook; see NA, AIR 20/2950, Directorate of Public Relations, Progress Report for the nine months ended 30 September, 1941, p. 5; AIR 41/9, Propaganda and Publicity, f. 28.
7. *Daily Telegraph*, 18 August 1941, p. 3; *The Times*, 14 August 1941, p. 6; see also e.g. *Monthly Film Bulletin*, 31 August 1941, p. 97; *Daily Herald*, 12 September 1941, p. 2. On *Dangerous Moonlight* at the box-office see *Kinematograph Weekly*, 8 January 1942, p. 41; see also Guy Morgan, *Red Roses Every Night: An Account of London Cinemas Under Fire* (London: Quality, 1948), p. 71.
8. See Glancy, *Hollywood Loved Britain*, p. 121.
9. *To-Day's Cinema*, 8 October 1941, p. 10; *Monthly Film Bulletin*, 31 October 1941, p. 134; *Picture Show*, 31 January 1942, p. 10; *Manchester Guardian*, 2 December 1941, p. 6; see also *The Times*, 3 November 1941, p. 8; *Daily Telegraph*, 3

November 1941, p. 3. On the lack of impression at the box-office see *Kinematograph Weekly*, 8 January 1942, pp. 40–1, 14 January 1943, p. 47. A little footage of real Spitfires from 602 Squadron was also used in *Mrs Minever* (MGM, 1942), set in 1939–40 but dealing for the most part with civilian life.

10. See Glancy, *Hollywood Loved Britain*, pp. 117–22.

11. *The Times*, 29 December 1941, p. 2; *Daily Telegraph*, 29 December 1941, p. 3.

12. *To-Day's Cinema*, 24 October 1941, pp. 7–8; *Monthly Film Bulletin*, 30 November 1941, p. 156; see *Kinematograph Weekly*, 8 January 1942, p. 6; see also *Picture Show*, 14 February 1942, p. 8; Julian Poole, 'British Cinema Attendance in Wartime: Audience Preference at the Majestic, Macclesfield, 1939–1946', *Historical Journal of Film, Radio and Television* 7 (1987), p. 22; Morgan, *Red Roses*, p. 46.

13. *Monthly Film Bulletin*, 31 August 1942, p. 99; see Glancy, *Hollywood Loved Britain*, pp. 122–6.

14. *To-Day's Cinema*, 5 August 1942, p. 9; *Daily Telegraph*, 3 August 1942, p. 2; *The Times*, 3 August 1942, p. 8; see Glancy, *Hollywood Loved Britain*, p. 127; Poole, 'British Cinema Attendance', p. 22; *Kinematograph Weekly*, 14 January 1943, p. 47. On the reaction to the film of real Eagle Squadron pilots see Philip D. Caine, *Eagles of the RAF: The World War II Eagle Squadrons* (Honolulu: University Press of the Pacific, 2002), pp. 250–1.

15. On British critics thinking that films about fighters in the RAF ought to be made at home, see e.g. *Daily Telegraph*, 3 August 1942, p. 2; *Manchester Guardian*, 2 December 1941, p. 6.

16. 'The Aeroplane', *The Royal Air Force at War* (London: John Murray, 1941), pp. 17–18. On the origins of the Mitchell film see Ronald Howard, *In Search of My Father: A Portrait of Leslie Howard* (London: William Kimber, 1981), p. 105. On Spitfire Funds see Angus Calder, *The People's War: Britain 1939–1945* (London: Jonathan Cape, 1969), pp. 148–9. The prominence of Fighter Command is illustrated by the way in which in the first nine months of 1941 a total of 441 permits were issued for press and newsreel visits to RAF fighter stations for publicity purposes, far more than for the stations of any other RAF command. See NA, AIR 20/2950, Directorate of Public Relations, Progress Report for the nine months ended 30 September, 1941, p. 7.

17. *Kinematograph Weekly*, 5 December 1940, p. 23; see Howard, *In Search*, p. 105.

18. *Kinematograph Weekly*, 27 March 1941, p. 23; see also e.g. *Kinematograph Weekly*, 6 March 1941, p. 25, and 6 February 1941, inside cover promotion.

19. Imperial War Museum [hereafter IWM], 96/58/1, P. I. Howard-Williams papers, clipping from *Sunday Express*, 23 August 1942; see Howard, *In Search*, pp. 105–6.

20. 364 HC Deb. 5s, cols 1166–7; see *Kinematograph Weekly*, 16 January 1941, p. 39. On the words not having much impact at the time they were uttered see John Colville, *The Fringes of Power: Downing Street Diaries*, Volume One: *1939–October 1941* (London: Sceptre, 1987), p. 267. Churchill would later use the phrase to close the chapter in his war memoirs dealing with the Battle of Britain. See Winston S. Churchill, *The Second World War*, Volume Two: *Their Finest Hour* (Boston: Houghton Mifflin, 1949), p. 340.

21. IWM, 96/58/1, P. I. Howard-Williams papers, clipping from *Sunday Express*, 23 August 1942; see ibid., 'Filming "The First of the Few" ', as told by Peter Howard-Williams to his brother Jeremy; Howard, *In Search*, pp. 107–11; Graham Wallace, *R.A.F. Biggin Hill* (London: Putnam, 1957), p. 227; *Kinematograph Weekly*, 16 January 1941, p. 39, 18 September 1941, p. 17, 16 October 1941, p. 29; NA, AIR 41/9, f. 28.

22. See Adrian Brunel, *Nice Work: The Story of Thirty Years in British Film Production* (London: Forbes Robertson, 1949), pp. 190–2; Howard, *In Search*, pp. 108–9; Michael Kennedy, *Portrait of Walton* (Oxford: Oxford University Press, 1989), p. 117; Graham Lord, *Niv: The Authorized Biography of David Niven* (New York: Thomas Dunn, 2003), pp. 148–9. It appears that the journalist Charles Graves was at one point considered as a possible script collaborator as well. See Charles Graves, *Off the Record* (London: Hutchinson, 1942), pp. 195, 203. Derrick De Marney, who had appeared in both *Dangerous Moonlight* and *The Lion Has Wings*, would play the part of the squadron leader in charge of the RAF High Speed Flight in *First of the Few*.

23. BFI, *First of the Few* pressbook.

24. See e.g. Neil Rattigan, *This is England: British Film and the People's War, 1939–1945* (Madison, NJ: Farleigh Dickinson University Press, 2001), pp. 53–4, 58. On Leslie Howard as English intellectual hero see e.g. Anthony Aldgate and Jeffrey Richards, *Britain Can Take It: The British Cinema in the Second World War* second edition (Edinburgh: Edinburgh University Press, 1994), pp. 53–5. On the 'Deep England' tendency in general see e.g. Angus Calder, *The Myth of the Blitz* (London: Jonathan Cape, 1991), *passim*, ch. 9.

25. IWM, 96/58/1, P. I. Howard-Williams papers, 'Filming "The First of the Few" ', as told by Peter Howard-Williams to his brother Jeremy, p. 4. On the good time the pilots had while guests of the company see also Charles Graves, *Londoner's Life* (London: Hutchinson, 1942), p. 27.

26. Introduction by Dr Gordon Mitchell to DVD version of *The First of the Few* (Classic British Film Collection, 2002); audio interview of Geoffrey Quill by his daughter, 1996, track on DVD version of *The First of the Few* (Classic British Film Collection, 2002); BFI, *First of the Few* pressbook, 'Exploitation' column; see Gordon Mitchell, *R. J. Mitchell* (Olney, Bucks: Nelson and Saunders, 1986), ch. 33. On R. J. Mitchell's character and career see also the video biography *First of the Few: The True Story* (Doughty Group, 1997). Some of the gull footage came from *Conquest of the Air*.

27. H. E. Browning and A. A. Sorrell, 'Cinemas and Cinema-going in Great Britain', *Journal of the Royal Statistical Society* 117 Pt II (1954), p. 134; Wartime Social Survey, *The Cinema Audience: An Inquiry Made by the Wartime Social Survey for the Ministry of Information*, L. Moss and K. Box, new series no. 37b, 1943.

28. *The Spectator*, 28 August 1942, p. 194; *Manchester Guardian*, 6 October 1942, p. 3; *Daily Telegraph*, 24 August 1942, p. 2; see also e.g. *The Times*, 20 August 1942, p. 2.

29. *Evening Standard*, 22 August 1942, p. 6; *Evening News*, 21 August 1942, p. 2; *Daily Express*, 22 August 1942, p. 2; *News of the World*, 23 August 1942, p. 6.

30. *Documentary News Letter*, vol. 3, September 1942, p. 128; *Monthly Film Bulletin*, 30 September 1942, p. 111; *Picturegoer*, 3 September 1942, p. 5; *Picture Show*, 12 September 1942, pp. 3–7, 10.

31. See NA, AIR 20/4200; INF 6/345; *Daily Express*, 15 September 1942, p. 1; *Daily Telegraph*, 15 September 1942, p. 3; *Daily Herald*, 15 September 1942, pp. 1, 2; *The Times*, 15 September 1942, p. 2; *Manchester Guardian*, 15 September 1942, p. 3. Coverage extended to America, on which see e.g. University of South Carolina Newsfilm Library, RC 1869, 'RAF in Mass Review' section of 'News Events of the United Nations' (Movietone News, 1942).

32. *To-Day's Cinema*, 21 August 1942, p. 9; *Picturegoer*, 29 November 1941, p. 5; see *Kinematograph Weekly*, 14 January 1943, pp. 46–7; Jeffrey Richards and Dorothy Sheridan (eds), *Mass-Observation at the Movies* (London: Routledge and Kegan Paul, 1978), pp. 220–89; see also e.g. Poole, 'British Cinema

Attendance', p. 22; J. P. Mayer, *British Cinemas and their Audiences: Socio-logical Studies* (London: Dennis Dobson, 1948), p. 177.

33. On the *Why We Fight* series see Joseph McBride, *Frank Capra: The Catastrophe of Success* (New York: Simon and Schuster, 1992), pp. 453–501; David Culbert, ' "Why We Fight" ', in K. R. M. Short (ed.), *Film and Radio Propaganda in World War II* (London: Croom Helm, 1983), pp. 173–91; T. W. Bohn, 'An Historical and Descriptive Analysis of the "Why We Fight" series' (PhD thesis: University of Wisconsin, 1968).

34. Calder, *Myth*, pp. 246–48; see also *Manchester Guardian*, 22 September 1943, p. 4.

35. *Daily Telegraph*, 27 September 1943, p. 3; *Monthly Film Bulletin*, 31 October 1943, p. 112; *Daily Express*, 25 September 1943, p. 2. On the absence of much impression at the box office by *The Battle of Britain* see *Kinematograph Weekly*, 11 January 1945, p. 45, 13 January 1944, p. 52. On the comparative box-office weakness of critically acclaimed documentaries see e.g. *Kinematograph Weekly*, 11 January 1945, p. 90.

36. BFI, *First of the Few* pressbook, 'Exploitation'. Reg Whitley described the picture as 'a war film of distinction and all the better for having so few actual war scenes in it'. *Daily Mirror*, 21 August 1942, p. 7. On the belief that the critics and public were growing tired of war films see e.g. *Kinematograph Weekly*, 25 June 1942, p. 22; ibid., 2 July 1942, p. 17, 14 January 1943, p. 103, 3 June 1943, p. 10; *Daily Mirror*, 16 April 1943, p. 7; see also George H. Gallup (ed.), *The Gallup International Public Opinion Polls: Great Britain, 1937–1975* vol. 1 (New York: Random House, 1976), p. 81. RAF Public Relations were renowned for their superiority over the other services. See e.g. NA, ADM 1/19195, Report on history of Naval Information, 25 July 1945, p. 4; AIR 20/2950, undated memo, c. 1942, p. 1; Imperial War Museum Sound Archive 4579, Hugh St Clair Stewart TS, p. 64; Richard Hough, *One Boy's War* (London: Heinemann, 1975), p. 83. On press coverage of Battle of Britain day through the rest of the war see e.g. *Daily Telegraph*, 15 September 1943, p. 4, 15 September 1944, p. 4, 15 September 1945, pp. 2, 4; *Daily Herald*, 16 September 1944, p. 2, 17 September 1945, pp. 2, 3; *The Times*, 15 September 1943, p. 2, 16 September 1944, p. 2, 15 September 1945, pp. 4, 5; *Manchester Guardian*, 15 September 1945, p. 5. The RAF certainly took the associated parades with some seriousness. See e.g. J. R. D. Braham, *"Scramble!"* (London: Muller, 1961), pp. 201–2. There was also media coverage of the opening of a Battle of Britain memorial chapel at Biggin Hill in 1943. See e.g. relevant footage incorporated into *Aviation Heroes of World War II: The Battle of Britain* (Greenwich Workshop, 1990).

37. On *The Way to the Stars* see Aldgate and Richards, *Britain Can Take It*, ch. 12; see also Robert Murphy, *British Cinema and the Second World War* (London: Continuum, 2000), pp. 27, 29, 110–11, 147, 149–50, 161; Chapman, *British at War*, pp. 199–200. On *Canterbury Tale* see e.g. James Howard, *Michael Powell* (London: Batsford, 1996), pp. 46–50. The RAF Film Unit, it is worth noting, chose 15 September 1940 as the subject of its last wartime documentary in 'The Gen' series. See *Royal Air Force Victory* (IWM/DD Video, 1995). On the unit see Keith Buckman, 'The Royal Air Force Film Production Unit', *Historical Journal of Film, Radio and Television* 17 (1997), pp. 219–44.

FIGURE 4 Batchy (Humphrey Lestocq), Moon (Michael Denison) and Baird (John Gregson) relax in *Angels One Five* (Templar Productions, 1952).

BFI Stills, courtesy of Canal+ Image UK.

3

One for All: *Angels One Five* (1952)

We are making a story about people who fought in the Battle of Britain.

Co-producer John Gossage, June 1951[1]

Though there were relatively few British films about the war experience in the immediate aftermath of victory, the 1950s would prove to be the heyday of the British war picture. In the years after the war, those participants who had interesting experiences to relate and the means to do so were often either putting pen to paper or hiring writers to tell their stories. Many of the resulting works were sought after by a reading public eager to find out more about what had actually happened than had been possible under wartime news censorship restrictions. British film-makers in turn hoped to cash in on popular interest by bringing these stories and their fictionalised counterparts to the big screen; and did so with consistent success at the box office throughout the 1950s. Explanations for the success of these war films have varied over the years, ranging from nostalgia for a period of bygone national glory to a desire to reflect on what had, after all, been a huge and comparatively recent upheaval in people's lives. Whatever the reasons, there was no doubt that large numbers of cinema-goers were willing to pay to see war pictures of all kinds as long as they dealt with the British experience.[2]

Given the position it had already achieved during the war, and the way in which the Air Ministry continued to remind the public of what was being framed as the RAF's definitive wartime triumph – thanksgiving services, march-past parades, airfield open days and, of course, flypasts – each year on 15 September, it is hardly surprising that the Battle of Britain should have been viewed as one of the first war subjects seen as fit for feature film development in the 1950s.

Indeed, as early as June 1951, production had started on what was to become *Angels One Five*.[3]

The man who first broached the possibility of a film about the Finest Hour was Cecil Tenant who wanted to find a marketable project for two of the harder-up producers he represented, John Gossage and Derek Twist. 'Why don't you two boys form a company and make a film about the Battle of Britain?' he suggested one day. 'You were both in the R.A.F., weren't you?' With financial backing from their agent, Gossage and Twist formed Templar Productions and set about selling the idea of a drama that would focus on a new pilot – they already had Scots actor Richard Todd in mind – adjusting to life on a fighter station during the Battle of Britain. On the understanding that the film would be made on a relatively small budget with only limited outlay by the studio, Robert Clark, head of Associated British, gave what was initially titled *Battle of Britain* the green light.[4]

Gossage and Twist were by no means the only people involved in the production with links to the wartime Royal Air Force. Given that this was to be a picture on a subject that had an aura of sanctity about it – as the critic Paul Holt wrote in *Picturegoer* before shooting began, the film 'must not fail' on account of the emotional investment many people still had in the battle – a deliberate effort was made to involve as many other industry figures with links to the wartime RAF as possible. Though he was better known for his work in television, George More O'Ferrall happened to have served as an army liaison officer at Fighter Command HQ and was chosen to direct the picture. Some of the actors were also ex-RAF. Ronald Adam, who played an 11 Group controller, actually had been a sector controller at Hornchurch during the Battle of Britain. Cyril Raymond, who played a sector controller in a more in-depth reworking of the same role he had assumed in *First of the Few*, had been a real-life sector controller at Kenley. Better known as a radio comedian, Humphrey Lestocq found himself playing the kind of slightly fatuous Hurricane pilot he had been for real a decade earlier.[5]

Given all this, it seemed clear that the picture promised to be the kind of story that could 'be expected to enhance the prestige of the Service' and also might 'possess a recruiting value', so the Air Ministry was happy to offer assistance when asked. RAF Kenley, one of the most famous fighter stations of the battle and still operational, was made available to the production for location shooting, along with the original 11 Group operations room. Three members of the Women's Royal Air Force, who could convincingly play operations-room WAAFs, were allowed to participate in the film. The last Hurricane in RAF service, normally flown only for the Battle of Britain Day fly-past over London, was also made available, as was a specimen preserved by the manufacturer, now the Hawker Siddley Group. A pair of aircraft, of course, cannot simulate an entire squadron. Luckily for Gossage and Twist, the Portuguese air service was just about to phase out its Hurricanes and, when five Portuguese planes paid a goodwill visit to England in the spring of 1951, the producers were able to persuade the Portuguese government to leave these aircraft at Kenley for the duration of filming. An assortment of other aircraft, including a Harvard trainer and a Spitfire, as well as everything from fuel bowsers to operations-room headsets, rounded out the period equipment assembled for the film.[6]

As for the screenplay, written by Twist, it was based on an original story solicited from Pelham Groom, a hard-up author who had penned a substantial series of tales of adventure in aviation who also happened to be an ex-group captain in the RAF and served as technical adviser on the film. By the time Twist had finished with it, however, the plot and dialogue had become rather more mature and reflective than the Biggles-style stories commonly associated with its original author.[7]

Though the producers had managed to assemble a handful of airworthy Hurricanes, they knew that this would not be enough to stage a battle epic, which may have been why *Battle of Britain* was dropped as a title. When film reviewer Paul Holt asked Gossage what sort of film he was making, the co-producer stressed that the emphasis would be on people rather than on machines, going on to emphasise the very small number of Hurricanes with which Templar had to work. This was to be an ensemble piece involving half-a-dozen major, and a dozen more minor, characters interacting during the summer of 1940 on and above a fictional sector station, 'RAF Neethly', undergoing trials and tribulations similar to those experienced at Kenley and Biggin Hill during the actual Battle of Britain: a growing number of calls to action, losses in the air, and enemy bombing attacks on the airfield and its operations room. Though there would be a certain amount of personality conflict involved, every character would demonstrate the characteristics commonly associated with the battle, above all understated bravery and stoic endurance.[8]

Once the title *Battle of Britain* had been abandoned, various alternative titles were bandied about. *Hawks in the Sun* was adopted and then discarded because it made the film sound like a desert war picture. *Angels Fifteen*, the code phrase for flying at fifteen thousand feet, doubtless sounded better insofar as it suggested communication between the ground and air rather than just aerial exploits. But this was eventually changed to *Angels One Five* which presumably eliminated any fears that potential audiences would think the film had something to do with rugby.[9]

Twist, meanwhile, had completed the screenplay that would be filmed. After the radar network – omitted from *The Lion Has Wings* and *First of the Few* for security reasons but public knowledge since the later stages of the war[10] – and ground control system are explained through a montage sequence, the plot of *Angels One Five* gets underway. Amid a scramble from RAF Neethly in July 1940 newly minted and terribly keen RAF Volunteer Reserve pilot and former Scottish medical student Pilot Officer T. B. Baird (John Gregson who was parachuted in when it became clear that Richard Todd was already committed to another film)[11] is introduced. Baird is under orders to deliver himself and a new Hurricane to Neethly but he crashes on landing while trying to avoid a battle-damaged aircraft skidding across his path, and is slightly injured.

The rather priggish Baird, nicknamed 'Sceptic' by happy-go-lucky Flight Lieutenant 'Batchy' Salter (Humphrey Lestocq), is disappointed to learn that he will not be allowed to commence flying with 'Pimpernel' squadron immediately but will instead serve in the operations room under the experienced eye of Squadron Leader Peter Moon (Michael Denison).[12] When the unhappy Baird tries to argue the toss with the fair but occasionally volatile station commander, Group Captain 'Tiger' Small (Jack Hawkins),[13] his superior lays down the law:

> Understand this, Baird. I'm not in the least interested in whether you get shot down or not. All I'm interested in is the efficiency of the squadrons under my command. A squadron is a team. Each member must have complete confidence in every other member in attack or defence. It takes quite a time to build such a team. And I'm not going to jeopardise one of the finest squadrons in Fighter Command just so that you can poop off your guns. Is that clear?

Baird is then introduced to the operations room by the avuncular Squadron Leader Barry Clinton (Cyril Raymond). And though the Pimpernel CO, Squadron Leader Bill Ponsford (Andrew Osborn), has made it clear he blames Baird for the loss of a badly needed replacement aircraft, other members of the squadron, led by Batchy, along with Clinton and his wife, Nadine (Dulcie Gray), whose cottage garden Baird ploughed into on his arrival, try their best to be friendly towards a new arrival who is both literally and figuratively stiff-necked.

Meanwhile, there have been a couple of scenes in which the station commander lays out to subordinates just how serious the position of the Royal Air Force really is as the Battle of Britain begins to hot up. Though Fighter Command has several strengths, above all 'radio location [RDF, better known as radar] and ground control', the odds are still six-to-one against the RAF in numerical terms. 'If he can flatten our fighter defences,' Small grimly reminds his operations room and squadron commanders, 'then all the rest of it is a piece of cake to him, invasion and all.'

Shortly thereafter the audience is led to infer that Ponsford is killed in action when he fails to return to finish his sherry after Pimpernel is scrambled during a mess party, and Small makes Moon the new CO. A montage sequence shows the days turning into weeks with the ops room and the squadrons doing their job but the *Luftwaffe* coming back time after time. A scene in a pub indicates that other members of Pimpernel squadron are now no longer among the living, and that Fighter Command in general is feeling the strain. 'I'm not so worried about aircraft,' Small tells Moon after a sortie in which his Hurricane comes back full of holes, 'it's pilots we need so desperately.'

Baird, who has performed well in the ops room and warmed up to both the Clintons and Betty Carfax (Veronica Hurst), the sister of a pilot from another squadron, is declared to be ready to fly operationally by Small. While still in the operations room, however, Sceptic, like everyone else, sees that, because the fighter squadrons are occupied elsewhere, Neethly is about to be hit by an enemy raid. Before the bombs actually start to drop and explosions shatter vehicles, buildings, and the ops room itself, he rushes out to take off in a spare Hurricane, narrowly beating out Small who has had the same idea.

Finally able to do what he has waited to do for so long, the young Scots pilot engages and shoots down an Me 110 over the airfield. After inspecting the wreck, a happy Sceptic is lifted up and cheered

by his fellow fighter pilots: only to find himself confronted in the
dispersal hut by a seething Peter Moon.

> MOON: You come bursting in here, grinning all over your face. Did
> you report to intelligence?
> BAIRD: I'm sorry sir, in the excitement I must have forgotten.
> MOON: This is an operational squadron, not a flying circus. We've
> no time for personal jamborees.
> BAIRD: I realise that, sir.
> MOON: Perhaps you also realise that you left your radio on transmit
> the whole time you were in the air.
> BAIRD: I did sir?
> MOON: Yes you. The textbook pilot who knows all the answers.
> You jammed the channel so that Operations couldn't speak to
> any pilot on your frequency. Pilots returning from a gruelling
> action. Shot up. Short of juice. Not even knowing that their base
> had been bombed.

In a subsequent debriefing with 'Tiger' Small, a now very crest-
fallen Baird is forcibly reminded that, though he has scored a kill, he
is not yet a team player.

> I hope you've learned a lesson, Baird. Discipline and procedure are
> just as important as courage and skill. Every man and woman on
> this station has a part to play and a strict set of rules to play it by.
> Now I warned you before that we don't take kindly to people who
> break the team's rules. The others are all trying to help you do your
> job, and it's up to you to help them do theirs.

Small does, however, add that he understands why Baird acted so
impulsively, confessing to his own dash for the Hurricane and how 'I
lost my temper and grabbed hold of a Lewis gun and starting
pooping off at the Jerry planes.' This, however, was not the right
thing to have done – 'I'm a station commander, not an ack-ack
gunner!' – in light of the need by one and all not to let 'personal
feelings get the better of service training.'

A second montage sequence and another bombing raid on Neethly
indicate the battle continuing over the following days and weeks,
with the strain beginning to tell even more on all concerned. But
everyone still does his or her duty. As Small remarks in conversation
with Mrs Clinton: 'We keep going because . . . well, we've got to keep

going, isn't that it?' Late one afternoon, on the very day that Baird is going out on his first date with Betty Carfax, Pimpernel squadron is scrambled yet again and – in an extended sequence – Sceptic receives a bullet wound that slowly proves to be mortal despite the best efforts of Moon in the air and Small in ops to guide him down to a safe landing. The crash is not shown: instead, the audience gets the perspective of those in the operations room as Baird's voice grows weaker, culminating in a stiff-upper-lip farewell exchange between Sceptic and the 'Tiger'. The film ends with Mrs Clinton lighting the lamp in her ruined cottage to give returning pilots a fix, followed by a shot of the runway over which are superimposed the familiar words: 'Never in the field of human conflict was so much owed by so many to so few.'

From the perspective of the early twenty-first century, *Angels One Five*, with its highly restrained emotional content, focus on officers, and primitive model and travelling matte work, is clearly something of a period piece. When *Angels One Five* first appeared on cinema screens in the spring of 1952, however, the events it portrayed had happened only twelve years earlier, and all concerned had done their best to make it as authentic as possible. The premiere, significantly, was attended by a number of actual Battle of Britain pilots, including Al Deere, Bob Tuck, and Douglas Bader.[14]

Bader, who himself would be immortalised on screen within a few years, was pleasantly surprised. 'I went to the film with my tongue in my cheek', he explained. ' I came out amazed. I can't fault it in any detail. "Angels One Five" depicts life on any fighter station in the South of England during the Battle.' The film critics, however, were rather more divided in their opinion of the picture.[15]

Some reviewers thought *Angels One Five* fully lived up to its subject matter. 'An extremely well-directed and acted picture' was the verdict of the fan magazine *Picturegoer*:

> Every character from the Station C.O. to the lowliest mechanic helps you become absorbed in the activities of the airfield. You find yourself living among these men who are ready to give their all for squadron and country. The backgrounds of the operations room and other component parts of the air base add to this realism.

Picture Show also thought it excellent while, for the more sophisticated cineastes, there was also a strong endorsement of *Angels One Five* in the British Film Institute's *Monthly Film Bulletin*. Here the reviewer commented on how by concentrating on one particular squadron, a few combats and a handful of people out of such a vast canvas as the Battle of Britain, the makers of the film have achieved a great deal. Heroics have been avoided (the bombing of the station, for example), the human element is there, even if the accent is on boisterous good spirits and the impact of outside events is overshadowed.

All in all this was a truly 'worthwhile' film. For those in the film industry, the positive endorsement expressed in the pages of *Cinema* doubtless confirmed the sense that *Angels One Five* was well made and 'enjoyable dramatic entertainment.'[16]

Some of the mass circulation newspaper reviewers were also enthusiastic. 'I wish I had columns and columns to sing the praises of "Angels One Five"', Ewart Hodgson exclaimed in the *News of the World*: 'In its simple way it is an awe-inspiring picture. I came away from it a little misty-eyed and very proud that I belong to the same race as The Few who saved the world in the summer of 1940.' Jympson Harman, writing for the *Evening News* (which was to serialise the story-line),[17] agreed that 'this suspenseful, dignified tribute to "The Few"' was 'splendid entertainment', and that those responsible 'deserve our heartiest thanks'.[18]

Most critics, however, were rather less enthusiastic about *Angels One Five*. Those writing for the quality press were not slow to express their disappointment.

The *Guardian* reviewer thought that the plot was rather weak, and that the film lacked ambition: 'one day, surely, one of our great directors – say Carol Reed or David Lean – will take up this great, nostalgic, and deeply poignant subject and will turn it to fuller and more daring account'. The *Times* critic also thought the story lacking in depth, though suggesting in contrast to *The Guardian* that 'no fictional reconstruction can live up to the drama of the historical facts'. Patrick Gibbs, writing for the *Daily Telegraph*, added his voice to those who believed the story 'slender' and thought there was an excessive degree of understatement in the dialogue. Like the *Times* reviewer, Gibbs wondered if it was still too soon to try to tackle a subject as resonant as the Battle of Britain: 'it hangs now too uncertainly between memory and history'.[19]

The upmarket journals were equally unimpressed. In the pages of the *New Statesman* William Whitebait wrote that, in trying to be authentic, the makers of *Angels One Five* had produced a film that was essentially lifeless. 'The excitement and psychological tension that such a film should engender', he reflected, 'seem to have been whittled away by that passion for understatement which in the end rules out everything.' Virginia Graham of *The Spectator* also thought *Angels One Five* an oddly detached film, its stiff-upper-lip understatement allowing, in her view, for only two scenes of real drama: the bombing of the ops room and the death of Baird. As Eleanor Wintour put it in *Time and Tide*, the overall effect was 'deadening'.[20]

Many of the critics writing for more middlebrow papers were also dissatisfied with *Angels One Five*. Though the film was a 'worthy effort' in the eyes of Dick Richards, writing for the *Sunday Pictorial*, it nevertheless 'just fails to come off'. Milton Schulman of the *Evening Standard* damned the film with faint praise by labelling it 'a minor but sincere effort' that mimicked in form dozens of wartime British features, a point echoed more bluntly by Richard Winnington in the *News Chronicle*. In his review for the *Daily Herald*, Paul Holt also took note of the number of stiff upper lips, as did Leonard Mosley in the pages of the *Daily Express*. 'One big grumble', Mosley added: 'The Battle of Britain *was* won in the air. Couldn't we have seen more of the actual dogfights?' Not surprisingly Thomas Spencer of the communist *Daily Worker*, while acknowledging that *Angels One Five* was 'on the whole a decent and moving British tribute to the Battle of Britain fighter pilots', objected to the way in which the lower classes were parodied in the film.[21]

Luckily for the careers of those involved, the public tended to side with the reviewers who praised *Angels One Five*. Teamwork and a stiff upper lip were what people imagined had helped win the Battle of Britain, and Jack Hawkins and the rest of the cast played their roles with complete conviction and occasional subtlety. *Angels One Five* therefore did very well in terms of drawing in audiences. According to Josh Billings in his annual survey of the British box-office for *Kine Weekly*, the film had been 'an outstanding British effort that made a packet of money'.[22]

*   *   *

Within months of *Angels One Five* appearing on the big screen, thought was being given within the BBC to the first attempt to depict the Battle of Britain on the small screen. It would not be until the later 1950s and 1960s that television in Britain truly began to eclipse the cinema in terms of mass appeal. Nevertheless, spurred on by the example of the American documentary series, *Victory at Sea*, the BBC, with the help of the Air Ministry and other government departments, was determined to make the case for British airpower in a series of films that was eventually titled *War in the Air*. As was to be expected, one of the fifteen episodes was devoted to the Battle of Britain. Drawing heavily on wartime documentary footage, the second half-hour episode, *Battle for Britain*, was, in essence, a more restrained version of Capra's *Why We Fight* film on the same subject, with great emphasis being placed on the air battle of 15 September 1940. When the episode was aired in mid-November 1954, the television critics were not always kind. In the pages of *The Spectator*, John Metcalfe wrote that it was at best a 'limited success', while Reginald Pound, writing for *The Listener*, thought it succeeded only in 'reviving sentimental memories rather than in sharpening one's sense of recent history'. Some reviewers, though, including the radio critic of the *Manchester Guardian*, were more willing to accept a rehash of wartime documentaries and the moods they conveyed. According to the BBC audience research department the people agreed with those who liked *War in the Air*. When *Battle for Britain* was first broadcast almost 60 per cent of the viewing public, making up 17 per cent of the entire adult population, tuned in. A precedent had been set, though it would be some years before such a large-scale documentary series would be screened again on British television.[23]

Meanwhile, the Battle of Britain remained a likely, yet critically problematic, subject for big screen treatment. *Angels One Five* had received some rough handling from certain reviewers, many of whom seemed to think it either did not rise to the grandeur of its subject or go beyond the established stiff-upper-lip, we're-all-in-it-together tropes of the war years. This was a rather paradoxical position insofar as the film-makers involved had valiantly tried, within budget and equipment constraints, to be as faithful to the words, actions and, indeed, spirit of the Battle of Britain as possible. Some reviewers had considered the level of authenticity insufficient; others, in a way, too old-fashioned.

Whatever the truth of 1940, a new decade seemed in at least some minds to demand an angle of attack at variance with an ensemble approach now considered overdone. Within the film industry, war pictures continued to be lucrative. *Angels One Five* had made good money at the box-office, yet was still small enough in scale not to overshadow any further stab at the general subject matter made within the next few years. And, though few critics recognised it at the time, the next film in which the Battle of Britain played a key role would in certain respects be the polar opposite of *Angels One Five*.

Notes

1. *Picturegoer*, 23 June 1951, p. 8 (author emphasis).
2. For the most recent survey of the 1950s British war film phenomenon and what others have written about it see Robert Murphy, *British Cinema and the Second World War* (London: Continuum, 2000), ch. 8. See also, in reference to the appeal of the genre, Sue Harper and Vincent Porter, *British Cinema of the 1950s: The Decline of Deference* (Oxford: Oxford University Press, 2003), pp. 268–9. On the translation of war stories from book to film see John Ramsden, 'Refocusing "The People's War"': British War Films of the 1950s', *Journal of Contemporary History* 33 (1998), p. 36.
3. See *Picturegoer*, 23 June 1951, p. 8. On press coverage of 15 September in the latter 1940s see e.g. *Daily Express*, 16 September 1946, p. 3, 16 September 1949, p. 1; *Daily Telegraph*, 16 September 1946, pp. 1, 4, 15 September 1947, p. 5, 15 September 1948, p. 1, 16 September 1948, p. 1, 15 September 1949, p. 5, 16 September 1949, pp. 1, 8; *Daily Herald*, 16 September 1946, p. 3; *The Times*, 16 September 1946, pp. 2, 6, 15 September 1947, p. 2, 16 September 1946, pp. 2, 8, 22 September 1947, p. 8, 16 September 1948, p. 10, 19 September 1949, p. 2; *Manchester Guardian*, 16 September 1946, p. 5, 15 September 1947, p. 3, 16 September 1947, p. 6, 16 September 1948, p. 3, 15 September 1949, p. 4. On Air Ministry policy regarding the commemoration of the Battle of Britain into the post-war years see National Archives [hereafter NA], AIR 2/6557; AIR 16/672; MEPO 2/8651; AIR 2/12799; AIR 20/6441; AIR 2/7002; AIR 2/9875; AIR 20/7075; see also Jeremy A. Crang, 'Identifying "The Few": The Personalisation of a Military Elite', *War and Society* 24 (2005), pp. 13–18. That it was not just the RAF that was keen to commemorate the event is demonstrated by the decision by Southern Railways to introduce 'Battle of Britain'-class locomotives named after famous places, people and later squadrons associated with the battle. See NA, RAIL 1188/208; AN 157/218.
4. *Picturegoer*, 26 May 1951, p. 10.
5. Trevor Popple, 'Angels One Five', *After the Battle* 30 (1980), p. 11; *Picturegoer*, 23 June 1951, p. 8.
6. NA, AIR 2/12261, 1C, Notes of meeting on 23 December 1946 to consider the provision of RAF facilities in the making of commercial films, para. 2(a); see AIR 20/7400, loose minute, DOps(1) to DDO(A), 26 May 1951; *Picturegoer*, 23 June 1951, p. 8.
7. On Groom's involvement see *Picturegoer*, 26 May 1951, p. 10. For Pelham Groom stories featuring characters and units that bore the same names, if not always the same traits, as those in the screenplay – Moon (spelt Mohune), Batchy, Beeswax, Pimpernel, and so forth – see e.g. Pelham Groom, *What Are Your Angels Now?* (London: Jarrolds, 1943), ch. 1.
8. On the Gossage-Holt exchange see *Picturegoer*, 26 May 1951, p. 10. The similarities with Biggin Hill during the Battle of Britain – everything from the code word 'Sapper' to a frustrated officer blazing away with a Lewis

gun – can be found in Graham Wallace, *R.A.F. Biggin Hill* (London: Putnam, 1957), *passim*.

9. See Popple, 'Angels One Five', pp. 11–18.

10. See e.g. the 1944 *Daily Sketch* pieces on the Battle of Britain collected in Arthur Bryant, *The Battle of Britain* (Manchester: Grove, 1948), p. 20.

11. Though in his early thirties by this point, Gregson, in what was his first leading film role, played a man in his early twenties with amazing facility. On Gregson replacing Todd see *Picturegoer*, 26 May 1951, p. 10.

12. Denison found his role 'reasonable but not too exciting', and took exception to the way in which the part of his real-life wife, Dulcie Gray, was whittled down in order to reduce the length of the final cut. See Michael Denison, *Double Act* (London: Michael Joseph, 1985), pp. 24–5

13. This would turn out to be the first of many similar roles for Hawkins; something of a mixed blessing in the long run from his own perspective. See Jack Hawkins, *Anything for a Quiet Life* (London: Elm Tree, 1973), p. 94. 'Tiger' Small was apparently based on two real wartime station commanders, Group Captain Dick Brice (RAF Biggin Hill) and Group Captain Oliver Bryson (RAF Manston). See Ramsey, 'War Films', p. 11. There are also perhaps traces of Wing Commander Victor Beamish, on whom see Doug Stokes, *Wings Aflame: The Biography of Group Captain Victor Beamish* (Manchester: Crecy, 1988).

14. *Evening News*, 19 March 1952, p. 2.

15. Bader quoted by Ewart Hodgson in *News of the World*, 23 March 1952, p. 6. With regard to *Angels One Five* as one of the quintessential war films of the 1950s, it is worth noting that it was fairly recently presented as such in Stephen Poliakoff's complex, nostalgia-laden BBC television drama *Perfect Strangers* (first aired in May 2001): though, in point of fact, it resembles in many ways (except for the emphasis on middle-class officers to the relative exclusion of lower-class NCOs and other ranks, which was quite characteristic of war films in the decade in which it was made) the war features of the 1940s, with themes such as the need for co-operation and emotional restraint. As a reviewer for *Cinema* put it, 'The acting is a matter of unselfish teamwork rather than star performances.' *Cinema*, 5 March 1952, p. 9. On the war films of the 1950s see note 2.

16. *Cinema*, 5 March 1952, p. 9; *Monthly Film Bulletin*, May 1952, p. 63; *Picturegoer*, 5 April 1952, p. 16.

17. *Cinema*, 18 March 1952, p. 11.

18. *Evening News*, 20 March 1952, p. 2; *News of the World*, 23 March 1952, p. 6; see *Picture Show*, 2 August 1952, p. 10.

19. *Daily Telegraph*, 24 March 1952, p. 6; *The Times*, 21 March 1952, p. 2; *Manchester Guardian*, 22 March 1952, p. 3.

20. *Time and Tide*, 29 March 1952, p. 314; *The Spectator*, 21 March 1952, p. 366; *New Statesman*, 29 March 1952, p. 373.

21. *Daily Worker*, 22 March 1952, p. 2 [this was also a point made by Eleanor Wintour in *Time and Tide*, 29 March 1952, p. 314]; *Daily Express*, 21 March 1952, p. 6; *Daily Herald*, 21 March 1952, p. 4; see *News Chronicle*, 22 March 1952, p. 2. Though Spencer of the *Daily Worker* was well within his rights to critique the treatment of class present in *Angels One Five* and most other war films of the period, it is worth noting that, although officers predominate and the other-rank ground-crew characters are stereotypical in their lower-class accents and behaviour, Batchy does point out to Baird, albeit in passing, a sergeant pilot he admires – 'he's a jolly good type; he's got four [kills] already' – and that 'Tiger'

Small in a couple of scenes underlines the importance of good work by other
ranks ground personnel.
22. *Kinematograph Weekly*, 18 December 1952, p. 10. On audiences see Sue Harper
    and Vincent Porter, 'Cinema Audience Tastes in 1950s Britain', *Journal of
    Popular British Cinema*, 2 (1999), pp. 66–82.
23. BBC Written Archives Centre, R9/8/2, Audience Research: Television Weekly
    Summary, Week 47, 16 November 1954; *The Listener*, 16 December 1954, p. 1088;
    The Spectator, 19 November 1954, p. 610; see *Manchester Guardian*, 16 No-
    vember 1954, p. 5; *TV Mirror*, 6 November 1954, p. 8. On the making of *War in
    the Air* see BBC Written Archive, T6/301/1–2, T6/295–311.

FIGURE 5 Kenneth More as Douglas Bader in front of his 242
Squadron Hurricane.
BFI Stills, courtesy of London Features International plc.

4

All for One: *Reach for the Sky* (1956)

Rather good, old boy.
Douglas Bader, c. 1966[1]

As previously noted, stories about the Second World War were among the most bankable subjects for film-makers in the 1950s, particular subjects becoming especially attractive if they had already achieved success in print. This was certainly the case with *Reach for the Sky*, the authorised biography of the legless air ace, Douglas Bader, that had achieved best-seller status immediately after its initial publication in March 1954. Once developed into a feature film released in the summer of 1956, *Reach for the Sky* would show the Battle of Britain in a fashion superficially similar to, yet profoundly different from, the version on display in *Angels One Five*.[2]

Despite having lost both his legs in a pre-war flying accident, Bader had managed to force his way back into the air force when war came. Thereafter he had risen rapidly to command first a Hurricane squadron and then a multi-squadron fighter wing during the summer and autumn of 1940. By the following year, thanks to press interest in his remarkable struggle against adversity, he had become one of the most publicly recognised of the RAF fighter aces. Shot down in the summer of 1941, Bader had made himself a constant headache for the Germans as a prisoner of war before being liberated from Colditz Castle and given the task of leading the Battle of Britain Day fly-past over London on 15 September 1945.[3]

As related in the fast-paced *Reach for the Sky*, a hit both with book critics and book buyers (100,000 copies were sold at once and another 72,000 within the next few weeks), this was a tale with obvious commercial potential for the cinema. Quickest off the mark was independent producer Daniel Angel who, even before reading

the book, purchased the screen rights for £15,000. Having secured
financial support from the Rank organisation, which would distri-
bute the finished product, Angel turned to Lewis Gilbert – with
whom he had worked on two previous war pictures – to write and to
direct the film version of *Reach of the Sky*.[4]

The first problem Gilbert faced was condensing into a feature-
length script several hundred pages of text that spanned more than
thirty years and dealt with a large number of events and people. 'We
chose the high-spots and human incidents which lent themselves to
film reconstruction and rejected the rest', he explained. Events and
characters that were not left out entirely might still receive only
passing attention or undergo amalgamation. Thus, *Reach for the Sky*
as filmed leaves out childhood and adolescence entirely, skims over
the period after Bader learnt how to walk again and the outbreak of
the war, and pretty much ignores his years in captivity at Colditz
Castle. To take the prime instance of combining actual people,
'Johnny Sanderson' is based on Geoffrey Stephenson, an RAF contemporary of the lead character, but also at various junctures stands
in for other friends of Bader and serves the additional function of
narrator when big jumps in time occur. This sort of thing did not go
down well with Bader himself who eventually refused to attend the
premiere in protest against what he saw as the slighting of some of
those who had played important parts in his life. It is difficult,
though, to see what else could have been done. 'There was enough
material for four films' Gilbert explained in his own defence. Bader
eventually saw the film on television in the 1960s and admitted he
had liked it.[5]

As for casting, it was Richard Burton who was initially approached to play the part of Douglas Bader. If he had accepted,
the character on screen might have been rather more abrasive, and
thereby true to life, than was in fact the case. As it was, Burton
declined and the bluff-yet-sensitive Kenneth More, who had very
much wanted the part, was cast in the lead role. Others contracted to
play supporting roles included Muriel Pavlov – who had also fought
for the part – as Bader's wife. Holdovers from *Angels One Five*
included Ronald Adam, who was promoted to play Bader's superior,
Air Vice-Marshal Trafford Leigh-Mallory, along with Sam Kydd, now
an RAF warrant officer instead of a mess waiter.[6]

Sets and props proved a more daunting challenge. Bader's life was
about flying, not least in wartime, and for that a suitable airfield and
period aircraft would be necessary. The Air Ministry once again
allowed shooting to take place at RAF Kenley, which stood in for a

variety of locales ranging from Cranwell to Tangmere. By 1955, however, finding authentic and airworthy aeroplanes was even more of a problem than it had been when *Angels One Five* went into production a mere four years previously. The Shuttleworth Collection was able to provide a single Avro 504 trainer for the Cranwell days, while the Science Museum loaned out their Bristol Bulldog for the scenes in which, as a young fighter pilot, Bader ignores advice and crashes while doing low-level aerobatics in 1931. Full-size mock-ups of each were built for travelling-matte close-ups in the studio at Pinewood and to provide dressing background for outdoor scenes.[7]

Much more difficult to resolve was the problem of finding enough wartime aircraft to resemble a squadron of Hurricanes or Spitfires. By this point the only Hurricane in Britain in flying condition was the one that the RAF had lent for *Angels One Five*, an aircraft that, along with two unserviceable Hurricanes, was loaned out again for the making of *Reach for the Sky*. These, together with a full-size replica, some models, and a piece of footage borrowed from *Angels One Five*, would represent 242 Squadron during the Battle of Britain. As for Spitfires, which Bader had flown before he took command of 242 and while he was a wing leader in 1941, there were more of them still about but, unfortunately, those still in flying condition were of the Mark XVI variety, very different in appearance – four-bladed propellers and teardrop canopies, among other things, instead of three-bladed props and a canopy that backed into the fuselage – from the Marks I, II and V flown during the period in question. The RAF provided four airworthy Spitfires along with six others that were used for ground shots and cockpit close-ups. Unfortunately, the budget, though big by the standards of British films of the day, would not accommodate attempts to modify the appearance of the Spits beyond the paint scheme and markings; and even then, those in the know noticed some fairly basic mistakes.[8]

The air war, though, was not the only subject to be covered in the film. A good deal of screen time is given over to how Bader recovered from his flying accident and learned to walk again. In the opinion of Lewis Gilbert, some of these scenes were 'the best in the picture'.[9] Indeed, the central thread of the screenplay that Gilbert developed was the triumph over adversity achieved by a truly remarkable individual, as the synopsis accompanying the post-production script, very similar in outline to that provided to the press, makes clear:

For Douglas Bader, life is a challenge. And to each challenge he responds with the determination to succeed. As a rugger player,

cricketer, boxer he excels. In whatever he tackles he is determined
to be unbeaten. But above all else, he excels as a flyer. Within
weeks of his arrival at the Royal Air Force College, Cranwell,
cadet-pilot Bader has earned an accolade. 'His progress', reports
his instructor, 'is remarkable.' So remarkable, that before long he is
demonstrating his skill at the Hendon Air Display. He is a wizard
of the air. And among flyers, his reputation soars. But it brings
Bader to the biggest challenge of his life. At the Reading Aero Club
on December 14th, 1931, some high-spirited civilian pilots con-
gratulate him on his ace-performance at Hendon and challenge
him to give them a 'show'. Bader declines: for already, two pilots
have lost their lives through low-flying in Bulldog aeroplanes. But
the civilian pilots scoff. Their tone is sarcastic. 'These boys', says
one, 'only perform when there's a crowd.' Taunted, Bader gives
them their 'show'. He puts the aeroplane through dazzling aerobatics. And the Bulldog, overstrained, crashes. In hospital, Bader's
determination remains. The doctors expect him to die: he defies
them. They amputate first one leg, then the other. They expect
horror from the athlete-flyer: instead they find stoical determination to go on living . . . and flying. During convalescence, the
challenge grows. He will live normally, despite it all. With peg-leg
and crutches, he drives a car to the country. At a hotel, he flirts
with a waitress named Thelma. And he is determined that before
long he will dance with her. At Roehampton hospital, Bader is
fitted with his 'tin legs'. With ferocious tenacity he practices [sic]
walking with them. He endures pain, suffers exhaustion, in his
effort to walk unaided. He will do it, quickly, quickly. He will
dance with the girl he met in the country. And he will fly again. For
to Bader, living and flying are inseparable. He succeeds. Soon, he
dances with his girl. He drives a sports car, fast. At the Central
Flying School, he proves that a legless man can still fly with the
skill of an ace. And he marries Thelma. But there is bitter
disappointment for Bader. The regulations, the Air Ministry re-
grets, do not provide for a man without legs. And Bader is
grounded. The succeeding years are torment. In the offices of a
petroleum company he sits, day in, day out, 'flying a desk'. But
there is still the challenge of living and playing normally. Then –
war. This time, the regulations are forgotten. Eagerly, Bader flies
again. And still he has the same skill. He is as quick off the mark as
the next man. And in the air, he is a fighter with swift, cool
intelligence. A brilliant tactician. Fearless. Determined to be unbeaten. He wins promotion. He wins respect from men who do not

give it readily. He creates crack fighting units to blaze through the Battle of Britain. His tenacity never deserts him. Over France he is shot down. His 'tin legs' save him. As his blazing plane plunges to earth, his legs are trapped. He unstraps them – and bales out. And in German hands, his first thought is for escape. Once, he succeeds. And even when recaptured and sent to the escape-proof Colditz, his desire for freedom persists. When liberation finally comes, Bader's spirit is as tenacious as ever. He returns to his wife. But he is determined to have a 'last fling' at battle. The war ends before he gets his fling. He has responded to the challenge of life as no one thought possible. He has come through, triumphantly. On September 15th, 1945, 300 aircraft fly in triumph over London. And at their head, in a Battle of Britain Spitfire, flies Wing Commander Douglas Bader, DSO, DFC – the legless hero who was determined that nothing should beat him. The man who reached for the sky and made it his empire.[10]

At the same time, however, it is clear in synopsis, as in the film, that the Battle of Britain – or, more accurately, the role of Douglas Bader therein – is an important part of *Reach for the Sky*.

In this the film, over the course of about thirty minutes, follows the book quite closely. After having proved himself in the skies over Dunkirk, Bader is given command of 242 Squadron, a Hurricane unit composed mainly of Canadians suffering from low morale. In the weeks prior to the battle, Bader quickly wins their trust through a display of his own flying skill and a determination not to let anything stand in the way of turning the squadron into a first-class unit ready to face the looming *Luftwaffe* onslaught. Using his own instinct as much as direction from ground control, Bader goes into battle with his squadron and they collectively down twelve enemy aircraft. He is congratulated by Leigh-Mallory, but explains that he would have done better in command of three squadrons. The AOC 12 Group accepts his logic – 'if we'd had three times the number of aircraft we'd have shot down three times as many' – and Bader gets command of a wing. More action follows, along with various further suggestions by Bader to his superiors. 'Douglas's new tactics proved so successful that very soon he was leading a unique formation of five squadrons: this became known as the Duxford Wing', Sanderson narrates. 'His pilots looked on him as a superman, and his breezy confidence in the air was so reassuring to young pilots flying into battle for the first time.' Bader, it seemed, had been first among the few.[11]

Reach for the Sky was similar in many technical respects to the films that had come before that dealt with the Battle of Britain. The Air Ministry had provided necessary support, and monochrome rather than colour film stock had been used – no doubt partly because newsreel and other footage could thereby be used to supplement what was shot on location and at Pinewood. Furthermore, thanks to the fact that Brickhill and Gilbert knew Bader and had been in the RAF, the terminology and slang used by the central character ('old boy' at the end of every other sentence) as well as that of pilots and personnel had the ring of authenticity. The same things had been true of *First of the Few* and *Angels One Five*.

In thematic terms, however, *Reach for the Sky* was perhaps closer to *First of the Few* than it was to *Angels One Five*. As noted in the previous chapter, a central message conveyed in *Angels One Five* was the need for co-operation and teamwork, rather than individual heroics, to win the battle. In *Reach for the Sky* the opposite almost seems to be the case; success in battle coming through the efforts of a single inspiring figure rather than from bureaucratic group-think. Indeed, while *First of the Few* also focuses on a visionary battling against bureaucratic inertia, at least in this case the role of teamwork in the Battle of Britain itself is emphasised through the plotting table scenes and the number of different pilots briefly showcased at the start and near the end of the film. It is the squadron leader who more often than not tells the controller what to do in *Reach for the Sky* rather than the other way round as in *Angels One Five* and *First of the Few*. Radar is not even mentioned. If *Angels One Five* had been about The Few, *Reach for the Sky* was about The One.[12]

This was deliberate. The book on which the film was based had, after all, been a biography, and its author had stressed to the writer/director 'the importance of making the film the story of one man'. What was more, the way in which the battle was portrayed in *Reach for the Sky* was an accurate reflection of how Bader himself saw things. In later years there would be a good deal of debate about just how effective the 'big wing' approach had really been, some observers arguing that, in fact, Bader had done more harm than good because he disobeyed instructions and the wing took too long to get where it was needed. In the mid-1950s, though, there was no open controversy; and, indeed, it might even be argued that this more egocentric retelling of the Battle of Britain neatly reflected the apparent shift in values away from wartime communalism and toward individual consumerism that was taking place as the decade advanced.[13]

After *Reach for the Sky* first reached the big screen in July 1956 there were a few critics who judged it rather tepidly. John Gillet, who wrote for *Sight and Sound* as well as for the *Monthly Film Bulletin*, thought the film workmanlike but rather two-dimensional in its portrayal of Douglas Bader: 'it falls somewhat short of the complete portrait'. So, too, did Eleanor Wintour in the pages of *Tribune*, arguing that it was 'just another story of an R.A.F. hero' complete with 'dialogue that sounds like the echo of a hundred other films'. Perhaps predictably (but not without some justification) the reviewer for the communist *Daily Worker* zeroed in on the class dimension. 'Bader is built up as an egocentric superman bashing on through life with a set of rudimentary emotions', readers were told, 'while less gifted colleagues form an admiring chorus and lower orders radiate mute devotion.' Others found the writing rather facile and some of the scenes banal because of their similarity to other war films.[14]

Most reviews, though, were positive enough to verge on the ecstatic. *Reach for the Sky* was 'vividly exciting and deeply moving' (*Daily Herald*); an inspiring story 'told simply and well' (*Daily Telegraph*); an 'outstanding film' (*Manchester Guardian*); a 'complete success' (*News Chronicle*); 'entertainment of the choicest kind' (*News of the World*); and 'a film you must see' (*Sunday Express*). Though most critics concentrated their attention where Gilbert had intended, on Kenneth More and the way he portrayed his character, especially in hospital, a number also mentioned in passing the 'vivid and exciting scenes of air battles' (Milton Shulman) and how the Battle of Britain section 'conjures up the whole flavour of that brilliant summer' (Isabel Quigly). Not surprisingly the trade press thought they had a success on their hands. 'No exhibitor should on any account miss this one', advised *To-day's Cinema*. 'Stirring true-life, good direction, first-class acting and "U" certificate', as the reviews for showmen section of *Kinematograph Weekly* summed up the points of appeal in *Reach for the Sky*. The public agreed with those who liked the film, ticket sales making it the top box-office attraction in Britain for 1956 and a 'colossal money-maker' according to industry observer Josh Billings.[15]

*   *   *

While *Reach for the Sky* was in the process of dominating the big screen, the first effort at mounting a Battle of Britain drama for the small screen was coming to fruition. This was an adaptation of the widely admired 1942 autobiographical work *The Last Enemy*, in which Richard Hillary – killed in a flying accident in 1943 – reflected in depth on his experiences learning to fly, serving in an auxiliary air force squadron, going on operations, being shot down in flames on 3 September 1940, and the long and painful process of recovery from extensive burns to his hands and face. The ninety-minute teleplay version of *The Last Enemy* was the work of director Peter Graham Scott, working on behalf of Associated-Rediffusion, one of the new independent television (ITV) companies set up in the mid-1950s to offer an alternative to BBC television.[16]

Graham Scott was able to assemble a strong cast, including the relatively unknown Peter Murray to play Hillary himself, John Robinson as the famous plastic surgeon Archie McIndoe, and Patricia Discroll as Denise, the former fiancée of a dead friend with whom Hillary develops a bond. Though much of *The Last Enemy* would be shot on interior sets and broadcast live, a teleplay about a Battle of Britain fighter pilot, especially one who was shot down in flames, would lose out in terms of credibility if there were not exterior sequences showing the climactic dogfight. Footage from the war could flesh out the combat scenes but, for obvious reasons, this would not help with close-ups or indeed the necessary aerobatic shots. Once again the Air Ministry proved willing to help, lending a Spitfire and pilot for an afternoon of manoeuvring filmed from the ground, as well as a Spitfire fuselage for the scenes in which the camera would record Hillary trapped inside a flaming cockpit. 'We put a sheet of flameproof glass between Peter and a conflagration of oily rags,' remembered Graham Scott. 'He reacted with true terror until the heat became unbearable and he was forced to smash his way out.'[17]

After a number of other close calls involving an industrial dispute and the distinct possibility that the *Daily Express* would denounce the programme before it was aired (opining that commercial television was not a suitable venue for such a serious subject), *The Last Enemy* was broadcast more or less to schedule on the evening of 10 September 1956. Like *Reach for the Sky*, it was essentially a story of individual heroism – albeit of somewhat more self-critical kind than in the Bader story – rather than the collective effort, an outstanding example of 'the indestructibility of the human spirit', as the director later put it.[18]

The critics were duly impressed. 'Sixteen years rolled away last night when television recreated that terrible glorious first Battle of Britain week in the words of one of the immortal Few,' was how Robert Cannell of the *Daily Express* described *The Last Enemy*, going on to argue that it 'evoked for millions moving memories of the days when the blue skies above London were filled with battle and the nights shattered by bombs'. Philip Purser of the *Daily Mail* was just as effusive in his praise. 'The air battles were there, in brilliantly edited combat film, the surgical battle was there, and the spiritual battle was there,' he explained. The *News Chronicle* concurred, describing the play as 'a courageous attempt to capture the very spirit of the Battle of Britain pilot's view of life from a hospital bed'. Television viewers were also enthralled, 70 per cent of all households with sets in areas where ITV was broadcasting tuning in to *The Last Enemy* in preference to the alternative offered by the BBC.[19]

*   *   *

The Battle of Britain, it seemed, was still very much a part of popular consciousness, with *Reach for the Sky*, *The Last Enemy* and, of course, the official commemorative activities mounted each year to mark Battle of Britain week and its climax, Battle of Britain day, on 15 September. In the week prior to Battle of Britain day the Air Ministry mounted a display of period and contemporary aircraft, including examples of the *Luftwaffe* types that had been shot down in 1940; while, on the day itself through much of the 1950s, hundreds of RAF jets, along with the odd Spitfire and Hurricane, flew in formation low over London. Despite the passage of more than fifteen years it seemed as if the public would never grow tired of harking back to the Finest Hour.[20]

The emotional investment was certainly strong enough to generate some opposition to any German being allowed to share the limelight with The Few. The same year as *Reach for the Sky* and *The Last Enemy* appeared on screens, the Air Ministry, in order to pre-empt an outcry from the jingoistic Beaverbrook press, made sure that a *Luftwaffe* pilot, who had shot down twenty Allied planes during the war and was now serving on a NATO exchange with a Fighter Command squadron, did not participate in the Battle of Britain day fly-past. The director of *The One That Got Away*, a film based on the true story of a German pilot shot down 'at the height of the Battle of Britain', as the pressbook put it, but who subsequently escaped, which came out a year after *Reach for the Sky*, found himself under fire. 'There was lot of opposition to my making it;' Roy Ward Baker remembered: 'I was heavily criticised.'[21]

Yet even before the decade drew to a close there were signs that attitudes to the battle, as well as to how it should be remembered, were changing in some quarters. As early as 1956, the Foreign Office had been pressing for an end to the Horse Guards display because of fears that the *Luftwaffe* trophies would offend the West German government, and in 1960 it was quietly shelved. The following year, much to the fury of the *Daily Express*, the RAF fly-past was scaled back radically to a mere three fighters because of noise complaints and on the premise that 'the spectacular qualities' of the event 'must inevitably diminish with the advent of faster-type aircraft'. Fighter jets would return in reduced numbers for the rest of the decade and on into the 1960s, but the old triumphal mood was gone.[22]

As for the Spitfire and Hurricane that had traditionally led the way and were intended to continue to provide an overhead presence of a 'token nature', there was talk among the civil contingent at the Air Ministry of retiring these overaged planes as early as 1957 'because of the risk of engine failure and the adverse publicity which any untoward incident would create'. Though traditionalists demurred at the time, two years later even the Chief of Air Staff was admitting that:

It was becoming increasingly difficult to maintain the Hurricane and the Spitfire which traditionally led the Battle of Britain Fly-Past. Spare parts were increasingly difficult to obtain and it must be recognised that there would ultimately be a risk of one of the aircraft defaulting from flight because of technical trouble or having to leave the formation because of engine failure.

He added: 'The consequences of such an incident could be very serious.' In September 1959 the fly-past Spitfire did, indeed, develop engine trouble and the pilot was forced to belly-land on a cricket pitch near Bromley. Despite protests, and in line with a decision previously announced, the remaining aircraft of what was now the RAF Memorial Flight were dropped from future fly-pasts over London in the immediate future.[23]

The authorities and the press might still kick up a fuss when the established version of what had happened in 1940 was challenged, as Richard Collier found to his discomfort before and after his revisionist study of the evacuation of the British Expeditionary Force, *The Sands of Dunkirk*, appeared in 1961. Yet the passage of time and, in particular, the emergence of a generation of young men and women with no personal memory of the war, meant that, for many people, the Battle of Britain was really part of history rather than a collectively life-altering event. Moreover, the 1960s would turn into a decade of tumultuous social and cultural change within the United Kingdom, generating shifts in attitude that would in turn help produce rather more critical versions of the battle on screen. Just as *Angels One Five* had seemed in some eyes too old-fashioned for the age, so too the individualistic approach taken in *Reach for the Sky* would become a byword for dated ideas.[24]

Notes

1. Laddie Lucas, *Flying Colours: The Epic Story of Douglas Bader* (London: Hutchinson, 1981), p. 246.
2. On Bader accepting Brickhill, who had also been a wartime pilot and POW and successfully recreated the people and atmosphere of Stalag Luft III in *The Great Escape* (London: Collins, 1950) and of 617 Squadron in *The Dam Busters* (London: Collins, 1951), as the man to write his story see John Frayn Turner, *Douglas Bader: A Biography of the Legendary World War II Fighter Pilot* (Shrewsbury: Airlife, 2001 edn), pp. 154–5.
3. On press coverage of Bader during the war see Royal Air Force Museum, Department of Information Services, MF10027, Bader press clippings book; see also e.g. L. E. O. Charlton, *The Royal Air Force: From September 1939 to December 1940* (London: Hutchinson, 1941), p. 266.
4. Trevor Topple, 'Reach for the Sky', *After the Battle* 35 (1982), p. 39. On positive press reaction to Paul Brickhill's *Reach for the Sky: The Story of Douglas Bader* (London: Collins, 1954) and sales figures see advertisements in *The Times*, 18 March 1954, 13 May 1954, 9 June 1954. On Daniel Angel see Sue Harper and Vincent Porter, *British Cinema of the 1950s: The Decline of Deference* (Oxford: Oxford University Press, 2003), pp. 173–7.
5. Lewis Gilbert in *Films and Filming*, September 1956, p. 9. On Bader seeing the film on television see Turner, *Douglas Bader*, p. 158; Lucas, *Flying Colours*, p. 246. On Bader being upset see Lewis Gilbert in Brian McFarlane (ed.), *An Autobiography of British Cinema* (London: Methuen, 1997), pp. 221–22; Turner, *Douglas Bader*, pp. 157–8. On not attending the premiere see e.g. Leonard Mosley in the *Daily Express*, 5 July 1956.
6. Kenneth More, *More or Less* (London: Hodder and Stoughton, 1978), pp. 168–9; Muriel Pavlov in McFarlane, *Autobiography*, p. 452. It seems likely that Burton would have brought to the role the kind of edge he displayed in a Battle-of-Britain era fighter pilot cameo appearance in *The Longest Day* (Twentieth Century-Fox, 1962). At least one contemporary thought More came closer to replicating another Battle of Britain ace, Al Deere, than he did the abrasive Bader: see Richard C. Smith, *Al Deere: Wartime Fighter Pilot, Peacetime Commander: The Authorised Biography* (London: Grub Street, 2003), p. 122. On the darker side of Douglas Bader see National Sound Archive, *Secret Lives: Douglas Bader* (Twenty-Twenty Productions, 1996).
7. Popple, 'Reach for the Sky', pp. 40–3.
8. Ibid., pp. 44–7. The most curious mistake is the code lettering on the Hurricanes which was that of 501 Squadron – as seen in *First of the Few* – rather than LE, the correct code letters for 242 Squadron.

9. Lewis Gilbert in *Films and Filming*, September 1956, p. 9.
10. British Film Institute library [hereafter BFI], S14922, *Reach for the Sky* post-production script, pp. 1–2. See also BFI, *Reach for the Sky* pressbook. There are some errors in this account compared to the film and book. Bader in fact lost only one of his tin legs when his Spitfire went down, for instance, and it was not a Battle of Britain machine that he flew on 15 September 1945.
11. The scenes in question appear in reels nine to twelve (see BFI, S14922).
12. See Christine Geraghty, *British Cinema in the Fifties: Gender, Genre and the 'New Look'* (London: Routledge, 2000), pp. 184, 186, 189–90.
13. See e.g. Malcolm Smith, *Britain and 1940: History, Myth, and Popular Memory* (London: Routledge, 2000), pp. 115–16; see also Dominic Sandbrook, *Never Had It So Good: A History of Britain from Suez to the Beatles* (London: Little, Brown, 2005), ch. 4. On the big wing debate see e.g. John Terraine, *The Right of the Line: The Royal Air Force in the European War 1939–1945* (London: Hodder and Stoughton, 1985), pp. 194–205.
14. BFI, *Reach for the Sky* reviews on microfiche, *Daily Worker, Tribune, New Statesman, Time and Tide, Evening Standard*; *Monthly Film Bulletin*, July 1956, pp. 87–8; see also *Sight and Sound*, 26 (1956), pp. 97–8; *The Times*, 9 July 1956, p. 12.
15. On box-office performance see *Kinematograph Weekly*, 13 December 1956, p. 7; *Kinematograph Weekly*, 7 June 1956, p. 17; *To-day's Cinema*, 6 June 1956, p. 12; *The Spectator* (Isabel Quigley), 13 July 1956, p. 67; BFI, *Reach for the Sky* reviews on microfiche, *Sunday Express* (Milton Schulman), *News of the World, News Chronicle, Manchester Guardian* (Manchester edn); *Daily Telegraph*, 7 July 1956, p. 8; *Daily Herald*, 6 July 1956, p. 6.
16. Peter Graham Scott, *British Television: An Insider's History* (Jefferson, NC: McFarland, 2000), pp. 78–95; see Richard Hillary, *The Last Enemy* (London: Macmillan, 1942); see also David Ross, *Richard Hillary: The Definitive Biography of a Battle of Britain Fighter Pilot and Author of* The Last Enemy (London: Grub Street, 2000).
17. Graham Scott, *British Television*, pp. 85–6.
18. It should be noted that, though the focus was mostly on an individual hero, the screenplay that Graham Scott developed did include the book's semi-fictional ending, in which what Hillary has had to endure is meant to represent the suffering of the British people in general. Graham Scott, *British Television*, p. 78; see Hillary, *Last Enemy*, p. 212 ff.; Samuel Hynes, *The Soldiers' Tale: Bearing Witness to Modern War* (New York: Allen Lane, 1997), pp. 126–7.
19. Graham Scott, *British Television*, pp. 94–5.
20. On the fly-past see e.g. *Daily Telegraph*, 16 September 1953, pp. 5, 8, 16 September 1954, p. 7, 16 September 1955, p. 5. On the Horse Guards display see National Archives [hereafter NA], PREM 11/3087; see also AIR 8/2144, ACPC(58)1.
21. Roy Ward Baker in McFarlane, *Autobiography*, p. 51; BFI, *The One That Got Away* pressbook; see *After the Battle* 2 (1973), pp. 44–50; Roy Ward Baker, *The Director's Cut: A Memoir of 60 Years in Film and Television* (London: Reynolds and Hearn, 2000), p. 95; see also John Ramsden, *Don't Mention the War: The British and the Germans since 1890* (London: Little, Brown, 2006), ch. 8. On the *Luftwaffe* ace and fly-past incident see *Daily Express*, 15 September 1956, p. 1.
22. NA, AIR 2/13320, encl. 1A, extract from SC(56)25, 15 October 1956; see *Daily Express*, 16 September 1957, p. 5; PREM 11/3087.
23. For the CAS's comments see NA, AIR 2/15690, extract from SC 25/5/1959. For

the 'token nature' comment see AIR 2/15690, S4d to D of Ops (AT&O), 4 May 1959. On concerns about safety as early as 1957 among the civil contingent at the Air Ministry see AIR 2/13320, encl. 15A, extract from AC(57)17, 18 July 1957. On the crash and withdrawal from future fly-pasts see *The Times*, 21 September 1959, p. 10; *After the Battle* 4 (1974), p. 43.
24. See Richard Collier, *The Past is a Foreign Country: Scenes From a Life* (London: Allison and Busby, 1996), pp. 202–8.

FIGURE 6 Spitfire in trouble, *The Battle of Britain* (United Artists, 1969).
BFI Stills, courtesy of MGM.

5

The Big Picture:
The Battle of Britain (1969)

It must be equal to the occasion.
Marek Piotrowski,
Battle of Britain pilot, 1968[1]

In the years following *Reach for the Sky*, it was by no means clear that there would be at any time soon another big-screen film dealing with the Battle of Britain. This was not because its success deterred other film-makers from tackling some of the same subject matter; war films, after all, continued to make money into the first years of the next decade. Rather, a combination of cultural and demographic factors made a film less likely in the 1960s.

By the end of the 1950s it was increasingly obvious that watching television at home was supplanting going out to the cinema as a prime recreational habit for young and old in Britain. This, in turn, had led to serious shrinkage both in the number of operating cinemas and in film production within the United Kingdom. And, as the 1960s unfolded, what film output there was came as often as not to be financed by the more affluent American studios with an eye on the wider world market where the Battle of Britain did not resonate.[2]

The battle itself, what was more, was starting to fade into history. Twenty years on, a generation, whose members had no memories of the event, was starting to come of age. The war itself was something increasingly associated among teenagers with parents and their values and, while some youths helped perpetuate the national mythology surrounding the conflict through avid consumption of war-related items in bookstalls and on the screen, others sought to distance themselves from their parents by adopting different, often rebellious, styles and tastes up to and including attitudes towards 1940. Symptomatic of a shift towards a more jaundiced outlook was the send-up of The Few contained in the comedy sketch 'Aftermyth of

War', part of the hit satirical revue *Beyond the Fringe*, staged by four bright young men at the beginning of the 1960s. So, too, was the widely publicised sit-down rally staged by the youth-attracting Campaign for Nuclear disarmament in Trafalgar Square during the annual Battle of Britain service of thanks in Westminster Abbey on 17 September 1961.[3]

Even within the Air Ministry there were those who wondered if harking back to the Battle of Britain every year was really in the best interests of the RAF. In January 1960, for instance, the Permanent Under-Secretary of State for Air, Maurice Dean, had circulated a memorandum in which he had questioned the recruiting value of annual celebrations on the grounds that the Royal Air Force needed aircrew with very different skills and attitudes to the devil-may-care Fighter Boys of 1940. Commemorative events – everything from memorial services to staged fly pasts – were repeated annually each September through the first half of the 1960s, but on a reduced scale and with more emphasis on the contemporary RAF than on The Few. The possibility of an official Battle of Britain memorial was periodically raised but always allowed to fizzle out. And, by the time the twenty-fifth anniversary of the Battle of Britain rolled around, it was brand-new supersonic jets rather than long-retired piston-engined fighters that were most prominent both in the air and on the ground.[4]

The way in which both the battle and the war itself meant something different – or worse still nothing at all: 'at least half the world had forgotten it or had never even heard of it', one 1940–vintage pilot reflected on the situation by the late 1960s – to the younger generation was sometimes problematic for those who had actively participated and did not want what had for them been one of the defining experiences of their lives to be dismissed or forgotten. 'There must be many others who feel that 20 years ago is as yesterday', as journalist Drew Middleton put it. This was certainly true of Ben Fisz, an independent film producer who had flown with one of the Polish fighter squadrons in the RAF during the war. He had been struck by the way in which, by the 1960s, young people did not seem to recognise a Spitfire or a Hurricane when they saw one. There were 'countless children who had never heard of the Battle of Britain', as he put it to a fellow veteran flyer. Another project having fallen through, Fisz decided in the late summer of 1965 to try to organise a new film about the Battle of Britain.[5]

What he had in mind was something along the lines of *The Longest Day*, the sprawling 1962 epic in which the story of the D-Day landings had been told from the perspective of a wide range of characters drawn from both sides and speaking in their native tongues. Fisz believed he could pitch this idea successfully to the Rank Organisation, which had financed his previous film, because *The Longest Day* had made a mint at the box office, restored the fortunes of Twentieth Century–Fox, and made a lot of money for Rank as well. What was more, he soon discovered, Rank already owned the rights to a book that dealt with the Battle of Britain that could be used as source material – *The Thin Blue Line* by Charles Graves – and Fisz was quick to make initial contact with those he thought would be a good fit as writer and director for such a task. Freddy Thomas, head of the production division at Rank, expressed cautious enthusiasm for the idea of a wide-screen colour epic on the battle and, by mid-October 1965, the producer was confident that he had a commitment from the Ministry of Defence to supply period aircraft, that playwright Terrence Rattigan had agreed to write the script, and that veteran war-film director Lewis Gilbert had signed on to a picture that would be ready for release by September 1967.[6]

Then complications set in. Towards the end of 1965, it emerged that the New York agent representing Rattigan wanted a much larger fee for his client than the producer had envisioned, and that the playwright was already involved in other projects to the point where it would be impossible for him to finish a Battle of Britain script by the intended deadline (March 1966). Freddy Thomas, meanwhile, perhaps worried that an independent producer could not handle such a big and potentially expensive project (Fisz had already requested an advance of £5,000 to cover various costs he had incurred), wrote a letter indicating that, as Rank owned the rights to *The Thin Blue Line*, the film ought to be primarily a Rank production. 'You are trying to take over my project,' Fisz heatedly replied, and something of a deadlock ensued. Ever the optimist, Fisz nevertheless put a new scriptwriter, James Kennaway, to work on the project and sent Hamish Mahaddie, a specialist in the movie aviation business, in search of period aircraft.[7]

The project might still have come to nothing – Lewis Gilbert had to drop out because of the continuing delay – if it had not been for the intervention in May 1966 of another independent producer, Harry Saltzman. A comparative heavyweight in the film industry as a result of acting as co-producer with Cubby Broccoli on the first four immensely successful James Bond films, Saltzman was growing bored and looking for something new with which to grapple. Recognising that Saltzman possessed the clout necessary to assuage fears within Rank about committing a large amount of money to an independent film and also to raise the necessary extra cash, Fisz swallowed his pride and agreed to a co-production deal when Saltzman met him and said 'I would like to come in on The Battle of Britain'. With Saltzman in on the picture, Rank was eager to offer financial help, and it was Saltzman who brought in Guy Hamilton, with whom he had recently worked, as director.[8]

Unfortunately, the new deal with Rank fell through in September 1966 over the question of what percentage the organisation would get from overseas distribution of the film. Saltzman then turned to Paramount for backing and, by November, the press was announcing that an agreement had been reached. A change in the front office at Paramount, however, put the film in jeopardy yet again. The new studio chief found the script Kennaway had written 'awfully English' and wanted more American content. Saltzman, however, refused to make a film that would pretend the Yanks had led the way in the manner of Errol Flynn in Objective Burma, a 1944 Hollywood movie that had caused outrage when it was released in Britain. In March 1967 it was announced that Paramount was withdrawing the £3 million it had pledged to the production. Saltzman continued to pay the bills for some of the pre-production work being undertaken by Spitfire Productions, as the company was now known, but it was not until Saltzman convinced United Artists many weeks later to fill the funding hole left by the departure of Paramount that the future of the project, with an $8.5 million budget, was assured.[9]

Meanwhile, progress had been made on other fronts. To give it the necessary epic quality and distinguish it from early black-and-white films where only a few planes, wartime gun-camera footage, and rather uninspiring models had been used, Fisz wanted the Battle of Britain to be filmed in colour using large numbers of period aircraft. Thanks to intensive lobbying, the Ministry of Defence agreed at the end of 1966 to lend whatever vintage planes it still owned to Spitfire Productions for the duration of filming.[10]

Fisz had imagined this would be enough but it quickly became apparent to Mahaddie that twenty-odd Spitfires, three or four Hurricanes, and the odd example of a period German aircraft would not be sufficient. The majority of the planes were not in flying condition and most of the Spitfires were versions that did not closely resemble those that had flown in 1940. The same was true for the dozens of aircraft obtained by Mahaddie from civilian sources. This problem was solved by employing Simpson Aero Services, which specialised in maintaining vintage aircraft, to bring as many planes as possible back to flying or at least taxiing condition and to modify the late-model Spitfires so that they roughly resembled those of 1940. This was accomplished over the winter of 1966–67 at RAF Henlow by eliminating tear-drop canopies and cannon mountings, installing three-blade propellers in place of four-bladed propellers for static-shot scenes, and rounding out the wingtips and tailfins. Life-sized replicas, that could be used for set dressing, might be blown up on the ground or even, with the aid of a lawnmower-type engine, taxied, were built at Pinewood. Though only three Hurricanes proved airworthy, the production company eventually held over twenty Spitfires that could fly. The Ministry of Defence again helped by agreeing to allow serving RAF pilots to be trained to fly the restored fighters.[11]

Finding planes for the film's *Luftwaffe* presented additional problems. The RAF could provide only single examples of various German types, none of which was flyable. Plans to use a civilian Proctor aircraft modified to resemble a Stuka dive-bomber had to be abandoned because of air-stability problems. And, while it was possible to envision using one-eighth scale radio-controlled models for the dive-bombing sequences, the complete absence of full-scale aircraft which looked like the real thing in the air was unthinkable.[12]

Luckily it was ascertained that the Spanish air force still operated a fleet of over thirty Heinkel bombers dating from the 1940s that, though powered by British engines since the 1950s, otherwise closely resembled the He 111s that had flown against Britain in 1940. With Anglo-Spanish relations then at a low ebb over the Gibraltar question it was by no means certain that the Spanish air force would allow Spitfire Productions to use this bomber fleet but, with the support of Rolls Royce, the company which supplied the parts for the engines, the Franco government not only lent out the aircraft but also provided crews and fuel free of charge.[13]

Mahaddie was also able to purchase in Spain enough parts from recently retired and dismantled HA 1112 M1Ls – a modified version of the Messerchmitt 109 powered by a Rolls-Royce engine – to build a force of eighteen airworthy fighters that bore more than a passing resemblance to the Me 109Es that had escorted *Luftwaffe* bombers during the Battle of Britain. Another six HA 1112s were reassembled to the point where they could taxi, and four more airworthy machines bought by the American preservation group, the Confederate Air Force, were also made available alongside a Spitfire purchased in 1965. Arrangements were made to modify the HA 1112s to resemble the Me 109E more closely by clipping the wingtips, adding tailplane struts and fake gun mountings, and, for static ground scenes,

replacing four-bladed propellers with the three-blade variety. As
with the He 111s, it was agreed that the Me 109s would be serviced
and flown – except for the four now belonging to the Confederate Air
Force, which would be piloted by their owners – by Spanish air force
personnel. An American B-25 bomber, with its gun positions subsequently remodelled to maximise the view, was acquired for use as
an aerial camera ship.[14]

In Spain the authorities made available airfields at Tablada and El
Corpero outside Seville and assorted other locations, such as Huelva
(the beach of which would double for the sands of Dunkirk) and San
Sebastian (which would stand in for Berlin during a night raid). In
England, the Ministry of Defence lent Spitfire Productions not only
RAF Henlow (along with some RAF technicians) for the purposes of
collecting and modifying airframes but also the now inactive Battle
of Britain aerodromes at Hawkinge, Debden, North Weald, and most
importantly, Duxford, from which to fly and film ground scenes.
Arrangements were also made with the Greater London Council to
take advantage of the council's slum clearance plans to simulate the
Blitz by setting fire to and blowing up parts of certain East End
streets due for demolition along with a condemned warehouse in the
St Katherine's Dock area. London Transport, in turn, agreed to allow
Aldwych underground station, the terminus of a branch of the
Piccadilly Line, to be dressed for one night in 1940 fashion and
filled with extras seeking shelter from the bombing.[15]

Aircraft and locations, however, would count for nothing without
a script. James Kennaway who, among other accomplishments, had
written the screenplay for the successful film version of his novel
Tunes of Glory, originally conceived of the story covering the entire
battle, from the channel convoy attacks of July to the fighter-bomber
sorties of October, told largely through the experiences of three
fictional characters. These were to be a United States war correspondent, loosely based on Ed Morrow, a British intelligence officer
who would be an amalgam of various true-life civilian and RAF
figures, and an enemy reporter-photographer roughly modelled on
three real Germans. The overall goal, as Kennaway explained in a
letter addressed to the producers and director in October 1966, was
'the examination of the moral fibre of the British people'.[16]

In early November 1966, a first draft screenplay was passed on to
the film-makers and, for the next ten months, Hamilton worked with
Kennaway on improving the script. The producers and the director
had read a lot about, and talked to a large number of people involved
in, the Battle of Britain. And Hamilton, in particular, as he later put it

in interviews, aimed to 'destroy the myth' of the battle by showing 'it the way it was – really was, I mean, with real human beings flying those machines instead of starry-eyed knights of the air doing daring deeds to the sound of soulful music'. This meant a film in which bickering at the top plus everything from issues of class to fatigue, fear, hatred, and what it meant to be trapped in a burning cockpit, would be explored. The resulting script, however, was not to everyone's liking.[17]

To make sure the scenes involving the Germans were as accurate as possible, as well as to generate publicity for the project, Fisz had brought in former wartime *Luftwaffe* ace General Adolf Galland as a high-profile consultant on *The Battle of Britain*. In August 1967 he was shown a copy of the script as it had evolved thus far. Galland, who had been assured that the film would tell the story of the battle from both sides without prejudice, was infuriated by what he read. So too, apparently, were four other ex-*Luftwaffe* fighter pilots to whom he showed the script. To their minds, as he explained in a detailed reply sent in mid-September, what had been written was one sided, shallow and littered with inaccuracies. Among other things, he took strong exception to a sequence in which an RAF pilot is attacked while dangling from a parachute. All in all 'the film [script] has a strong anti-German tendency'. Kennaway and Hamilton were quite irritated by this missive but recognised that at least some of the points Galland had made might be valid. A subsequent threat to resign as consultant unless changes were made also had to be taken into account. 'I think we'd better take another look at that script', as Hamilton put it.[18]

Kennaway did his best to adapt the screenplay to take account of the points the ex-*Luftwaffe* general had made and, by November, a revised script had been developed and 'Dolfo' Galland was back on a first-name basis with 'Ben' Fisz. Unfortunately, it turned out that in smoothing one set of feathers the film-makers had ruffled another. One of the conditions of RAF participation in the making of the film was that the relevant public relations committee within the Ministry of Defence would have some say in how Fighter Command was portrayed. And, as Squadron Leader Sam Flood explained in a letter to Fisz in January 1968 with reference to the revised screenplay, the consensus was 'that in firming up the Luftwaffe image without a corresponding adjustment on the British side the overall impression of the RAF and British attitudes tends to be one of shoddy amateurism'.[19]

Harry Saltzman was keen to avoid a confrontation – 'don't let's stir up too many wasps' nests', as he told Hamilton on one occasion:

'We're relying on RAF co-operation, remember.' The director, however, who was by now firmly committed to a vision of the film in
which the harsh realities of the battle would be revealed, was
unwilling to yield to Ministry of Defence sensibilities. 'We don't
have to worry about the RAF,' he replied. 'They need our film more
than our film needs them.' In the end a compromise was hammered
out in which incidents for which plenty of documentation existed
were nevertheless dropped in order to keep the peace. Just as some of
the more objectionable sequences from the perspective of Galland
and his friends, such as an RAF pilot being attacked while hanging
from a parachute, were deleted from the final script or cut during
editing, so too were the most controversial scenes from the standpoint of the RAF, including one in which a German flying boat with
Red Cross markings is shot down.[20]

By the time shooting began in March 1968 the plot of The Battle of
Britain, which had been worked on not only by the director but also
for several months by a second screenwriter, Wilfred Greatorex, bore
almost no resemblance to what Kennaway had originally proposed.
The main factual source through successive drafts was a detailed
day-by-day account of the battle written by Derek Wood – who was
on hand during the actual shooting of the film – and Derek Dempster,
The Narrow Margin, first published in 1961, along with a small host
of technical and other advisers. On the German side there were two
other ex-Luftwaffe officers, Hans Brustellin and Franz Frodl, as well
as Galland. On the British side the substantial number of ex-RAF
types connected with the production included Battle of Britain
fighter pilots such as Tom Gleave, Bob Tuck, and Ginger Lacey,
along with former controller Ronald Adam, Claire Legge to represent
the Women's Auxiliary Air Force (WAAF), and Robert Wright,
personal assistant to Hugh Dowding during the late stages of the
battle.[21]

Quite apart from the difficulties encountered with Galland, Guy
Hamilton sometimes had mixed feelings about the advice constantly
offered by the experts. 'They mean well, I know,' he commented at the
time, 'but they have a tendency to talk terrible rubbish,' by which he
evidently meant nit-picking over details at the expense of the big
picture. When presented with something that he thought he could
use in reference to his desire to uncover previously hidden truths,
however, Hamilton paid attention. Robert Wright, for instance, was
co-operating with Dowding on a book about the role of the C.-in-C.
Fighter Command in the battle; and through Wright, as well as
through his own intervention and that of his former deputy, Keith

Park (who had commanded 11 Group), Dowding was able to help shape the screenplay in ways that favoured his policies and called into question the Big Wing tactics advocated by Trafford Leigh-Mallory of 12 Group. 'The hero of the *Battle of Britain* is the story itself', one press release suggested, adding: 'And one man, Lord Dowding'.[22]

As both the shooting script and the finished film make clear, however, *Battle of Britain* was by no means the Dowding Story in the manner that *Reach for the Sky* had been the Bader Story. Though the C.-in-C. Fighter Command was a central figure (a role that was supposed to go to Alec Guinness but, owing to delays and scheduling problems one that was played by Laurence Olivier), he was far from alone. Senior commanders on both sides – everyone from Goering (Hein Reiss) and Kesselring (Peter Hager) to Park (Trevor Howard instead of Rex Harrison, again due to delays and scheduling problems) and Leigh-Mallory (Patrick Wymark) – were featured to a greater or lesser extent.[23]

Moreover, while the three semi-fictional characters originally envisioned by Kennaway had fallen by the wayside, there were more than a dozen major and minor replacements by the time shooting began, especially on the British side. To allow more latitude for character and plot development, it had been decided that the squadrons, airfields and those who operated from them in *Battle of Britain* should not be directly identified with their real-life equivalents. It was quite obvious, nonetheless, that the bullish squadron leader identified only as 'Skipper' and played by Robert Shaw, was modelled on Sailor Malan, and that the part of the cigar-chomping *Major* Falke given to Manfred Reddeman was a version of none other than Dolfo Galland.[24]

Whether recognisable or not as based on particular individuals, there were on the British side alone major parts for Michael Caine (as Canfield, a well-to-do squadron leader), Christopher Plummer (playing Colin Harvey, an irascible Canadian squadron leader), Susannah York (as Harvey's independently minded WAAF wife, a part loosely modelled on Dame Felicity Peake), and Ian McShane (as an NCO pilot from the East End), as well as smaller roles for Kenneth More (this time as a rather stuffy station commander), Edward Fox (playing an upper-crust public-school educated pilot officer), Robert Flemying (11 Group's suave senior controller), Barry Foster (as the harassed commander of a Polish squadron), and – in a cameo appearance – Nigel Patrick (as a group captain briefing new controllers). There were also character roles for the likes of Nicholas Pennell (playing

'Simon', a frightened and under-trained Spitfire pilot), Myles Hoyle (as 'Peter', a young pilot who becomes a veteran in a matter of weeks) and James Cosmo (as 'Jamie', a Scottish pilot in a similar position), as well as several other young English actors.[25]

FIGURE 7 Heinkel bomber under attack in *The Battle of Britain* (United Artists, 1969).
BFI Stills, courtesy of MGM.

The finalised screenplay developed by early 1968 was lengthy and complex. It opened with sequences set on a temporary RAF airfield in France in the third week of May 1940, with Skipper and Harvey flying off with the remnants of their Hurricane squadrons just in time to escape strafing 109s. The scene then shifts to Whitehall, where Dowding makes the case that no more fighters should be sent as reinforcements to France if Britain's own defences are not to be fatally weakened. There follow shots of Dunkirk and the littered beaches after the evacuation, a BBC news announcer in voice-over repeating in truncated form Churchill's opinion that 'The Battle of France is over: the Battle of Britain is about to begin.' The title credits then appear against a background of line after line of German bombers being inspected on their newly acquired aerodromes in

France. This is followed by a scene set in Switzerland in which the British ambassador defiantly rejects the peace offer presented by the German ambassador on behalf of Hitler but privately admits to his wife that the British position has become very precarious: 'We're on our own. We've been playing for time. And it's running out!'[26]

The next sequences, in which the lack of training of newly minted RAF fighter pilots is emphasised as Skipper tries to teach a hapless Simon how to survive in the air, are specifically identified as taking place in June 1940. There follows an important scene in which the senior controller, played by Nigel Patrick (Group Captain 'Hope' in the script), briefs new controllers – including an officer who has obviously had plastic surgery on his face because of burns[27] – on how the air defence of Britain is organised. As the viewers learn, radar is 'the ace up our sleeve'. The *Luftwaffe* is then shown to be confident and eager to start the battle. This is in marked contrast to Dowding in the next scene as he forces a cheerful government minister to face up to the fact that 'our young men will have to shoot down their young men at a rate of four to one if we're to keep pace at all'. There follow some scenes establishing the less-than-harmonious relationship between Harvey and his wife, the death of an over-eager RAF pilot at the hands of Falke over the English Channel, and German preparations for invasion.

The next several sequences are identified as taking place on Eagle Day, the start of the full-scale *Luftwaffe* assault on Fighter Command, and involve dive-bomber attacks on radar stations along with the bombing of a sector airfield. Though a group of unescorted Stukas is interrupted in its task to great effect by Canfield's squadron, the sector station – where Maggie Harvey and the station commander played by Kenneth More suddenly have to come to terms with death and destruction – is badly mauled. Even before this sequence, Park opines: 'This is only the beginning – they won't stop now.' The truth of this is demonstrated in the next few scenes in which, apparently due to failure on the part of 12 Group, Skipper's squadron is caught on the ground during a bombing raid: several aircraft are shown blowing up while taxiing to try to take off and, once in the air, the luckless Simon is picked off by a 109 coming out of the sun. As the day comes to an end the 11 Group controller notes the damage done and wonders if the remaining planes ought to be pulled back north of the Thames, a suggestion to which Park replies: 'That is precisely what they want us to do.' As the personnel of the sector station where Maggie Harvey works try to pick up the pieces that evening, a BBC announcer explains that

Fighter Command has shot down forty-seven enemy aircraft in the course of the day.[28]

In the next scenes German intelligence is shown to be confident enough that half of Fighter Command has been wiped out for the *Luftwaffe* to launch an unescorted bomber raid from Norway against northern England. This is intercepted and broken up by Colin Harvey and his new squadron without loss but Dowding is shown to be preoccupied with the growing shortage of fighter pilots. That the RAF is in difficulties is demonstrated in scenes chronicling subsequent escorted bomber raids against 11 Group. German air-craft are shot down but so too are Spitfires after being bounced by 109s. Andy Moore, the flight-sergeant pilot played by Ian McShane, parachutes to safety in one dogfight but Canfield, the squadron leader played by Michael Caine, is killed along with others. The airfields are also left in a mess, including – in a scene strongly reminiscent of *Angels One Five* – the operations room of the sector station commanded by Kenneth More's Group Captain Baker. Park blames Leigh-Mallory of 12 Group for trying to assemble big wings instead of using squadrons to protect 11 Group airfields but Dowd-ing remains more concerned about the pilot shortage: 'we don't need a big wing, or a small wing, we need pilots: and a miracle'.

The miracle occurs when, as witnessed by the Harveys in a hotel room as they try to patch up their fractured relationship, an off-course Heinkel accidentally unloads its bombs on London, causing a retaliatory raid to be launched against Berlin by the RAF. This in turn prompts an enraged Hitler to announce that British cities are to be a prime *Luftwaffe* target. In the next scenes, which are shown to be taking place on 7 September 1940, Goering watches from the Pas de Calais as huge formations of bombers and fighters pass overhead towards London, and arrive unopposed because the RAF controllers believed they were once more aiming for the airfields. Flight Sergeant Moore witnesses the resulting inferno that evening while trying, but ultimately failing, to rescue his family from the East End. The following day a Polish squadron in training successfully attacks an enemy formation and is consequently made operational along with the other foreign squadrons. Park and Dowding, it emerges, though unable to do anything about night attacks, are pleased by the switch in enemy targeting by day: 11 Group airfields will have time to recover, the *Luftwaffe* will spend more time over England and will also come in range of 12 Group squadrons. 'Turning against London', Dowding reflects, 'could be the Germans' biggest blunder.'[29]

As the *Luftwaffe* prepares to renew its assault on the capital, the

Fighter Command sector and group controllers assemble a wing from 12 Group and squadrons from 11 Group to intercept: 'This should give them something to think about,' the 11 Group senior controller comments. German bomber losses are high, causing an angry Goering to order the *Luftwaffe* fighter pilots to fly closer to the bombers. Further combat leads Goering to demand a decisive conclusion from his commanders. The climax then comes in a series of sequences dealing with the big attacks on London of 15 September. Harvey bails out in the morning but, as his wife – who has by this time has seen what this means – is informed, he is seriously burned. In the afternoon a weary Peter, now a combat veteran, gives advice to two new pilots before leading them into the fray. As the second attack develops we hear the 11 Group controller and Park discuss the fact that all reserves have been committed, Park adding that this is what he has just told the Prime Minister (Churchill and his staff having just been shown looking down at the plot table in a brief long shot). There is almost no dialogue in the following air battle but, as evening draws on and Londoners take shelter in the tube from night bombing, the BBC announces that 165 enemy aircraft have been shot down that day. The Air Minister tells Dowding over the telephone that questions are being raised in America about the success claims being made by Fighter Command. 'If we're right,' Dowding replies, they'll give up. If we're wrong, they'll be in London within a week.'[30]

The following scenes, taking place the next morning, again contain very little dialogue. The plotting table at 11 Group HQ is empty. Pilots, now very tired and tense – in one case so much so that he vomits when the phone rings announcing tea rather than another scramble – sit and wait. 'They're late this morning, sir,' the senior controller reports. 'The bastards are up to something,' Park replies; at which point the scene switches to shots of German troops abandoning their preparations for invasion and of an infuriated Goering telling Kesselring and other *Luftwaffe* subordinates that they have betrayed him. Against the background of Dowding looking out from his garden at Bentley Priory, the end titles begin with Churchill's by now de rigueur 'Few' remarks. These are followed by a list of the numbers and nationalities of the Allied pilots who fought and were killed in the battle, plus the German loss total; only then do the extensive credits for the film begin to roll.[31]

Shooting such a complicated epic proved to be a headache for many of those concerned. Hamilton continued to have problems with some of the advisers: 'when you get experts,' the director reflected decades later, 'they sometimes become so tied up with their knowledge that they have no sense of proportion about the whole picture'. Galland ended up walking off the set because he objected to Kesselring being shown using the Nazi salute. Filming formations and mock dogfights in the air proved to be much more technically challenging and time consuming than anticipated; roughly 3,000 people were on the payroll at one time or another, and bad weather (in Spain and in England where most of the filming occurred) drove up costs even further. By the time the last exterior shots had been taken in September 1968, forty-two weeks had elapsed and expenditure had ballooned to over $13 million. Trouble continued to dog the production in later months, what with Kennaway dying suddenly of a heart attack while driving at the end of 1968 and bad publicity arising in the spring of 1969 from the decision to replace a musical score written by the world famous William Walton with one by the comparatively unknown Ron Goodwin.[32]

Still, as Hamilton worked with editor Bert Bates and others to complete the film through the summer of 1969, he could know for certain that he had got much of what he wanted. For the first time in a film dealing with the Battle of Britain, scenes on the ground had indicated high-level squabbling over tactics, included a major WAAF character, dealt with the German perspective, and demonstrated a broad range of emotions among the men who had fought in the skies – fright, fear, horror, despair, and anger had all featured – along with some degree of class tension in relations between Andy and Archie. The presence, albeit in the comparatively minor role of a junior controller, of ex-RAF pilot Bill Foxley, whose extensive injuries – the result of efforts to save his crew mates after a plane crash during the war – were still shockingly evident more than twenty years on, meant that audiences would have no choice about seeing what a serious burn victim looked like even after plastic surgery. As the director later emphasised, 'everything in the script was based on a character that we either met or knew about'. Yet, while endeavouring to 'tell it like it was' in the midst of a decade during which established views on practically everything were being challenged, Hamilton was not trying to denigrate those who had flown in 1940 or their achievement. While aiming to undermine the conventional pieties of earlier films about the nature of aerial combat and the battle itself, he still wanted to make sure that *Battle of Britain* was 'a tribute to The Few'. As the director put it at the time, his goal was 'to destroy the myth, only to create a greater myth, because it's a *fantastic* story'. Just as importantly, despite all the difficulties that had been encountered, a huge amount of often very good aerial footage had been shot that could be cut and spliced along with cockpit close-ups to make up the forty-odd minutes of screen time that would be devoted to combat in the air.[33]

Finally, after years of work and a good deal of press scrutiny, *Battle of Britain* was ready to be given its high-profile premiere at the Dominion Theatre in aid of the RAF Benevolent Fund on the evening of 15 September 1969. What would veterans, critics and, above all, the public make of this costly, 130–minute, full-colour, wide-screen effort to capture the essence of the battle, warts and all?[34]

By and large, the former pilots of Fighter Command, who had fought in the battle back in 1940, seem to have been impressed. Though inaccuracies could be, and were later, picked out – everything from the way aircraft broke up to the apparent humourlessness of RAF fliers – the reaction was genuinely positive in the wake of the premiere to which many veterans of the battle had been invited. 'I think we all relived the special moments of our wartime days that evening,' Dennis David later reflected. 'Obviously I'm biased,' Max Aitkin admitted at the time, 'but "The Battle of Britain" is the greatest film I have ever seen.' The film critics, however, as the reviews that appeared the next morning and on subsequent days indicated, were often rather less euphoric in their reactions. Though almost everyone thought Laurence Olivier had done a fine job portraying Dowding, there were deep splits over *Battle of Britain* as a piece of cinema.[35]

There were some critics who were wholly unreserved in their praise for the film or at least mostly positive. According to Cecil Wilson of the right-leaning *Daily Mail*, it was an 'epic tribute' with the right mix of strategic and tactical explication, good combat scenes, and 'some telling touches of comedy, drama and plain humanity'. At the other end of the political spectrum, John Gritten, the reviewer for the Communist *Morning Star*, generally concurred: 'On the whole a worthy tribute to The Few'. It was in several ways a 'stunning achievement' according to Margaret Hinxman of the *Sunday Telegraph*. Patrick Gibbs, writing for the *Sunday Times*, described it as 'a model of clear exposition and worthy of its subject', while Ernest Betts of *The People* called the film 'a wonderful reconstruction of "The Few" in action, with some awe-inspiring shots of aerial combat'. Though finding *Battle of Britain* uneven in places, Dick Richards labelled the film 'a fine job' in the pages of the *Daily Mirror*, while David Nathan of *The Sun* thought it 'honest' and 'sometimes brilliant'. As Ian Christie explained in the *Daily*

Express he had found it 'a rewarding experience at an historical level'.[36]

That, however, was part of the problem for those critics who thought that human drama had been sacrificed on the altar of the quest for authenticity. Though the combat scenes were 'breathtakingly filmed', Derek Prouse explained in the *Sunday Times*, with so many players involved, character development was sketchy at best. David Nathan of *The Sun*, Robert Ottaway of the *Daily Sketch*, Philip French of the *Financial Times* and Penelope Houston of *The Spectator* all agreed on this point. Houston added that even the impressive aerial sequences began to blend together after a time into 'a steady series of doomed spins' – a view also expressed by John Russell Taylor in *The Times*. Others were more forthright in their criticism. *Battle of Britain* was 'bitterly disappointing' according to Eric Rhode, writing for *The Listener*, a film full of stereotypes rather than real people – mere 'waxwork dummies' in the opinion of *New Statesman* reviewer Nicholas Graham. 'Compared with machines,' Madeleine Harmsworth argued in the *Sunday Mirror*, 'human beings have a raw deal.' Among the multiple characters there was nobody with whom the audience could identify. 'You simply don't care when anyone is killed,' Graham added.[37]

More pertinent, perhaps, for those involved was how *Battle of Britain* performed in terms of drawing in audiences. Given its high production costs, the film would have to be a hit worldwide for United Artists to recoup its investment. 'It's a lot of dough to have to get back before starting a profit,' *Variety* noted. Unfortunately by early October 1969 it was becoming clear that the box office takings were probably not going to be as high as everyone involved had hoped. Within the United Kingdom the ticket sales had grossed in the region of £198,413. In the rest of Europe combined the figure was around £435,552 while, in the United States – where reviews were also mixed – the picture had taken in only the equivalent of about £838,422 by late January 1970. As Fisz admitted many years later, *Battle of Britain* had not turned out to be the kind of hit required to make a profit, at least in the short term.[38]

With the advantage of hindsight, it seems evident that *Battle of Britain* did not quite work either as drama or, to a much lesser extent, as history. As critics pointed out, it was often difficult to keep track of the large cast of characters (especially when they were as often as not faces half hidden behind flying helmets and oxygen masks). And the novelty of the combat sequences – streets ahead of anything seen before on screen in relation to air fighting – could pale after a while. *Battle of Britain* helped boost the reputation of Dowding and, in general, did a fair job of explaining the general shape of the battle: no mean feat for a non-narrated screen drama lasting just over two hours trying to illustrate a multi-phase engagement that went on for several months. On the other hand, there were some omissions, such the first phase of the battle over the Channel, plus a large number of individually minor, but cumulatively notable, technical and other inaccuracies: nearly two hundred by one count. Some, such as the way in which late-model Spitfires and modified Me 109s had to double for those of 1940, the fact that He 111s represented the entire twin-engine German bomber fleet of several types, and the way Hurricanes seemed to be rarer than Spitfires on screen though the opposite had been true during the battle, were an inevitable consequence of having to make do with what vintage aircraft were available. Others, such as the contemporary hairstyles sported and idiom used by one or two of the younger cast members – very different from the haircuts and slang of twenty-five years earlier – might have been avoided.[39]

It should be borne in mind, however, that the film-makers were trying to make their product appealing to younger viewers who, as the director admitted, 'don't care a care a damn about the Battle of Britain as such', but might relate to characters who looked and sounded something like themselves. In the event, to judge by box-office takings, this strategy did not work. 'Present-day youth,' John Fairhall reported for the benefit of *Guardian* readers on the reactions he had met with while questioning audience members after the London premiere, 'needless to say, tended to by cynical.' Many of those born after the war, reaching young adulthood in the context of a strongly anti-war and anti-establishment counter-culture, were apparently not that interested in celebrating, to borrow from Wordsworth, 'far off things, and battles long ago'.[40]

In a sense the problem with *Battle of Britain* was that it tried to be too many things to too many people. On the one hand, those involved tried to break with the past by introducing elements more in tune with a time in which war-making was being widely condemned by the younger generations: individual fear, class barriers, command squabbles, and horrific wounds among them. On the other hand, *Battle of Britain* had still to be a celebration of The Few that earlier generations might go to see, a panoramic victory feature in colour utilising large numbers of period aircraft. As it turned out, there were not enough representatives of the latter segment of the population among those going to the cinema for *Battle of Britain* to succeed in light of its high cost. As for younger people, many were evidently not convinced that the film marked a real break from sanitised and *ipso facto* old-fashioned versions of the air war of the *Reach for the Sky* variety.[41]

*   *   *

Battle of Britain turned out to be not only the biggest but also the last dramatic effort in the twentieth century to represent the battle for cinema audiences. Lack of success at the box office doubtless had a deterrent effect. And, in any case, what remained of the British film industry was generally so weak through the following decades that something new on the summer of 1940, which would not come cheap if vintage aircraft were to be used, was not on the cards. Hence, though one of the last of the many 'Carry On' lowbrow-but-cheap film comedies, *Carry On England* (Peter Rogers/Rank, 1976), ostensibly dealt with the Battle of Britain, the plot centred on the misadventures of an anti-aircraft gun battery crew rather than The Few. As for Hollywood, Paramount's refusal to buy into the Fisz-Saltzman-Hamilton concept for the *Battle of Britain* had turned out to be correct in financial terms, and it would be very difficult in future to interest an American production company in such a British subject. Hence, director John Boorman found it next to impossible in the 1980s to get the financial and other backing necessary to make *Hope and Glory*, the film version of his wartime childhood experiences (which included a scene in which his alter ego watches a Spitfire shoot down an Me 109 during the Battle of Britain). Indeed, there were several points at which it seemed that what turned out in the end to be a hit would not get made at all. As with many other subjects, in future, any script dealing with the Battle of Britain seemed likely to involve the small rather than the big screen. What eventually emerged, almost two decades after the problematic *Battle of Britain* first appeared on screen, would look very different from what had gone before.[42]

Notes

1. Piotrowski (who, as well as having fought in the battle, was now working for the art department on the film) in conversation with Leonard Mosley. Leonard Mosley, *The Battle of Britain: The Making of a Film* (London: Weidenfeld and Nicolson, 1969), p. 146.

2. See Bill Baillieu and John Goodchild, *The British Film Business* (Chichester: John Wiley, 2002), pp. 88–9; Alexander Walker, *Hollywood, England: The British Film Industry in the Sixties* (London: Michael Joseph, 1974); John Spraos, *The Decline of the Cinema: An Economist's Report* (London: Allen and Unwin, 1962).
3. On the CND protest coverage see e.g. Jeremy Isaacs, *Look Me in the Eye: A Life in Television* (London: Little, Brown, 2005), pp. 46–7. On the youth appeal of CND see Frank Parkin, *Middle Class Radicalism: The Social Bases of the British Campaign for Nuclear Disarmament* (Manchester: Manchester University Press, 1968), p. 140 et al. On *Beyond the Fringe* see Alan Bennett, Peter Cook, Jonathan Miller, Dudley Moore, *Beyond the Fringe* (London: Souvenir, 1963); see also Humphrey Carpenter, *That Was Satire That Was: The Satire Boom of the 1960s* (London: Gollancz, 2000), pp. 113–14. On keeping war mythology going see Michael Paris, *Warrior Nation: Images of War in British Popular Culture* (London: Reaktion, 2000), ch. 7. On socio-cultural changes see Arthur Marwick, *The Sixties: Cultural Revolution in Britain, France. Italy and the United States, c. 1958–c. 1974* (Oxford: Oxford University Press, 1998).
4. On Lightnings and contemporary coverage see e.g. *Daily Express*, 16 September 1964, p. 7; *The Times*, 20 September 1965, p. 20, 15 September 1962, p. 6; National Archives [hereafter NA], AIR 8/2260, Souvenir booklet for 20th anniversary; AIR 8/2420, Battle of Britain 25th anniversary souvenir book; AIR 2/17151, encl. 83A, APS to VCAS. On the memorial question see CAB 21/3879; AIR 19/909; PREM 11/3525; UGC 7/209; AIR 20/12191. On the reduction in scale of events, e.g. open days at RAF stations, see AIR 8/2420, Annex to AFB(64)24, p. 1. See also, with reference to the low number of vintage aircraft maintained by the RAF at the start of the 1960s, Warren James Palmer, *Battle of Britain Memorial Flight* (Epsom: Ripping, 1996), p. 9; J. C. Scuts, 'The Battle of Britain Memorial Flight', *After the Battle*, 4 (1974), p. 43. For the PUS memo see NA, AIR 8/2144, Brief for CAS for AC meeting, 4 February 1960.
5. Dennis David, *My Autobiography* (London: Grub Street, 2000), p. 31; Drew Middleton, *The Sky Suspended: The Battle of Britain* (London: Secker and Warburg, 1960), p. 11; Peter Townsend, *Time and Chance: An Autobiography* (London: Collins, 1978), p. 307. Fisz claimed inspiration struck while watching a Spitfire and Hurricane practising for the 1965 fly-past and seeing the puzzlement of young observers: see Mosley, *Battle of Britain*, p. 15; British Film Institute library [hereafter BFI], *Battle of Britain* press material microfiche, S. Benjamin Fisz, 'A Dream of Battle', *Briefing One*. As vintage aircraft had not flown over London to commemorate the battle since 1959, however, it seems likely he was thinking of another time or place: see Robert J. Rudhall, *'Battle of Britain': The Movie* (Worcester: Ramrod, 2000), pp. 10–11. It should also be noted that the 1960s, despite the great upheavals that took place, was a decade in which the people of Britain were 'obsessed' by the past. Bernard Levin, *The Pendulum Years: Britain in the Sixties* (London: Pan, 1972), p. 417. It is possible that the decision to go ahead with *Battle of Britain* may have contributed to the decision not to proceed with a film version of *The Last Enemy* that London Films had been contemplating around the same time. See BFI, Special Collections, London Film Productions Collection, B/021. It should be noted that in the early 1960s the Battle of Britain and the war in general remained a staple subject of the *Commando* comic series aimed at adolescent boys. See e.g. *Achtung! The Ultimate Guide to Commando Comics* 1 (1999), pp. 22, 29, 3 (2001), p. 25.
6. Mosley, *Battle of Britain*, pp. 15–16; François Prins, 'Battle of Britain', *FlyPast* 98

(1989), p. 14. *The Thin Blue Line* (London: Hutchinson, 1941) was a fictionalised account, supported by the Air Ministry, of the training and first operations in 1940 of seven assorted RAF pilots designed to appeal to possible recruits still in school, the rights to which were bought by Rank. See Charles Graves, *Off the Record* (London: Hutchinson, 1942), pp. 36–207; Charles Graves, *Londoner's Life* (London: Hutchinson, 1942), p. 119. On *The Longest Day* – in which Richard Burton, playing Flying Officer David Campbell, an RAF fighter pilot of 1944 who fought in the Battle of Britain, utters the arresting phrase, 'the thing that's always worried me about being one of The Few is the way we keep on getting . . . fewer' – see Lawrence H. Suid, *Guts & Glory* new edn (Lexington, KY: University Press of Kentucky, 2002), pp. 168–87.

7. Mosley, *Battle of Britain*, pp. 17–18.
8. Ibid., pp. 19–21. On Saltzman and the Bond films see e.g. Walker, *Hollywood, England*, pp. 178–85.
9. Mosley, *Battle of Britain*, pp. 22–8, 48; *The Times*, 11 September 1969, p. 8; Trevor Royle, *James and Jim: A Biography of James Kennaway* (Edinburgh: Mainstream, 1983), pp. 201–2; *The Times*, 23 November 1966, p. 17, 11 March 1967, p. 10; see also Elaine Gallagher, *Candidly Caine* (London: Robson, 1990), p. 117.
10. Mosley, *Battle of Britain*, 39. On Air Ministry help see NA, AIR 2/18162, AIR 2/18163; see also AIR 2/16547.
11. Rudhall, '*Battle of Britain*', pp. 15–18, 21, 27; Mosley, *Battle of Britain*, pp. 45, 112; NA, AIR 2/18163, minute 1, DDE9(RAF) to DofE3(RAF), 23 February 1968, encl. 111/2, memo of 21 October 1968.
12. On not wanting to rely on models see Mosley, *Battle of Britain*, p. 40. On scale model work see Rudhall, '*Battle of Britain*', pp. 63–5. On the Proctor experiment see ibid., pp. 107–8, 126.
13. Rudhall, '*Battle of Britain*', pp. 20–1. Though most of the shooting of the He 111s took place in Spain, two were purchased from the Spanish government so that they could be used for additional shooting in Britain. Spanish air force pilots and mechanics were imported to fly both these aircraft and the Me 109s despite some quibbling by the Foreign Office because of the Gibraltar dispute (see NA, FCO 9/561).
14. On purchasing the HA 1112 parts see Mosley, *Battle of Britain*, pp. 41–5; Rudhall, '*Battle of Britain*', pp. 21–2. On the HA 1112 itself see e.g. Martin Caidin, *Me 109: Willy Messerschmitt's Peerless Fighter* (New York: Ballantine, 1968), pp. 158–9. On Confederate Air Force involvement in the film see Mosley, *Battle of Britain*, p. 63; *Battle for the Battle of Britain* (1969) attached Special Edition DVD version of *Battle of Britain* (MGM 2004); see also Nigel Moll, *Confederate Air Force* (Osceola, WI: Motorbooks, 1987), pp. 20, 59; Peter R. March, *Confederate Air Force* (Midland, TX: Confederate Air Force, 1997), pp. 45, 49. On the camera ship, dubbed the 'Psychedelic Monster' because of the odd-looking multicolour paint scheme used to allow the pilots of period aircraft to orient themselves to the camera plane, see Rudhall, '*Battle of Britain*', pp. 44–5; Mosley, *Battle of Britain*, pp. 75–81. A helicopter was also used.
15. Rudhall, '*Battle of Britain*', pp. 29, 32, 69–72; Mosley, *Battle of Britain*, ch. 9.
16. National Library of Scotland [hereafter NLS], Acc. 5440/23/4, Kennaway Papers, Kennaway to Saltzman, Fisz, Hamilton, 18 October 1966; see also Acc. 5440/23/4, Outline, 18 October 1966.
17. Mosley, *Battle of Britain*, p. 28–30 ['the way it really was']; Hamilton in *The Battle for the Battle of Britain*, 1969 television documentary, attached to *Battle of Britain* Special Edition DVD (MGM, 2004).

18. Mosley, *Battle of Britain*, pp. 30–4; NLS, Kennaway Papers, Acc. 5540/23/4, [Galland] Comments on the Script of 'The Battle of Britain'; see British Film Institute library [hereafter BFI], S8479, 'The Battle of Britain' Revised Draft Screenplay, 23 February 1967; NLS, Acc. 5540/23/4, Fisz to Galland, 18 September 1967, Kennaway to Saltzman, Fisz, Hamilton, 17 September 1967, Galland to Fisz, 2 October 1967.

19. NLS, Kennaway Papers, Acc. 5540/23/4, Flood to Fisz, 18 January 1968.

20. Hamilton-Saltzman exchange in Mosley, *Battle of Britain*, p. 65; see NA, AIR 2/ 18162, E133, minutes of meeting held on 8 November 1967, paras 1–2; BFI, S8479, pp. 93–4, 134, 138, 147 (compared to S1127).

21. BFI, *Battle of Britain* microfiche press material, *Briefing One* to *Briefing Five*; Imperial War Museum Sound Archive [hereafter IWMSA] 20486/6, J. R. C. Young. On *The Narrow Margin* see *After the Battle* 1 (1973), p. 50; Mosley, *Battle of Britain*, p. 119.

22. BFI, *Battle of Britain* medium pressbook, p. 10 (see also *Battle of Britain* small pressbook, 'The Story of the Film'; BFI), *Battle of Britain* microfiche press material, small pressbook, Hamilton comment; see Robert Wright, *Dowding and the Battle of Britain* (London: Macdonald, 1969), pp. 280–1; see also, with reference to Hamilton's desire to expose the plotting that went on against Dowding, Mosley, *Battle of Britain*, pp. 29, 64, 154–7. On reassuring Park and Dowding see ibid., pp. 157–69; Royal Air Force Museum, Department of Research and Information Services, Park Papers, X002–9394/003, Park to Howard, 22 July 1968; see also X002–9343/004, Park to Dowding, 22 July 1968. Though reassured that his and Dowding's perspective would be shown accurately, Park was not, in the end, entirely happy with how Trevor Howard portrayed him in the film. See BFI, Special Collections, Cinema (Granada TV, 1964–75) Collection, Trevor Howard (TX 21 February 1971), p. 5. It helped that, while Park and Dowding were still alive, Leigh-Mallory had been killed in an air crash in 1944.

23. Other senior figures portrayed in the film, albeit often in cameo appearances, included Air Vice Marshal D. C. S. Evill (Michael Redgrave), German ambassador to Switzerland, Baron Von Richter (Curt Jurgens), General Erhard Milch (Dietrich Frauboes), General Theo Osterkamp (Wilfred van Aacken), *Luftwaffe* chief of staff Hans Jeschonnek (Karl Otto Alberty), Under-Secretary of State for Air Sir Francis Stokes (Harry Andrews), the British ambassador to Switzerland, Sir David Kelly (Ralph Richardson), and the Secretary of State for Air, Sir Archibald Sinclair (Anthony Nicholls).

24. On Robert Shaw in a part written for, and shaped by him to resemble, Sailor Malan see BFI, S8479, *Battle of Britain* revised draft screenplay, p. 30; Mosley, *Battle of Britain*, pp. 60, 136. (There may have been some confusion in viewers' minds as to whether Shaw came closer to portraying Douglas Bader than he did Malan. See Karen Carmean and Georg Gaston, *Robert Shaw: More Than a Life* [Lanham, MD: Madison Books, 1994], p. 186.) On 'Falke' as Galland see David Baker, *Adolf Galland: The Authorised Biography* (London: Windrowe and Greene, 1996), p. 304; Mosley, *Battle of Britain*, p. 30. Maggie Harvey, played by Susannah York, was loosely based on Felicity Peake. See Hamilton in *A Film For the Few* featurette (MGM Home Entertainment, 2004) attached to *Battle of Britain* Special Edition DVD (MGM, 2004). The film also featured the recreation of a real incident involving New Zealander Al Deere. See David, *Autobiography*, p. 31.

25. On what it was like to be an actor on *Battle of Britain* see e.g. Michael Caine, *What's It All About? An Autobiography* (New York: Turtle Bay, 1992), pp. 290–2; Kenneth More, *More or Less* (London: Hodder and Stoughton,

1978), p. 215, and Mosley, *Battle of Britain*, pp. 173–81 on Susannah York. On York's character being based on Felicity Peake see Felicity Peake, *Pure Chance* (Shrewsbury: Airlife, 1993), p. 49. On the cast in general see BFI, *Battle of Britain* pressbook and briefings.

26. BFI, S1127, '*Battle of Britain*' domestic script.

27. Squadron Leader Tom Evans was played by Bill Foxley, whose face and hands had been seriously burned while trying to rescue fellow crew members from his Wellington bomber after it crashed and went up in flames during a training flight. See E. R. Mayhew, *The Reconstruction of Warriors: Archibald McIndoe, the Royal Air Force and the Guinea Pig Club* (London: Greenhill, 2004), p. 187.

28. Eagle Day, oddly, is identified in a subtitle as occurring on 10 August 1940. That was the day it was supposed to happen but, in fact, it was postponed until 13 August. The figure for the number of German planes shot down on Eagle Day was the correct one, as opposed to the much higher figure announced in 1940.

29. Though not identified as such, this initial attack on London is clearly meant to represent what happened on 7 September 1940. See Derek Wood and Derek Dempster, *The Narrow Margin: The Battle of Britain and the Rise of Air Power* (London: Hutchinson, 1961), pp. 334–9.

30. As was known secretly even during the war, RAF claims were in fact heavily exaggerated. On 15 September 185 enemy aircraft were claimed as destroyed, whereas the true figure was 65. The invented remarks attributed to Dowding were a way of dodging the issue. The scene in which the commitment of all reserves is discussed in the 11 Group operations room is based on what Churchill remembered of his visit there that day. See David Reynolds, *In Command of History: Churchill Fighting and Writing the Second World War* (London: Allen Lane, 2004), pp. 184–5. The difficult marriage of Maggie and Colin Harvey is the clearest imprint left by Kennaway (who wrote elsewhere about the tension and emotional cost of relationships) on the screenplay. See e.g. James Kennaway, *Household Ghosts* (London: Longman, 1961).

31. The daylight fighting in fact petered out more gradually through into October, though Sealion, the projected German invasion of Britain, was postponed indefinitely on 17 September. See Wood and Dempster, *Narrow Margin*, pp. 356–406.

32. Hamilton speaking on the commentary track for DVD Special Edition of *The Battle of Britain* (MGM, 2004). On the tiff with Galland see Mosley, *Battle of Britain*, pp. 105, 119–21. On the mess surrounding Walton, Goodwin and the musical score for the film see Michael Kennedy, *Portrait of Walton* (Oxford: Oxford University Press, 1989), pp. 237–40; Neil Turney, *William Walton* (London: Hale, 1984), p. 153. On the death of Kennaway see Royle, *James and Jim*, pp. 207–8. On the budget and ballooning costs see Mosley, *Battle of Britain*, pp. 48, 49, 91, 117, 172, 182, 195. On the length of the shoot and the vast number of people employed – everyone from crowd scene extras to model builders – see BFI, *Battle of Britain* pressbook (small). On the weather, the flying and the budget see e.g. Freddie Young, *Seventy Light Years: An Autobiography* (London: Faber and Faber, 1999), p. 123; Bernard Williams and Gareth Thomas in *Authenticity in the Air* featurette (MGM Home Entertainment 2004) attached to DVD Special Edition version of *Battle of Britain* (MGM, 2004).

33. Hamilton in *The Battle for the Battle of Britain* (1969) promotional film and *A Film For the Few* (2004) featurette attached to *Battle of Britain* Special Edition DVD (MGM, 2004). On the class dimension see BFI, *Battle of Britain* microfiche material, *Briefing Five*; Mosley, *Battle of Britain*, p. 138. On the forty-minute figure see ibid., p. 39. On Foxley see note 27.

34. On press coverage of the making of the film see BFI, *Battle of Britain* microfiche collection, press cuttings 1967–69. On the premiere see *The Times*, 16 September 1969, p. 2; *The Guardian*, 16 September 1969, p. 1; David, *Autobiography*, p. 184.

35. Max Aitkin in *Daily Express*, 16 September 1969, p. 10; David, *Autobiography*, p. 184; see Dave Ross in *A Film For the Few* (MGM Home Entertainment, 2004) attached to Special Edition DVD of *Battle of Britain* (MGM, 2004); Christopher Foxley-Norris, *A Lighter Shade of Blue: The Lighthearted Memories of an Air Marshal* (London: Ian Allen, 1978), p. 28; Imperial War Museum Department of Documents, 86/61/1, R. A. Morton, p. 53; IWMSA 20486/3, John R. C. Young; Smith, *Al Deere*, pp. 135–6; Dilip Sarker in Rudhall, "*Battle of Britain*", p. 173; Philip Judge, *Michael Caine* (Tunbridge Wells: Spellmount, 1985), p. 59; Liddell Hart Centre HC, Maurice Dean Papers 3/2/8, Wright to Dean, 23 November 1977, p. 3.

36. *Daily Express*, 16 September 1969, p. 10; BFI, *Battle of Britain* microfiche press cuttings.

37. BFI, *Battle of Britain* microfiche press cuttings; see also *Monthly Film Bulletin*, 36 (1969), p. 228.

38. *Variety*, 17 September 1969, p. 13, 28 January 1970, p. 11, 8 October 1969, p. 17; see Francis Pins, 'Battle of Britain', *FlyPast* 98 (1989), p. 14. On American reviews see e.g. *Time* and *Saturday Review* in BFI, *Battle of Britain* microfiche, press reviews. On *Battle of Britain* not making back its costs see James Chapman, *Past and Present: National Identity and the British Historical Film* (London: I. B. Tauris, 2005), p. 253.

39. On the number of the errors see Tony Aldgate, 'The Battle of Britain on Film', in Paul Addison and Jeremy A. Crang (eds), *The Burning Blue: A New History of the Battle of Britain* (London: Pimlico, 2000), p. 207. On the film helping to boost Dowding's reputation see e.g. *Daily Express*, 18 September 1969, p. 3; David, *Autobiography*, p. 185.

40. *The Guardian*, 16 September 1969, p. 1; Hamilton in Mosley, *Battle of Britain*, p. 29; see also Townsend, *Time and Chance*, p. 307. On the mood and interests of youth at this time see Marwick, *Sixties*. 1969 was also the year in which *La Battaglia d'Inghilterra* was first released. This was an Italian espionage film set during the Battle of Britain in which the Spanish Me 109s used in the making of *Battle of Britain* stood in for Spitfires and Spitfires appeared in German markings. The dubbed version that appeared in Britain in 1971 was called *Battle Squadron*. See *Monthly Film Bulletin*, 38 (1971), p. 19.

41. On this conclusion see also e.g. Malcolm Smith, *Britain and 1940: History, Myth and Popular Memory* (London: Routledge, 2000), p. 123.

42. John Boorman, *Adventures of a Suburban Boy* (London: Faber and Faber, 2003), pp. 271–77. It is noteworthy that the director was able to use only a single Spitfire rather than the larger number of Spitfires and German aircraft the script had called for. See John Boorman, *Hope and Glory* (London: Faber and Faber, 1987), p. 62. On *Carry On England* – which did very badly at the box office – see Morris Bright and Robert Ross, *Mr Carry On* (London: BBC, 2000), pp. 185–7; Sally Hibbin and Nina Hibbin (comps), *What a Carry On* (London: Hamlyn, 1988), p. 124; Robert Ross, *The Carry On Companion: The Life and Work of Peter Rogers* (London: Batsford, 1996), pp. 118–21. On the British film industry in the 1970s and 1980s see e.g. John Walker, *The Once and Future Film: British Cinema in the Seventies and Eighties* (London: Methuen, 1985); see also Geoff Eley, 'Finding the People's War', *American Historical Review* 106 (2001), p. 824.

FIGURE 8 Some of the pilots of Hornet Squadron from *Piece of Cake*
(Holmes Associates/LWT, 1988), including Fanny (Tom Burlinson,
left), Moggy (Neil Dudgeon, *centre*), Rex (Tim Woodward, *centre-right*)
and Hart (Boyd Gaines, *right*).
BFI Stills, courtesy of ITV.

6

Catalogue of Error: *Piece of Cake* (1988)

It's a six-part sizzler that cost £4 million to make and promises everything. Excitement, adventure, brave and handsome heroes, magnificent flying machines . . .
Television writer Linda McDermott,
Liverpool Echo, October 1988[1]

In marked contrast to the weakening British film industry, the television business in Britain seemed to be going from strength to strength from the mid-1950s onwards. By 1960, five years after the advent of commercial television in Britain, the number of annual television licences issued had climbed to over ten million; by 1970, to over fifteen million; and by 1980 to over eighteen million. And, while only 2 per cent of households had a colour set the year after colour broadcasting began in 1969, a decade later the figure had jumped to 76 per cent; and a decade after that to 93 per cent.[2]

Meanwhile, the way in which the past was being interpreted was changing. As far back as the early 1950s, it had become evident that Air Ministry claims concerning the number of enemy aircraft shot down had, in fact, been greatly exaggerated. It was also becoming apparent by the 1960s that RAF pilots had on occasion shot down friendly aircraft, shot up German seaplanes bearing Red Cross markings with the blessing of higher authority, and even fired at German aircrew after they had bailed out. In order to retain the necessary technical and other support provided by the Ministry of Defence the makers of the epic *Battle of Britain* film had eventually dropped the scenes from the script in which such matters were touched on. By the 1970s, in the wake of the broadening of what were deemed acceptable attitudes and behaviour in the preceding years, and in the context of mounting national difficulties which successive British governments seemed incapable of solving – everything from economic decline and industrial strife at home to diminishing power and influence abroad – many members of the public had become significantly more suspicious of, and thereby openly less deferential towards, established authority. Seventy-one per cent of respondents in a 1973 British Gallup poll, for instance, complained that people like themselves did not have enough say in how the country was run, as against only 23 per cent who professed themselves satisfied with their ability to influence affairs. Among other things this shift in attitude meant a growing willingness to ask awkward questions about the past as well as the present, and also to see present problems reflected or originating in historical events.[3]

As the most recent and perhaps most consequential upheaval of Britain's twentieth century, the Second World War was a natural subject for revision, not least among those who had no adult or perhaps even childhood experience of the war. 'Distanced by a generation,' as Jeremy Isaacs, producer of the twenty-six part documentary series The World at War broadcast by Thames Television in 1973–74 put it, 'we were not interested in just another telling of our parents' old soldiers tales.' Interpretations, not least established views of events previously considered beyond dispute and even sacrosanct, began to come under attack by those determined to get at the hard truths behind the heroic myths. What exactly happened at Dunkirk was one such subject; the Battle of Britain was another.[4]

Thus, there is a willingness to counterpoint a fairly conventional view of air fighting conveyed by ex-fighter pilot Ray Holmes with footage in an early episode of the hugely popular The World at War of ex-fighter pilot Max Aitkin admitting that, as far as he was concerned, there had been no sense of chivalry at all in the Battle of Britain. Hence also there was the way in which best-selling writer Len Deighton sought to emphasise many of the less palatable aspects of the battle from the British perspective – everything from poor training and tactics and the absence of an air-sea rescue service to pilots accidentally shooting down friendly aircraft and fear leading to instances of a refusal to obey orders on the ground and even in the air – in his controversial but widely read 1977 book Fighter: The True Story of the Battle of Britain.[5]

Some of the fictional accounts of the battle now appearing in print were also becoming harsher and more graphic. Richard Hough, for example, who had flown as a fighter pilot later in the war, wrote a pair of novels in the late 1970s about the events of 1940 in which, among other things, bad pre-war fighter tactics and those who clung to them were highlighted, along with the killing of aircrew who had taken to their parachutes, the full horror of being caught in a burning

Hurricane, and surreptitious theft by airmen when the opportunity arose. As former chief film censor John Trevelyan had put it as early as 1973, 'I think we are now passed [sic] the time when war was presented as good fun and a glorious adventure.'[6]

Taking a satirical poke at The Few, meanwhile, had not ended with *Beyond the Fringe*. In the film version of the highly successful 1970s' Yorkshire Television comedy series *Rising Damp*, made at the end of the decade, much fun is made of the way in which a skilful con artist named Seymour (Denholm Elliott), posing as an upper-crust former Battle of Britain pilot, is able to manipulate the worshipful class and historical prejudices of his skinflint landlord Rigsby (Leonard Rossiter).[7]

It was in this context that Derek Robinson began work on the novel *Piece of Cake*. Though not a pilot, Robinson had served his national service as an 'erk' (lowest rank in the RAF) during the early 1950s, loved period aircraft such as the Spitfire, and had been shortlisted for the Booker Prize for his 1971 novel *Goshawk Squadron*. This well-researched work of fiction had contrasted in sometimes almost comic terms the harsh realities of aerial combat in the Great War with the heroic 'knights of the air' mythology developed by the likes of W. E. Johns in the Biggles books. *Piece of Cake*, a much longer novel that did not appear until 1983, was both stylistically and thematically similar. Robinson again mixed fiction with historical fact, making sure that he had his period and technical details correct, and lacing the plot and dialogue with increasingly dark comic touches. And the author again sought to attack head-on a piece of war mythology, this time the one surrounding The Few, through chronicling the affairs of a fictional fighter squadron over a period of twelve months.[8]

His time in the service had shown Robinson that the RAF had its faults, while extensive research for the book had revealed a variety of bigger ones – everything from poor aerial tactics and aircraft design to inflated combat claims and faulty command and control – among the fighter squadrons of 1939–40. 'Why did I write *Piece of Cake*?' the author asked rhetorically some years later: 'Because I believed it ought to written, and nobody else had written it.' This was perhaps unfair on at least some of the other writers who had tackled the subject. But Robinson may have had a point when he argued that 'far too many' earlier representations had 'led to a sort of comic-strip image that is grossly unfair to the men of Fighter Command in those days'. *Piece of Cake*, which would follow the fortunes of 'Hornet Squadron' from September 1939 through the Battle of France and end in September 1940 at the height of the Battle of Britain, could perhaps remedy that by depicting true-to-life, warts-and-all characters against a background of institutional failure. 'I tried to depict them [the men of Fighter Command] as they really were', Robinson added, 'human yet special'.[9]

When it first appeared in late 1983 under the Hamish Hamilton imprint, *Piece of Cake* received little coverage and rather mixed reviews. Some readers argued that Robinson was slandering the real versions of his fictional subjects by apparently making out some of them to be cowards, while others praised the author for a convincing portrayal of squadron life. It was much more favourably received in America – where nobody's honour was at stake – early the following year, and appeared in a Pan paperback edition in Britain in the autumn. Television producer Andrew Holmes, after hearing Robinson talking about the book on Radio 4 one day, had his staff read the book and confirm his instinct that it could be translated on to the small screen. 'Early on in reading *Piece of Cake*,' Holmes later explained, 'I decided that it would make a six-part television series.'[10]

Having already sold the projected mini-series to PBS in America and to an Australian broadcaster, Holmes Associates was then able to convince London Weekend Television in Britain to chip in £4.2 million. Costs would eventually reach about £5 million – 12 per cent over budget – because of poor weather conditions. Nevertheless, the budget was large enough for the series to be shot throughout using a special type of 35–millimetre film instead of relying heavily on videotape, as was common in television up to that time and beyond. Even this amount of money, however, could not guarantee that enough period aircraft in flyable condition would be available to represent a vintage RAF fighter squadron and its opponents.[11]

Even in the 1950s it had been difficult to find airworthy fighters of the right type and, by the 1980s, the scarcity problem had become more acute than ever. The fictional squadron that Robinson had created had been, in common with the actual fighter units sent to France in 1939–40, equipped with Hurricanes. Early hopes that this aircraft type might also be used in the television version of *Piece of Cake* were soon dashed. Only two airworthy Hurricanes were in the hands of the RAF's Battle of Britain Memorial Flight, and the 5/8th-scale models that were available in America had engines that made them look very different from the real thing. The only realistic alternative seemed to be to equip Hornet Squadron with Spitfires. These machines had not served on the Continent in 1939–40, and the remaining airworthy examples were in any case almost all late-model Spits rather than Battle of Britain-vintage Mark Is or IIs. On the other hand, they were still machines dating from World War II, and there seemed to be enough of them to show at least a section of fighters in flight. 'Spitfires', as Robert Eagle, the man tasked with finding the necessary aircraft, pointed out at the time the series was broadcast in the autumn of 1988, 'were the only option.'[12]

The Battle of Britain Memorial Flight had a total of four airworthy Spitfires in the early 1980s but, in part because of air show scheduling conflicts and also, perhaps, because of concerns about how the wartime RAF was going to be portrayed, the Ministry of Defence in the end decided against providing assistance by way of aircraft for *Piece of Cake*. Negotiations proceeded more smoothly with private owners and, with the assistance of the commercially operated Old Flying Machine Company, the film-makers were able to bring together a Mk I, a Mk XI, and three Mk IX Spitfires and pilots to fly them. Unlike those in service in the Battle of Britain, all but two of these aircraft had cannon mountings jutting from the wings. These might have been removed, but this would have cost £20,000. The decision was therefore taken to leave them as they were and, in fact, make them the 'standard' fighter in *Piece of Cake*. At a cost of £120,000 six Mk IX replicas were built at Elstree – three of which were equipped with small engines to spin the props and one of which could actually taxi as well – and cannon fairings were restored to the Mk XI.[13]

As for the *Luftwaffe*, three airworthy and privately owned HA 1112s – two of which had previously been used on *Battle of Britain* – were brought in to serve as Me 109Es in the air battles, along with a CASA 211 version of the He 111 courtesy of the Confederate Air Force. The remains of another Spanish He 111, owned by the Aces High company, could do service as a wreck, while a flyable Ju 52 briefly stood in for a *Luftwaffe* air-sea rescue plane. For background shooting three of the still relatively common Tiger Moth trainers were used, along with an example of the scarcer Dominie passenger plane. For filming in the air, arrangements were made with Aces High for a suitably modified B-25 Mitchell to serve as principal camera ship along with a helicopter from Castle Air, while shots of 109s attacking Spitfires from behind were engineered by painting a Harvard trainer from the Old Flying Machine Company to resemble a Spitfire and training a camera aft from the rear cockpit. Out-takes from 1969's *Battle of Britain* would be used for whatever sequences – large enemy formations, exploding aircraft, and so forth – that could not be filmed.[14]

A lot of time and effort also went into finding and dressing suitable locations. Much of the novel was set on an airfield near a requisitioned château in eastern France. Charlton Park, a Jacobean mansion in Wiltshire, was chosen to stand in for 'Château St Pierre', in large part because a grass airstrip that could be lengthened to take Spitfires lay before it and the owner, the Earl of Suffolk, happened to be a flying buff. Exterior filming also took place at Cambridge Airport, doubling for Le Touquet on the Channel coast, and on an old RAF station at South Cerney, representing the fictional 'RAF Kingsmere' where the story begins. Scenes were also shot at Duxford – now owned by the Imperial War Museum – while a lot of thought and energy went into converting the farmland near Eastbourne, that had once been RAF Friston overlooking the Seven Sisters cliffs, into 'RAF Bodkin Hazel', the satellite grass airfield from which Hornet squadron operates during the Battle of Britain. Assorted lorries, cars, carts, and other wartime RAF equipment were hired to help dress the locations, along with the erection of various huts and hangers where needed. Group Captain (retd) Peter Matthews, who had flown in the battle, was brought on board as historical consultant in order to add legitimacy to what was being attempted, while composer Peter Martin was contracted to write an appropriate score.[15]

Meanwhile, the award-winning screenwriter Leon Griffiths had been approached to turn a sprawling narrative of over 550 pages into a screenplay that could fit into six fifty-minute parts. Having specialised in writing about the world of contemporary petty criminals for his series The Minder, Griffiths was at first reluctant to get involved in what he assumed was just another action-oriented war picture. Holmes, however, got him to read the book, after which Griffiths agreed that the raw material was 'tremendous' and 'will make great television'. Many incidents, along with one major and a number of minor characters, either had to be dispensed with altogether or significantly altered in order to meet length and market requirements and the strict limit on the number of locations the company could afford. Nonetheless, the resulting 300-minute screenplay required actors for ten central roles and sixty other parts of greater or lesser importance, and, in general, stayed true to the spirit of the novel by reinforcing some aspects even as others were altered. Ian Toynton, the man who would direct Piece of Cake, recounted how, after reading only the first few pages of the resulting script, he could see its 'enormous', perhaps 'extraordinary', television potential. 'I loved its originality and its unpredictability,' Toynton explained, 'and I could believe in its characters.'[16]

The first episode of *Piece of Cake* opens with idyllic shots of plimsoll-shod aircrew on a cross-country run around the fictional RAF station at Kingsmere. They are over-flown at low level by two Spitfires, the pilots of which turn out to be Squadron Leader Ramsey (Jack McKenzie), the grizzled CO of the fictional Hornet Squadron, and young Pilot Officer 'Dicky' Starr (Tom Radcliffe), out together on a training flight in the early morning of 3 September 1939. Though the photography is lush and beautiful throughout, right from the start of the plot there are hints that the fliers in *Piece of Cake* do not match the standard heroic profile of The Few. The viewers glimpse one character, who turns out to be 'Moggy' Cattermole (Neil Dudgeon), smoking while riding on the back of a farm cart rather than running with the rest of the pilots. Subsequently the viewers learn that Starr is giving a less than stellar performance in the air because he is seriously hung over. Then, just before the opening titles appear against a photograph of squadron personnel, Ramsey is shown inadvertently taxiing into a slit trench and then unintentionally killing himself through getting his neck broken while trying to clamber to the ground without assistance. As a corporal exclaims, 'Well I'll be buggered!'[17]

Taking over as acting CO, Flight Lieutenant Keith 'Fanny' Barton (Tom Burlinson), an Australian, appears hesitant and unsure of himself, while some of the other pilots go off to the pub instead of waiting at readiness. The squadron is then called on to intercept a bombing raid on this first day of the war and in the subsequent rather confused engagement at least one aircraft is shot down without loss. But it soon becomes clear that, owing to problems with RDF, the ground controller sent Hornet chasing after RAF rather than *Luftwaffe* aircraft and that, in the heat of the moment when markings could not be made out, Fanny has shot down a Blenheim rather than a Ju 88. The replacement CO, the confident and rather lordly Squadron Leader Rex (Tim Woodward), sends Fanny off to take the blame for the incident and next day leads a reassured Hornet squadron to France. After being welcomed at Le Touquet, the pilots and ground staff move to St Pierre in eastern France where Rex has picked out a well-appointed château adjoining an airstrip as the squadron's new home. The happy country-life atmosphere that Rex seeks to develop within the squadron is marred by only three problems. There is the boredom of the Phoney War (which Moggy deals with by risking his life flying solo under a river bridge). There are the disconcerting questions posed at a mess dinner to visiting Air Commodore Bletchley (Michael Elwyn) by the squadron's volunteer reserve intelligence officer, Pilot Officer 'Skull' Skelton (Richard Hope) about Britain's war aims. And there is the posting to Hornet of an independently minded American pilot, Chris Hart (Boyd Gaines).[18]

The second episode opens on 13 October 1939 with Hornet Squadron comfortably ensconced at Château St Pierre and Rex playing the role of country squire. Though there is no enemy activity, the CO is determined to make his pilots 'think, fly, and fight as a one-man team'. The official multi-aircraft attack formations designed to hit enemy bombers will become second nature through intensive training. 'The key to these attacks', Rex explains to the assembled pilots, 'is tight, close, precise formation flying.' Hart, based on his experiences flying against the *Luftwaffe* in the Spanish Civil War, is not convinced that this is such a good idea, and is less than impressed with the wooden propellers with which the aircraft of Hornet Squadron are equipped when his shatters in flight and forces him to make an emergency landing. While 'Flash' Gordon (Nathaniel Parker) and 'Fitz' Fitzgerald (Jeremy Northam) become closely acquainted with two local English teachers, Nicole (Corinne Dacla) and Mary (Helena Mitchell), needling by Moggy drives two other pilots to lay bets that they can repeat his unauthorised stunt involving flying under a local bridge. 'Pip' Patterson (George Anton), a Scot, balks at the last moment but claims he succeeded; 'Dicky' Starr then has a go, making it under the bridge but then crashing into the riverbank. Pip is very upset, but Moggy cold bloodedly rifles through the dead man's belongings in search of the money he claims to have won. The consequent burial ceremony is marred by poor co-ordination and by the insistence of the local priest that Starr, a non-Catholic, be disinterred and taken elsewhere. The episode ends with an Me 109 buzzing the château without opposition and dropping a Made-in-England chamber pot. 'The Luftwaffe are obviously feeling pretty bored as well,' as the adjutant, 'Uncle' Kellaway (David Horovitch), subsequently observes.[19]

Episode 3 begins in December 1939 with Ulsterman 'Flip' Moran (Gerard O'Hare) giving members of his section an aircraft recognition test, the results of which are collectively less than totally encouraging. Morale is boosted when elements of the squadron, led by Rex, shoot down a lone He 111. The only pilots who seem to be at all discontented are Fitz, who is having difficulties in bed with Mary, and Hart, who believes that Hornet squadron's first kill was a fluke. As he and Fanny – now back with the squadron – inspect the enemy wreck, Hart points out how few bullets actually hit the plane and how the official gun harmonisation range of 400 yards is to blame. Designed to compensate for pilot error, this 'Dowding Spread' is to the American a tacit admission that 'the average RAF pilot is a lousy shot'. Hart explains that to stand a real chance of shooting down the enemy he has quietly had the guns of his plane harmonised at 250 yards.[20]

At this stage, such views are disregarded by Rex and most of the other pilots, Hart having made no friends by disregarding the class-based gulf between officers and other ranks by inviting his fitter, Leading Aircraftman Todd (Neil Clarke), to play a game of squash in episode 2. A survival exercise set up by Rex goes awry after Moggy is arrested for stealing a chicken – he subsequently seduces Mary while Fitz is on leave – and when it emerges that, instead of living off the land, Hart has taken a number of other pilots into Switzerland for some rest and recreation. A major aerial dogfight subsequently occurs in which Hornet Squadron is comprehensively outfought by attacking 109s. 'Moke' Miller (Mark Womack), flying as tail-end-charlie, burns to death after his plane is hit and catches fire, while Pip and Flash are both forced to bail out after their machines are hit by cannon and machine-gun fire. In the aftermath of this debacle, majority opinion about Rex and his rigid formation flying suddenly starts to change, with Flash in particular coming back to St Pierre in a drunken rage over what happened to Miller. 'He's a disaster, that man', he says of Rex, going on to advise newly arrived Pilot Officer Trevelyan (Jason Calder) that 'if the CO asks you to be tail-end-charlie, just shoot him!' Pip, it emerges, has been mildly injured but seriously unnerved by the dogfight, so much so that Uncle suggests he drown his sorrows: 'Seems to work with Flash.'[21]

The fourth episode opens with a second disastrous encounter with the *Luftwaffe* for Hornet Squadron. With everyone concentrating on tight formation flying around Rex, nobody sees Trevelyan, flying tail-end-charlie, bounced and shot down by a diving Me 109. When the rest of the squadron dives to intercept some German bombers, 'Mother' Cox (Patrick Bailey) is hit so badly in one hand by shells from an Me 109 that he is barely able to make an emergency landing before passing out. Things seem to be looking up by the time of the joint wedding of Fitz to Mary and Flash to Nicole in the second week of May 1940, but the reception at Château St Pierre is ruined when the *Luftwaffe* pay a strafing visit and leave much death and destruction in their wake, the engineering officer, Marriot (Stephen Mac-Kenna), being the most prominent fatality. Hornet squadron attempts to get off the ground as the attack continues but a new pilot, Dutton

(Sam Miller), is hit while taxiing and crashes into the dispersal hut with spectacular and fatal results. When the rest of the squadron returns to base, it is clear that the air battle did not go well and that Rex is now far from popular as a leader. Though he has been seriously wounded in the back, the CO, with the aid of morphine, insists on leading the next sortie. This time, however, when he dives towards a massive enemy force, only another new pilot, Lloyd (Timothy Lyn), follows him down: the rest remain above and watch Rex and Lloyd blown to pieces. Fanny takes over what is left of the squadron, and Air Commodore Bletchley absolves him and the others of responsibility for Rex's death: 'Forget him, that's my advice.' Always unpopular because of his habit of peeing on unsuspecting people's legs and now unendurable because of his mournful howling, the CO's dog, Reilly, is shot dead by Fanny.[22]

Episode 5 opens with Fanny giving Flip and others practical advice on air fighting far removed from that which Rex had once advocated: now the rule is 'get in close, hammer the buggers, and get out quick'. Most do just this but, while 'Sticky' Stickwell is killed in battle, Pip abandons his aircraft before he is attacked. Uncle, meanwhile, has the unenviable task of telling Flash that, as was shown in the previous episode, Nicole was killed in a strafing attack while trying to flee to England with Mary. When Pip returns to the château he gets into a fist fight when Moggy indirectly accuses him of funk. Air Commodore Bletchley pays another visit and indicates that France is on its last legs and that what remains of Hornet squadron is to be withdrawn to England.[23]

The scene then shifts to the south coast in the high summer of 1940 where, at 'RAF Bodkin Hazel', the squadron is in the process of being reconstituted with new as well as veteran pilots under the direction of Fanny Barton. Clearly all is not well. News of the death of Nicole has apparently driven Flash to behave rather oddly and, as for the rest, they are, as Skull tells the adjutant, 'behaving exactly as one would expect: the old sweats have ganged up on the new faces [and] of course they're all deeply suspicious of the foreigners'. These foreign pilots consist of a Czech, 'Haddy' Haducek (Ned Vukovic), and a Pole, 'Zaddy' Zardonowski (Tomek Bork), described by Uncle as 'bloody keen' and by Skull as 'obsessional – they're real killers'. The vindictive nastiness of 'Moggy' Cattermole is confirmed by his taunting of a new pilot, Steele-Stebbing (Julian Cartside), and by the way he forces him to shoot down a German air-sea rescue plane with Red Cross markings and remonstrates with him for not shooting at a group of downed *Luftwaffe* personnel he sees in a dinghy. The behaviour of 'Flash' Gordon, meanwhile, has become so eccentric – he patrols with his Spitfire inverted – that the CO decides to have him looked at by an RAF doctor. Though Gordon quotes Churchill's speeches with a curious intensity and behaves rather oddly, the doctor decides that while Flash is a bit off his head, he should not be grounded. 'Have I got this right?' Fanny asks as he moves toward yet another sortie, 'he's batty but he can fly.' Flash's flight commander, 'Flip' Moran, already starting to show signs of fatigue, is killed in a subsequent dogfight, and the episode closes with Bodkin Hazel being plastered with *Luftwaffe* bombs.[24]

The sixth and final episode of *Piece of Cake* opens in August 1940. 'We're taking a hammering,' the squadron adjutant admits, 'and I don't know how long we can carry on.' One of the grimmer realities of air fighting is underlined when Uncle prevents relatives of Flip Moran from viewing his charred remains. Fitz is killed in the next dogfight, and Moggy is forced to jump from a crippled Spitfire. It turns out that his machine was pointing towards a built-up area and in fact crashed into a house, killing several civilians. Moggy, however, is utterly unrepentant when confronted by Skull:

SKULL: It didn't occur to you to sit tight and try and miss the houses?

MOGGY: No. I think you're trying to say something. 'Anyone with an ounce of gallantry would have stayed at the controls and tried to miss the innocent civilians.' Is that what you're saying?

SKULL: Something like that. Obviously I'm not a pilot.

MOGGY: No you're not. And I haven't got an ounce of gallantry. And I don't intend to get myself killed to save three and a half oiks. It's their war as well, you know. They're always saying this is a people's war. Well, now they know what it's like.

SKULL: That's a rather callous attitude.

MOGGY: Is it? Why give civilians a special status?

SKULL: Because they're non-combatants. They used to say women and children first.

MOGGY: Did they; but they can't fly Spitfires, can they?

Skull finds himself unable to rebut this argument, while Air Commodore Bletchley wants the matter swept under the carpet. 'Just tell your chaps to forget it ever happened,' he tells Fanny.[25]

Hornet Squadron as a whole does not seem to be acquitting itself as well as it thinks. In the previous episode Skull had voiced doubts about some of the kill claims being made by Hornet pilots and now demonstrates, with the aid of developed cine-gun film, that they have sometimes been firing at *Luftwaffe* bombers at too great a range while misidentifying and shooting at other RAF fighters during dogfights. Fanny sums up the situation: 'I reckon we've got three good pilots, two or three not bad, and the rest – they couldn't hit the floor if they fell out of bed.' After the next sortie Moggy indicates that Zaddy has been killed. While Hart still tries to educate the new pilots ('watch your tail . . . always watch the sun'), Fanny adopts a fatalistic attitude and is shown privately taking tablets washed down with whisky in order to keep going. In the next dogfight Flash is mortally wounded. Uncle tries to cheer up members of the squadron that evening by reading them Churchill's 'Few' tribute, but they are all tired and indifferent. The next day, later identified as 7 September 1940, Moggy once again causes distress, first by needling Haddy about the value of freedom to the point where he is physically attacked, and second by verbally abusing and driving off Mary, whose 'black widow' presence at the end of the airstrip each day in the hope that Fitz might return has become unnerving to all.[26]

In the climactic aerial dogfight that follows, Haddy, Hart, and Moggy are killed in succession, leaving Fanny and Pip as the only surviving Hornet pilots after one year of war. A new pilot asks the exhausted CO if it was a hectic engagement, to which Fanny smiles weakly and replies 'piece of cake'. The numerous personal, technical, and doctrinal problems demonstrated over the course of the series add up to a damning catalogue of error that cannot be reversed by Uncle announcing in voice-over as the end credits roll the point that 'this day was the turning point in the Battle of Britain'.[27]

'It was never my intention to debunk the Battle or to belittle the men of Fighter Command,' Robinson claimed in the author's note appended to *Piece of Cake*. He had done a good deal of research into the things that had gone wrong before and during the Battle of Britain, and presented what he believed to be a solid case: 'The characters I have portrayed *did* exist', he later argued, albeit 'not all in one squadron'. Yet, as Robinson admitted, 'anyone who tries to write honestly about that period risks the wrath of those who prefer the simpler [heroic] version'. The television adaptation of *Piece of Cake*, though differing in detail from the novel on which it was based, was still very much a revisionist account of The Few. Though London Weekend Television did its best to promote the series in advance, how critics and the viewing public would react to it would become clear only after the series began to be broadcast in early October 1988.[28]

Among the reviewers there were those who liked almost everything they saw in the first episode of *Piece of Cake*. Ian Christie, writing for the *Daily Express*, thought the series had got off to a 'flying start', what with the 'exhilarating' flying sequences not overshadowing plot and character development. 'The series might be about war in the air', he added, 'but it seems to have its feet on the ground.' In a review for the *Times Education Supplement* Robin Buss took a similar position. 'The models and aerial effects are brilliant, and there is the expected attention to detail of atmosphere and props,' he explained, 'but they are not allowed to become more interesting than the personalities.' Peter Lennon, reviewing the episode for *The Listener*, latched onto and praised 'confident ambiguities' – i.e. indications of revisionism – that Griffiths had written into the script, and pronounced it to be 'high-class entertainment' of 'irresistible' quality.[29]

Other critics were slightly more reserved in their endorsements of *Piece of Cake*. While impressed by the 'spectacular' flying and by the pilots' repartee, Richard Last informed *Daily Telegraph* readers that, despite the death of Ramsey, 'the Biggles element for the moment predominates over harsher realities'; so much so that Last admitted that he half expected to see Kenneth More put in an appearance. Moira Martingale, writing for *The Sun*, came to the same conclusion. '*Piece of Cake* has faultless acting, splendid filming and some pretty little planes': but so far, 'it's indistinguishable from those all-male, Boy's Own, war films of the Forties and Fifties.' The anonymous reviewer for the *Mail on Sunday* seemed to agree, commenting that while 'the flying shots are exciting' the first episode seemed to indicate that *Piece of Cake* might end up being 'a useful addition to the "We'll meet again, Scramble chaps, bandits at 11 o'clock wizard prang" school of drama'. In *The Guardian* Sandy Smithers admitted that the series had high production values – 'this is a quality job' – but seemed to take exception to what she labelled 'expertly marketed nostalgia'. Sandy Fawkes wrote that 'it is the Spitfires that are the stars' for the *Evening Standard*, going on to decry the flatness of the script and various errors in period detail. To Tony Pratt of the *Daily Mirror* it seemed that, while 'the old planes easily steal the show', the scenes between pilots on the ground were decidedly slow moving. Margaret Forwood in the *The People*, meanwhile, complained that 'I cannot distinguish between Fanny, Moggy, Dicky, Pip, Flip, Flash or Sticky, the callow boys in air force blue.'[30]

There were also a few critics who, on first acquaintance, unambiguously disliked *Piece of Cake*. William Holmes of *The Times* wrote that it 'spluttered into life, took off briefly and quickly sank to the ground again under the weight of sheer lack of interest.' A week later in the Sunday Times Patrick Stoddart wrote off Piece of Cake as a 'piece of half-baked tosh' complete with period errors and a formulaic plot. 'There's the usual kindly/irascible/cheerful/cynical squadron leader struggling to turn callow youths with names like Moggy, Spiffy [sic], Boffo [sic] and Basher [sic] into a crack fighting unit before they face the Hun,' he explained. 'Beyond that there's not a lot of characterisation and precious little sub-plot.'[31]

Other reviewers, who took the time to reflect or to watch a few more episodes before reporting on Piece of Cake, came back with mixed but generally negative opinions. In the Observer John Naughton judged the public-school atmosphere of Hornet Squadron to be authentic but disliked the use of Spitfires instead of Hurricanes; he thought that Charlton Park did not look a bit like a French château, and wondered if the inclusion of an American character and two willing-and-eager young women was not just an opportunistic marketing ploy. 'The worst, I fear,' he gloomily concluded, 'is yet to come.' Alan Coren, writing for the Mail on Sunday, argued in contrast that Charlton Park was acceptably 'done up to look like France', that Spitfires had to be used because of the shortage of flyable Hurricanes, and that this necessary evil 'should not interfere with enjoyment of seeing old planes whizzing about'. The real problem, Coren went on to write, was with the authenticity of the characters. They were 'cliches of cliches', yet at the same time 'in accent, in mannerism, in style,' too much of the 1980s to be believable in the 1939–40 setting. Tony Pratt, meanwhile, continued to report to readers of the Daily Mirror that he found the series 'disappointingly dull' and slow.[32]

Perhaps inevitably, some watchers objected strongly to the unfolding revisionist interpretation of The Few in Piece of Cake. There were, after all, plenty of people who still felt what Norman Shrapnel had earlier described as an 'understandable nostalgia' for an heroic past in the light of the dismal present. After the fourth episode, Charlie Catchpole took aim at the series in News of the World. 'I could overlook the little errors of detail: wrong aircraft, wrong armaments, wrong medals etc. if the feel of the programme was right,' he explained. But the feel was wrong: 'the ever-present air of world-weary, modern-day cynicism makes me see red. I don't imagine Battle of Britain pilots were all angels. But was there ever such a cruel, cowardly, cheating, boozing, bullying bunch of braggarts? Would an Air Commodore connive at murder (because that's what it was), saying "C.O. bought it. Happens all the time"?' All in all *Piece of Cake* 'stuck in my throat'. A rather more sympathetic Ron Lawrence, commenting on the series for the same paper as the final episode was about to be broadcast, noted that, while everyone seemed to like the Spitfires ('the undoubted stars'), *Piece of Cake* had 'upset some viewers who prefer their pilots to be super-heroes without feet of clay'.[33]

On the other hand there was Robert Hewison, writing for *The Listener* and making the case after watching the first three episodes that the script Griffiths had written was, in comparison to the novel on which it was based, too much of a compromise in relation to upholding rather than undermining Battle of Britain mythology. 'In the moral uncertainties of the 1980s', he argued, 'the myth is comforting, but corrupting.' The legend of The Few ought to have been 'challenged more forcibly' than was the case in the television version of *Piece of Cake*.[34]

By early November 1988, as *Piece of Cake* drew to a close, it seemed to have few overt supporters among the critics. 'You'd have thought it hard to miss with a series about R.A.F. fighter pilots during World War II,' Tony Pratt concluded in the *Daily Mirror*. 'But they've managed it here – apart from the occasional aerial scrap it's been tedious and disappointing stuff.' Patrick Stoddart, meanwhile, vented his very negative opinions once more in the *Sunday Times*.

> We also bid farewell, chocks way and tally-ho to *Piece of Cake* (ITV, Sunday), which took off for the wild blue yonder without ever having landed heavily enough to be noticed for anything but the historical clangers it dropped. I was more disappointed by its almost total lack of realism, which might have had something to do with the mock-period dialogue that tripped out of the actors' mouths with all the familiarity of Latin from a trawlerman.

In the *Financial Times* Christopher Dunkley wrote that it 'is at its most exciting and watchable when Spitfires are flying under bridges or dogfights are occurring', going on to argue that the mystique of the Battle of Britain had been undermined as long ago as *Beyond the Fringe*. 'If now, you want to re-write the myth and show that The Few were much like any other group of young men (which they presumably were) you need to do more than merely turn the whole thing upside down and make them out to be a bunch of shits.'[35]

How though, did the television-watching public, many of whom might never have read the metropolitan papers, react to *Piece of Cake*? The broadcast of the first episode drew 12.1 million viewers, placing the series at number thirteen among the top 100 programmes of the week, figures which held up for the second and third episodes. A prediction made by Linda McDermott of the *Liverpool Echo* that everywhere 'there will be grown men living out there boyhood fantasies' while their womenfolk swooned over Tim Woodward, seemed to be coming true in spite of the doubts expressed by some of the London critics. But then audience figures began to slip significantly. By the middle of October 1988, only 9.2 million people were still watching, placing *Piece of Cake* in thirty-ninth place. By the end of the month 200,000 fewer people were tuning in, which meant the series was now in forty-fourth place. The conclusion drew back 400,000 viewers, but *Piece of Cake* still achieved no higher than thirty-ninth place among the top 100 programmes in terms of viewing figures for the week ending 6 November 1988.[36]

Those involved in the making of the series were doubtless disappointed in the way *Piece of Cake* had failed to live up to expectations. Despite relatively high production values, the series had been damned for being too controversial as well as not controversial enough. The efforts to reproduce the attitudes and authentic atmosphere of 1940 had been dismissed in some quarters as so much scripting cliché while nits had been picked about the use of Spitfires instead of Hurricanes. Yet the series was not, it must be remembered, by any means a complete failure. Some critics had liked it and, more importantly, never less than nine million people – by no means a small number (even if fewer than sponsors may have hoped) – had been watching *Piece of Cake* in any given week. Evidently there were still plenty of viewers who were sufficiently intrigued by – or at least not sufficiently alienated by – this version of The Few to keep tuning in to the last. A revisionist approach to the RAF of 1940, in short, was not a complete bust as television subject matter.

Furthermore, as the next chapter indicates, whatever problems there may have been with the series, these did not deter others from tackling the Battle of Britain as a dramatic subject again within the space of only a few years. Indeed, *A Perfect Hero* was in many ways a reaction against *Piece of Cake*.

Notes

1. *Liverpool Echo*, 1 October 1988, p. 15.
2. Michael Svennevig, *Television Across the Years: The British Public's View* (Luton: University of Luton Press, 1998), p. 13; Patricia Perilli, 'Statistical Survey of the British Film Industry', in James Curran and Vincent Porter (eds), *British Cinema History* (London: Weidenfeld and Nicolson, 1983), p. 372.
3. Gallup, George H. (ed.), *The Gallup International Opinion Polls: Great Britain, 1937–1945:* Volume Two, *1965–1975* (New York, Random House, 1976), p. 1232. The negative result was three percentage points up over the figure for a similar poll taken in 1968. See ibid., p. 993. By 1984 those who thought that Britain's days as a world power were over for good outnumbered those who disagreed by more than two to one. See Lindsay Brook et al. (comps), *British Social Attitudes Cumulative Source Book: The First Six Surveys* (Aldershot: Gower, 1992), D-9. For the controversial material left out of *Battle of Britain* at the behest of the Ministry of Defence (see National Archives [hereafter NA], AIR 2 18162) see British Film Institute (hereafter BFI), S8479, 'The Battle of Britain' revised draft screenplay, 23 February 1967, scenes 289, 297, 432, 446–7, 466. On some of the less attractive aspects of the battle coming to light by the early 1960s see Derek Wood and Derek Dempster, *The Narrow Margin: The Battle of Britain and the Rise of Air Power* (Hutchinson: London, 1961), pp. 241, 255, 257, 348, 301, 317. On the origins of the public acknowledgement that the number of enemy aircraft shot down was in fact far lower than stated in 1940 see Denis Richards, *It Might Have Been Worse: Recollections 1941–1996* (London: Smithson Albright, 1998), pp. 115–16. On the way in which the difficulties of the late 1960s and early 1970s could generate new thinking about the Finest Hour and related events see e.g. Gavriel D. Rosenfeld, *The World Hitler Never Made: Alternate History and the Memory of Nazism* (Cambridge: Cambridge University Press, 2005), pp. 50–70. On the socio-cultural changes that allowed among other things for a more open attitude toward divergent attitudes and behaviour than had been the case through, say, much of the 1950s see Arthur Marwick, *The Sixties: Cultural Revolution in Britain, France, Italy and the United States, c. 1958–c. 1974* (Oxford: Oxford University Press, 1998). Arguably in the more permissive atmosphere of the late 1960s and 1970s, participants were more willing to admit to all they had felt and done in interviews and memoirs than would have been the case in the past. Furthermore, many hitherto restricted Air Ministry documents had become available early because of the changeover from the fifty-year to the thirty-year access rule starting in 1968.
4. Jeremy Isaacs, 'The Making of the Series *The World at War*' (1989) attached to the 2001 DVD Region 1 edition of *The World at War* (Thames Television, 1973–74). On the making of the series see Jeremy Isaacs, *Look Me in the Eye: A Life in Television* (London: Little, Brown, 2006), ch. 7; see also James Chapman, 'The World at War: Television, Documentary, History', in G. Roberts and P. M. Taylor (eds), *The Historian, Television and Television History* (Luton: University of Luton Press, 2001), pp. 127–44. On Dunkirk see e.g. Nicholas Harman, *Dunkirk: The Necessary Myth* (London: Hodder and Stoughton, 1980).
5. Len Deighton, *Fighter: The True Story of the Battle of Britain* (London: Jonathan Cape, 1977), pp. 142, 165–6, 170–1, 178–9, 185, 201, 220, 232, 202–3. See also, e.g., the piece on the battle by H. R. Allen in *The Times*, 15 September 1978, p. 14. It is interesting to note that it was A. J. P. Taylor, the ageing *enfant terrible* of the historical profession, who suggested that Deighton – who took six years to complete the work – tackle the battle of Britain and its 'patriotic myths'. See

Deighton, *Fighter*, pp. 294, 21. For reviews of *Fighter* see e.g. *Times Literary Supplement*, 28 October 1977, p. 1265; *The Guardian*, 15 September 1977, p. 16. After an initial print run of 40,500, *Fighter was* issued in paperback in Britain in 1979 by Triad/Panther. See Edward Milward-Oliver, *The Len Deighton Companion* (London: Grafton, 1987), pp. 322–3. For an example of a highly critical reaction to the book listen to Imperial War Museum Sound Archive 11716/1, Alfred Price interview of Douglas Bader; see also e.g. *The Spectator*, 14 November 1981, p. 19. The initial attempts at revisionism in relation to World War II, which appeared in the early 1960s, also met with the strongest criticism. See e.g. William Roger Louis (ed.), *The Origins of the Second World War: A. J. P. Taylor and his Critics* (New York: Wiley, 1972) on A. J. P. Taylor, *The Origins of the Second World War* (London: Hamish Hamilton, 1961) or – more specifically in relation to 1940 mythology – Richard Collier, *The Past is a Foreign Country: Scenes From a Life* (London: Allison and Busby, 1996), pp. 202–8; Richard Collier, *The Sands of Dunkirk* (London: Collins, 1961). On *The World at War* – which in a poll conducted among industry professionals by the British Film Institute in 2005 to determine the 100 greatest British television programmes ever made, came in at nineteen – see the *Making of the World at War* interviews attached to the thirtieth anniversary DVD edition; Noble Frankland, *History at War: The Campaigns of an Historian* (London: Giles de la Mare, 1998), pp. 189–92. The episode covering the Battle of Britain was the fourth, 'Alone, May 1940–May 1941'.

6. John Trevelyan, *What the Censor Saw* (London: Michael Joseph, 1973), p. 157. See Richard Hough, *The Fight of the Few* (London: Cassell, 1979); Richard Hough, *Angels One-Five* (London: Cassell, 1978). On this author's wartime career see Richard Hough, *One Boy's War* (London: Heinemann, 1975). It should be kept in mind, however, that, as early as the mid-1950s, novels could be a good deal grittier than the films of that decade (e.g. Elleston Trevor, *Squadron Airborne* [London: Macmillan, 1955]) and that, in the 1970s, novels dealing at least in part with the battle might not be that different from, say, *Battle of Britain* (United Artists, 1969) (e.g. Colin Willock, *The Fighters* [London: Macmillan, 1973]).

7. *Rising Damp* (ITC, 1979). The Battle of Britain connection was apparently absent from the television episode of *Rising Damp*, 'The Perfect Gentleman', on which the film was based: see Eric Chappell, *Rising Damp: The Complete Scripts* (London: Granada Media, 2002), pp. 205–23. For antecedents see Mark Connelly, *We Can Take It! Britain and the Memory of the Second World War* (Harlow: Longman, 2004), p. 108.

8. Compare Derek Robinson, *Piece of Cake* (London: Hamish Hamilton, 1983) with Derek Robinson, *Goshawk Squadron* (London: Heinemann, 1971). On this author's background and approach see Derek Robinson, 'Why I Wrote *Piece of Cake*', in Robert Eagle and Herbie Knott, *How They Made Piece of Cake* (London: Boxtree, 1988), pp. 16–25; 'Interview with Derek Robinson', in *DLB Yearbook 2002* Matthew J. Bruccoli and Richard Laymen, eds (Farmington Hills, MI: Gale, 2003), pp. 345–51; see also Robinson comments in François Prins, 'Taking the Cake! Slice One', *FlyPast* 87 (1988), p. 11.

9. Robinson, 'Why I wrote *Piece of Cake*', Eagle and Knott, *How they made Piece of Cake*, p. 25; see 'Interview with Derek Robinson' *DLB Yearbook*, Bruccoli and Laymen, pp. 345–51.

10. Prins, 'Taking the Cake! Slice One', pp. 11–12. On reviews see ibid., p. 11; see also e.g. *Books and Bookmen*, December 1983, p. 32, October 1984, p. 36; *Booklist*, 1 February 1984, p. 770; *Publisher's Weekly*, 17 February 1984, p. 72; *New Republic*, 14 May 1984, pp. 38–40; *New York Times Book Review*, 27 May 1984,

p. 18; *Best Sellers*, July 1984, p. 129. *Piece of Cake* was chosen as a Book of the Month Club main selection in the United States. Interestingly, at least one American reviewer mentioned that the book would make a good PBS television mini-series. *Time*, 9 July 1984, p. 85. For a 1940 RAF pilot's view of the book see Bob Doe, *Fighter Pilot* (Chislehurst: CCB, 2004), p. 39.

11. Prins, 'Taking the Cake! Slice One', p. 12. On the £5 million figure see *Sunday Mirror*, 2 October 1988, p. 2. On the cost overruns see *Broadcast*, 9 September 1988, p. 2 On the three-perf wide-screen 35 mm film used see Prins, 'Taking the Cake! Slice Two', *FlyPast* 88 (1988), p. 41.

12. Eagle and Knott, *How They Made*, p. 66.

13. Ibid., pp. 66–74; Prins, 'Taking the Cake! Slice One', p. 13.

14. Mike Jerram, 'Fighting Machines', in Eagle and Knott, *How They Made*, pp. 46– 51, 54–7, 61–2, 64–5.

15. Eagle and Knott, *How They Made*, pp. 76–83; Prins, 'Taking the Cake! Slice Two', pp. 41–2.

16. Eagle and Knott, *How They Made*, pp. 11–12; Prins, 'Taking the Cake! Slice One', pp. 12–13. The major character in the novel axed from the script was Jacky Bellamy, an American war correspondent. Perhaps it was considered redundant to have another American on screen given that United States interest would be piqued by the presence of Chris Hart, a Yank in the RAF perhaps loosely based on Billy Fiske. Other changes included making Keith 'Fanny' Barton an Australian instead of a New Zealander, presumably in order to help sell the series in Australia (a larger market than New Zealand).

17. The exclamation was the work of Griffiths. In the novel there is considerably more background on Ramsey prior to his accident. See Robinson, *Piece of Cake*, pp. 10–39.

18. The blue-on-blue incident in which Fanny kills a Blenheim pilot was based on a real incident in the first week of the war, the so-called Battle of Barking Creek in which two Hurricanes were shot down. See author's note, Robinson, *Piece of Cake*, p. 565. Due to problems with the squadron code letters stuck on to the Spitfires ('NS', actually used by a Sunderland flying boat squadron formed in 1944: see Michael J. F. Bowyer and John D. R. Rawlings, *Squadron Codes, 1937–56* [Cambridge: Patrick Stephens, 1979], p. 77), lines were added to the script in which Rex orders the letters to be obliterated after the blue-on-blue incident ('we don't want to get caught again, do we?'): see Eagle and Knott, *How They Made*, p. 68. Tim Woodward demonstrated his acting range in the part of the squire-like Squadron Leader Rex, having, among other roles, played a distinctly lower-class pilot in the World War I BBC television drama *Wings* a decade earlier.

19. Kellaway's comment is made during the voice-over introduction (done for episodes 2 to 6 with accompanying footage as a means of reminding the audience what had previously happened) to episode 3. Ray Hanna of the Old Flying Machine Company flew a Spitfire, at considerable risk, very low under a river bridge in Tyne and Wear for the scenes involving the attempts by Moggy, Pip, and Dicky. See Prins, 'Taking the Cake! Slice One', p. 10; Prins, 'Taking the Cake! Slice Two', p. 44.

20. In the previous episode, Hart was briefly shown installing ad hoc armour protection behind his cockpit seat, another indication of his lack of faith in official RAF air combat policy.

21. Pip Patterson developing the twitch is one of the additions made by Leon Griffiths to the original story, which does not feature anyone in France showing signs of cowardice.

22. In contrast to the book, Fanny Barton in the television series actively colludes in leaving Rex to his fate. See Robinson, *Piece of Cake*, pp. 357–8.
23. In the series Bletchley, as well as standing for the hypocrisies of Air Ministry brass-hats in general, serves the purpose of keeping Hornet Squadron and the audience apprised of how the war is going (which, in the case of episodes 4 and 5 usually means very badly indeed). Killed during an air raid under less than glorious circumstances in the book (see Robinson, *Piece of Cake*, p. 528), Bletchley survives in the series.
24. The credits for this and other episodes appear against an assembled squadron photograph background, the different photographs reflecting the state of the squadron at that particular time. This device – which works well – seems to have been developed from the single squadron photograph mentioned in the book. See Robinson, *Piece of Cake*, p. 464.
25. The exchange between Moggy and Skull in this episode is quite similar to that which appears in the book, though Robinson had Fanny and Hart asking the questions. See Robinson, *Piece of Cake*, pp. 488–89.
26. In episode 6 of the series the likelihood of a successful German invasion is stressed whereas, in the book, Jacky Bellamy, the American war correspondent, suggests that, whatever the RAF does, an invasion is unlikely because of the Royal Navy (see Robinson, *Piece of Cake*, pp. 548–51), a point later developed at length in Robinson's *Invasion 1940: The Truth About the Battle of Britain and What Stopped Hitler* (London: Constable, 2005).
27. The novel ends with the fight still going on and makes no mention of the significance of 7 September – the day the *Luftwaffe* turned against London – as a turning point.
28. Robinson, *Piece of Cake*, author's note, pp. 568–9; Robinson in Prins, 'Taking the Cake! Slice One', p. 11. On promotional publicity see e.g. *TV Times*, 1 October 1988, cover, pp. 4, 24; *Broadcast*, 30 September 1988, p. 7; *Today*, 1 October 1988, pp. 28–9; *Morning Star*, 1 October 1988, p. 9; *Daily Mirror*, 1 October 1988, p. 15; *Liverpool Echo*, 1 October 1988, p. 15; *Evening Chronicle* (Newcastle), 1 October 1988, p. 16; *Birmingham Post*, 1 October 1988, p. 45; *Yorkshire Evening Post*, 1 October 1988, Weekend Post section, p. 5; *Daily Record*, 1 October 1988, p. 19; *Western Mail*, 1 October 1988, p. 13.
29. *The Listener*, 6 October 1988, p. 45; *Times Education Supplement*, 14 October 1988, p. 28; *Daily Express*, 3 October 1988, p. 23. See also Jonathan Glancey, *Spitfire* (London: Atlantic, 2006), p. 206.
30. *The People*, 8 October 1988, p. 22; *Daily Mirror*, 9 October 1988, p. 19; *Evening Standard*, 30 September 1988, p. 31; *The Guardian*, 1 October 1988, p. 39; *Mail on Sunday*, 2 October 1988, p. 34; *The Sun*, 5 October 1988, p. 17; *Daily Telegraph*, 3 October 1988, p. 18.
31. *Sunday Times*, 9 October 1988, p. 20; *The Times*, 3 October 1988, p. 21.
32. *Daily Mirror*, 22 October 1988, p. 19, 15 October 1988, p. 19; *Mail on Sunday*, 9 October 1988, p. 35; *Observer*, 16 October 1988, p. 52.
33. *News of the World*, 6 November 1988, p. 26, 30 October 1988, p. 27; Norman Shrapnel, *The Seventies: Britain's Inward March* (London: Constable, 1980), p. 79. Robinson himself agreed that, though based on real people and incidents – see e.g. Richard Hillary, *The Last Enemy* (London: Macmillan, 1942), pp. 64, 79–80, for pilots killing themselves by undoing their straps and falling out of aircraft in the manner of Ramsey and flying under bridges in the manner of Moggy – the various characters in *Piece of Cake* would not all have belonged to the same squadron. See Robinson in Prins, 'Taking the Cake! Slice One', p. 11.

34. *The Listener*, 13 October 1988, pp. 14–15. The most obvious example of the message of the novel being compromised in the series is the postscript voice-over at the end of episode 6 in which 7 September 1940 is stated to be the turning point in the Battle of Britain.
35. *Financial Times*, 2 November 1988, p. 27; *Sunday Times*, 13 November 1988, p. 20; *Daily Mirror*, 5 November 1988, p. 15.
36. *Broadcast*, 25 November 1988, p. 28, 18 November 1988, p. 38, 11 November 1988, p. 32; *Liverpool Echo*, 1 October 1988, p. 15; *Broadcast*, 28 October 1988, p. 30, 21 October 1988, p. 32.

FIGURE 9 Nigel Havers as Hugh Fleming before being shot down.
Publicity still for *A Perfect Hero* (Havahall/LWT, 1991).
Image courtesy of ITV.

7

The Fighter Boys: *A Perfect Hero* (1991)

According to producer and director James Cellan Jones A Perfect Hero
(9 p.m., ITV) is not a war story. 'It's the story of a much older conflict –
the conflict between men and fire,' he maintains.
                    Graham Kael, *Northern Echo*, May 1991[1]

As the 1980s gave way to the 1990s, the myth-busting approach to
1940 And All That continued in the pages of the left-wing *New
Statesman* and in work of anti-establishment writers such as Clive
Ponting. They were soon joined by conservative revisionists, such as
John Charmley and Alan Clark, who argued that the Battle of Britain
had been a mistake and that the country would have been better off
in terms of global power and influence if Churchill had not rejected
peace overtures from Hitler. Yet, as some of the reactions to *Piece
of Cake* indicated, there were also those who thought that the
questioning of what had hitherto been admired had gone too far.
Traditional conservatives, among others, saw the memory of the
Finest Hour as part of the national heritage and an important
component in national identity that ought to be celebrated rather
than contemptuously discarded. Tory politicians, not least Mrs
Thatcher herself, became adept at associating their party in spirit
with the landmark events of 1940. It was therefore perhaps no
coincidence that much more was made of the fiftieth anniversary
of the battle by the RAF and in the press than had been the case for
some time, or that in the early 1990s, the long-delayed Battle of
Britain Memorial was finally was built near Folkestone.[2]
   Among those who thought that, on television, the radical-critique
approach in general had been overdone was scriptwriter Allan Prior
who deplored the preponderance of what he called '*against* plays',
especially those from the BBC. Nigel Havers, who had starred in a
successful television adaptation written by Prior of the Patrick
Hamilton novel *The Charmer* in 1987, was eager to see if the

screenwriter could adapt another story in which he might again play the lead, as was Prior himself if it could be something that would show 'the human spirit, at its best, in adversity'. Having served in the RAF during the war and being an admirer of those who had defended the skies over southern England in the summer of 1940, Prior decided that it might be worth reminding people what true heroism entailed: perhaps by adapting a story about a 'burnt RAF Pilot of the Battle of Britain?'[3]

The obvious choice was *The Last Enemy* but as noted in chapter 4, this had already been adapted with great success for television in the mid-1950s. The next best thing seemed to be a novel by a writer whom Nigel Havers's agent, Michael Whitehall, also represented and which both Havers and Whitehall had read and liked. The book was *The Long-Haired Boy* which, as the author Christopher Matthew freely admitted was 'inspired by the life of Richard Hillary' but used fictional characters, alternative settings, and drew on the experiences of other burned pilots, such as Geoffrey Page, as well.[4]

When it had first been published early in 1980 the novel had garnered a number of positive reviews. 'I have to acknowledge that a book which at first struck me as just another competent commercial product, another genre piece of Second World War fiction,' Anthony Thwaite reported in the *Observer*, 'came to disturb me and move me.' Jonathan Steffen of the *New Statesman* found the story 'clear, bold and uncluttered,' and argued that 'the novel convinces through its wealth of historical and technical details; so much so that it comes as a surprise to learn that the author was barely one year old when the Battle of Britain took place'. The reviewer for the *Times Literary Supplement*, A. N. Wilson, also praised *The Long-Haired Boy*. 'How refreshing to read a novel which has a moral, a good, strong, entirely believable story . . .' he wrote, 'and a beginning, middle and end.' Adaptation should, therefore, not be a problem.[5]

Alan Prior certainly liked what he read but eventually concluded that 'it was short, in length and substance, for a six-hour story'. As well as transposing characters and truncating or simplifying events for dramatic or practical reasons, the screenwriter also developed a major romantic interest not present in the book and added on substantial material dealing with what happens to the protagonist after the book comes to an end. As Prior subsequently explained, this latter task was one into which he poured his personal sentiments about The Few:

I extended the plot: I wrote a whole, new 'third act' [narrating the protagonist's return to flying], and I'm not sure, if I had not known the period and the setting from actual experience, that I could have done it . . . It was a time of heroes and heroics: everyone did live as if there was no tomorrow because very often there wasn't. Not the easiest thing to explain to young actors whose principal concern sky-wise is not the danger of the Hun in the Sun but the Hole in the Ozone Layer!

As another wartime veteran, Christopher F. 'Bunny' Currant, an ex-fighter pilot who had once played a supporting part in *First of the Few*, noted at about the time the new series was being made, the past really was becoming a foreign country as far as the young people were concerned:

I don't tell my grandchildren or children about it [the battle] unless they ask. And grandchildren never ask, at least my grandchildren don't, because they're at the age of fifteen to eighteen, and fifty years ago really doesn't grab their interest. 'The Battle of Britain? What's the Battle of Britain?' 'What was the War?' It's so remote in their minds. They're living now, in the youth of now, and they can't go back into the past and get any feel of it at all.

'It'll soon seem as remote as Agincourt, Trafalgar, and Waterloo', worried Christopher Foxley-Norris, chairman of the Battle of Britain Fighter Association. Prior saw it as part of his task to inform both the actors and the audience what it had felt like in those days.[6]

A change in title therefore seemed in order. *The Long-Haired Boy* was a reference to the way in which university air squadron recruits had been rather derisively known among regulars as 'the long-haired boys' in the 1930s; but it was a reference that would elude and mystify most viewers in the 1990s. Prior chose instead *A Perfect Hero*, a version of what Richard Hillary's mother had once said about her son – 'A Perfect Hero? Or perhaps a perfect fool?' – that came down heavily on the side of heroism over foolishness.[7]

A Perfect Hero would be a co-production of the new Nigel Havers company, Havahall Pictures, working with London Weekend Television. James Cellan Jones, who had done his national service in the Parachute Regiment (and therefore could explain to young actors who had never been in uniform something of what life was like in the services) was to produce the series. He would also direct six fifty-minute episodes that, despite certain cost-saving measures, such as limiting the number of sets and using videotape throughout, would end up costing around £4.2 million. Period aircraft were obviously a necessity and, once again, the Old Flying Machine Company came into the picture to provide a couple of airworthy Spitfires and pilots to fly them out of RAF Swanton Morley in Norfolk. Geoffrey Page, who himself had been shot down in flames and suffered extensive burns during the Battle of Britain, was employed as chief adviser, alongside a number of other historical and technical advisers. Cellan Jones also had to find a hundred extras to supplement the main cast which, in addition to Nigel Havers, included Bernard Hepton, Barbara Leigh-Hunt and James Fox.[8]

The first episode opens 'Somewhere in England' in September 1940 with Hugh Fleming (Nigel Havers), Julian Masters (Nicholas Pritchard) and other pilots of '89 Squadron' operating from 'RAF Woodfold' lounging about outside the dispersal tent awaiting the call to action. Julian is clearly nervous – he vomits after the phone rings for a call to breakfast rather than a scramble – while Hugh remains unperturbedly dozing in the sun. A brief exchange between them reinforces the sense that Hugh is far more confident than Julian, in love as well as in war, Julian remaking that 'You have all the luck', to which Hugh replies: 'Not luck old boy. It's called style. Some have it. Some don't.' A daydream in which Hugh recollects punting along the Cam with his sweetheart, Bunty Morrell (Fiona Gillies), is rudely interrupted by the call to scramble. In the subsequent dogfight between Spitfires and Me 109s, Hugh shoots down an enemy aircraft but is in turn hit from behind, causing his reserve petrol tank to catch fire. As the script explains, '*As Hugh turns his head, suddenly the cockpit erupts . . . A cannon shell has hit the aircraft . . . The cockpit is suddenly a mass of flame! HUGH is "frozen". He looks at his hands. They are being scorched. The control-panel is dissolving.*' He manages to bail out but, because he was not wearing gloves and did not have his goggles down, his hands and face are both very badly burned.[9]

Hugh Fleming's parents, Arthur and Iris (Bernard Hepton and Barbara Leigh-Hunt), receive a call from the squadron adjutant informing them that their son is in Ashford hospital. Lying in bed under sedation, Hugh, his face and hands swathed in bandages, recalls the pre-war day at Cambridge when he persuaded his circle of male friends – Peter Hemingford (Harry Burton), Jimmy Macdonnell (Nicholas Palliser) and Julian – to join in him signing on for the University Air Squadron ('a bit of a lark'). More flashbacks follow, alternating with brief scenes in the present suggesting how badly Hugh has been injured – 'he *is* a bit of a mess, isn't he?' comments the outwardly brisk but inwardly sympathetic Sister Grice (Rosalind Knight) to the more overtly upset Voluntary Aid Detachment (VAD) nurse Sarah (Tracy Kneale) – and how the news is being taken by his parents, Bunty, Julian and other members of his squadron, plastic surgeon Angus Meikle (James Fox), who play a central role in Hugh's recovery later on, as well as by Jean (Rachel Fielding), a land-girl Hugh has been seeing on the side. The flashback dream sequences, showing handsome Hugh's way with women and with flying – he is shown as the first among his Cambridge friends to go solo – illustrate the extent to which success in every aspect of life had come to him easily, seemingly without effort and without care in the eyes of his contemporaries. The contrast between his Golden Boy past and the grim realities of the present are underlined for Hugh when he first sees the state of his hands – 'Christ, what the hell's happened to my *hands*?' – and when he takes the opportunity offered by an air raid to stagger over to a mirror, unwind his bandages, and the viewers see just how disfigured his face has become (the final shot of episode 1).[10]

The second episode of *A Perfect Hero* begins with Meikle chatting with Hugh – described by Sister Grice as a 'rather difficult' patient – about his future, the surgeon pulling no punches about how plastic surgery will never restore the patient's former good looks. As Sister Grice explains to his mother, Hugh is understandably depressed, a mood not made better when Bunty – about whom he has been dreaming again – unexpectedly visits the hospital, sees his face while his dressings are being changed, and is so horrified that she immediately rushes out. It is Julian, with whom Bunty seemed to be getting close, who subsequently delivers her 'Dear John' letter to Hugh's bedside, while his squadron CO, 'Dickie' Bird (Thomas Wheatley), informs him that, while he is putting Hugh forward for a DSO, one of his Cambridge friends, Peter Hemingford, has been killed (in a dogfight shown earlier in the episode). There follows another dream sequence about the golden past at Cambridge, this time in connection with yet another girlfriend, Marg Fisher (Amada Elves), followed in turn by a visit from Hugh's parents and his sister, Susan (Fiona Mollison). Susan, who has always thought Hugh got what he wanted too easily, informs him when they are alone: 'Now you'll know who your real friends are'. Hugh dreams on about Bunty but it is Jean who makes contact by telephone and seems still to be in love with Hugh. They arrange to meet in London but, when Hugh arrives at the rendezvous during an air raid, he sees to his horror that it has been blitzed and Jean killed. 'It's all so bloody unfair,' he angrily comments to Meikle. 'Life's unfair, as I'm sure you've noticed,' the surgeon retorts. Miekle goes on to explain what Hugh now faces in the way of operations but it is clear once Hugh moves to the plastic-surgery hospital that he has yet to come to terms with his disfigurement: 'I feel like hiding away in a corner.'[11]

Episode 3 opens with another dogfight in which the viewers see that another Spitfire is lost. A visit by Julian to Hugh's hospital hut reveals that the pilot was Jimmy Macdonnell, another Cambridge friend. After another operation, Hugh is pleased to meet Tim Holland (Patrick Ryecart), his old flying instructor who has also been seriously burned, yet will not let this get him down, but is depressed by operations, the way in which Marg, who is now working as a physiotherapist for Meikle, refuses to resume their former relationship (shown again in flashback), and by the way people stare at him in public. Meikle counsels patience and a resilient attitude, pointing out that, though Tim's wife left him after the crash, he still always manages to maintain his spirit. Hugh admits that, with his disfigurement, he feels like 'packing it all in', to which Meikle responds that he will just have to 'work harder' at attracting women in future. Hugh makes some effort but is upset by the way in which Bunty refuses to see him (the viewers see that she is now sleeping with Julian) and Marg continues to keep their relationship entirely professional. A visit to the family home, initially a success, goes badly awry when one of Susan's small children sees Hugh and thinks he is a monster, and after Julian arrives and informs Hugh that he and Bunty are getting married. The episode ends with Hugh trying to kill himself that night by jumping off a boat and drowning, saved only by a watchful fisherman.[12]

The fourth episode begins with Hugh denying to Meikle that he tried to commit suicide, though this was clearly the case, followed by a conversation between Hugh and Tim in which Tim says he has no intention of trying to fly again: 'Why does everyone expect us to be perfect bloody heroes?' A concerned Marg, about whom Hugh has been daydreaming, still refuses to be anything other than his physiotherapist, noting that he still displays a photograph of Bunty on his night table. Loretta Stone (Joanna Lumley), a film star with whom Hugh had a brief fling during flying training and who visits the burns unit on an ENSA (Entertainers National Services Association) tour, seems more amenable to a physical relationship, and persuades him to work as a technical adviser on a film about Spitfire pilots during the Battle of Britain in which she is starring. This turns out to be a disaster, however, Hugh intensely disliking the high-flown dialogue given to the pilot-actors – shades of *First of the Few* – and refusing to accept that drama trumps reality at the pictures. Added to the pain of this debacle is Julian's wedding to Bunty (Hugh goes to the church accompanied by Tim but, in the end, decides it would be too painful to meet the happy couple), the withdrawal of an invitation to speak at his old school once they discover what he now looks like, and the refusal of the guard at RAF Woodfold to let him through the gate on an impromptu visit because he is civilian clothes and does not have a pass. 'His recovery', as Havers explained in an interview, 'is a case of two steps forward, three steps back.' Marg, who has been growing closer to Hugh, is horrified to discover that Hugh is now determined to return to the one thing he thinks he is still good at: flying a Spitfire.[13]

Episode 5 makes it clear at the outset that both Marg and Meikle think Hugh is not fit to fly, and that Hugh is immensely frustrated by their opposition, announcing drunkenly at a pub celebration of Tim's impending second marriage that 'Without them [Meikle and Marg] we'd be up there, dicing with death; that's where we ought to be; either that or bloody dead.' Thanks to some plain talking by Meikle, Hugh repairs his relationship with Marg whom he eventually takes home to meet his parents. His mother in particular is keen for Hugh not to return to flying, and he agrees to try working at her brother's advertising agency. This, too, ends badly when it becomes clear that, while his drawings are liked, his face is considered too alarming to allow Hugh to pitch ideas to clients. Relations between Marg and Hugh are still dogged by the question of his feelings for Bunty which, the viewers gather, are still unresolved when he goes out for dinner with Julian and his wife and later promises after a pub crawl with his old friend to look after her should anything happen to her husband.[14]

The sixth and final episode of *A Perfect Hero* opens with Hugh once more trying to persuade Meickle to pass him as fit to fly, something which the surgeon is reluctant to do beyond allowing Hugh to go before an RAF medical board and have them decide on his future. On a visit to Woodfold – this time in uniform – Hugh asks Dickie to put in a good word for him, which Dickie agrees to do; but then word arrives that Julian has been shot down: 'You're the last of the long-haired boys now', as Dickie puts it. Hugh visits Julian's distraught widow and offers to help, and they seem to be falling in love once again; but when Bunty discovers his plans to rejoin the war she rejects him: 'You'll get bloody killed, like he did!'[15]

Meikle continues to oppose a return to flying operations – 'You'd be a menace to everybody else; yourself too' – as becomes clear when Hugh goes before the RAF medical board. He asks for more time to recover strength in his hands before a final decision is taken as to discharging him from the RAF, to which the board agrees. 'An

FIGURE 10 Nigel Havers as Hugh Fleming after plastic surgery, *A Perfect Hero* (Havahall/LWT, 1991).
Image courtesy of ITV.

obvious suicide type', one board member remarks after Hugh has left; 'or a hero', another retorts. Relations between Hugh and Marg have improved over time to the point where they are living together; but things once more go awry when she catches him calling Bunty to see if she needs any help and Marg throws him out. His mother and father think that the break-up my be their fault – class differences had been painfully apparent during the visit by Marg and Hugh to his parents' country home – and try to bring them back together, eventually succeeding to the point where the couple get engaged and are married. Hugh, meanwhile, after a second medical board meeting, has been granted his wish to visit fighter stations, starting with Woodfold, in order to tell new pilots to 'take a good look' and listen to what he has to say about the importance of looking out for the enemy and wearing goggles and gloves if they do not want to end up looking like him. A montage sequence shows Hugh growing more confident in dispensing his advice and continuing to work to improve the strength of his grip. In voice-over the audience hears a letter dated 11 September 1942 in which Hugh is cleared to fly fighters and posted to Woodfold. The last shots are of Hugh sitting once more in the cockpit of a Spitfire and taking off into the wild blue yonder accompanied by Dickie. 'How does it feel?' asks the CO. 'It feels bloody wonderful, Dickie,' Hugh replies.[16]

Havers had been partly inspired to become an actor by watching Kenneth More, while Prior thought Havers was a sensitive and very English actor in the tradition of, among others, Leslie Howard. The screenwriter believed the story he had developed to be 'full of that stoicism that used to distinguish what Churchill called the Island Race'; *A Perfect Hero* was, in short, 'unashamedly a "for" play'. Indeed, in many ways it was something of a return to the films of the 1940s and 1950s such as *First of the Few* and *Reach for the Sky* in which the protagonist learns heroically to conquer adversity both for himself and for King and Country. It remained to be seen what critics and the viewing public would make of this when after, being delayed because of the first Gulf War, *A Perfect Hero* began to air on London Weekend Television in weekly instalments starting on Friday, 17 May 1991 amid a good deal of orchestrated media hype.[17]

Among the critics there were those who liked what they saw. Francesca Turn of the *Guardian* found it to be 'sensitively-made', 'atmospheric', and 'evocative'. Patrick Stoddart in the *Sunday Times* wrote after the first episode that Havers possessed 'quite enough charisma to make the story worth following', and remarked that James Fox was very good in the role of Angus Meikle (an opinion echoed in the *Daily Telegraph*). Jennifer Selwyn in the *Observer* added that in what was 'an unashamedly nostalgic piece' Bernard Hepton and Barbara Leigh-Hunt 'give touching performances as Hugh's parents'. *A Perfect Hero* was, in short, for at least some television critics a 'compelling popular drama', as Graham Keal put it in the *Liverpool Echo*. Most reviews, however, especially as the series continued, were far less charitable.[18]

The photography, especially the soft-focus used for the many flashback sequences, came in for a good deal of abuse, as did the script. 'Never before have frosted lenses been called upon to obscure so much', wrote John Lyttle for *The Independent*: 'the low budget, the laughable dialogue', going on to label *A Perfect Hero* 'sheer tack' and 'trashy', and, by June, 'Ghastly . . . Somewhere between camp and insulting'. The *Evening Standard* also took note of the 'irritatingly soft focus' so often used and the unconvincing dialogue. The down-market tabloids were even more scathing. With a strong cast and a good subject, *A Perfect Hero* ought to have had a lot going for it, argued Tony Pratt in the *Daily Mirror* after the first few episodes; yet 'in spite of having all the right ingredients, this series has yet to get off the ground'. In the same issue Hilary Kingsley agreed that the premise was good, but thought everything else was bad: Havers's acting, the writing, the action – the 'opening dogfight was the worst staged aerial combat I've seen on any screen' – were all not up to the subject matter. 'Definitely a Bad Show,' she complained in mock *Boy's Own* tones, 'not a Wizard one.' The *News of the World* got real-life Falklands War burn victim Simon Weston to point out the technical inaccuracies concerning how burn victims behave, while Garry Bushell in *The Sun* argued that 'this fictional Battle of Britain drama is shot full of holes – trite dialogue, dull direction and cheap, unconvincing dogfight scenes like something out of an arcade game'. As *The Independent* put it two weeks before *A Perfect Hero* drew to a close, Nigel Havers, like the character he played, had been 'badly burned by the reviews'.[19]

The public, however, was apparently not paying that much atten-tion. The opening episode of *A Perfect Hero* drew 10.3 million viewers, placing it at number thirteen among the top 100 pro-grammes broadcast that week. A few hundred thousand British television watchers failed to tune in subsequently, but the series never dropped below twenty-second place in the weekly rankings and, on average, drew over nine million viewers each week. Of the top fifty drama series broadcast in the summer of 1991, *A Perfect Hero* came in at a respectable eleventh from the top.[20]

However contrived and sepia toned such series might be, broad-casters knew that viewers, perhaps in reaction to the uncertainties of the contemporary world, still tended to lap up such nostalgic paeans with great enthusiasm, not least if they involved the war. The Battle of Britain, it seemed, when presented in the right form, might continue to generate considerable public interest though not much critical acclaim. Despite its potentially difficult subject matter, *A Perfect Hero* took an approach that was far less controversial, yet also far more melodramatic, than *Piece of Cake*. Despite its relatively low production values, it contained what many ordinary people seemed to like. *A Perfect Hero* had going for it an heroic yet troubled central character played by a recognised actor, a story set in a still widely recognised historical context, and a protagonist faced with a series of challenges in love and war which he ultimately overcomes. A fairly straightforward 'for' Battle of Britain story, in other words, was likely to – and did – do better than a relatively complex *Piece of Cake*-style 'against' plot. *A Perfect Hero* was 'typical of what of what viewers have come to expect from ITV', Angus Towler, no great fan of the series, admitted in *Television Today*, ' – and, to judge by the rating, what they appreciate'.[21]

*   *   *

There were no further efforts to chronicle dramatically the Battle of Britain on British screens in the last decade of the twentieth century beyond passing references in the 1998 BBC television play *A Rather English Marriage*, in which ex-fighter pilot Reggie Conygham-Jervis (Albert Finney) has to come to terms with old age.[22] Quite why this was the case remains unclear, though the critical roasting *A Perfect Hero* received, the costs involved, a belief among executives that the subject matter appeared to be increasingly irrelevant to a contemporary young audience, or was simply exhausted for the time being, may have played a role. The end result was to leave the field clear for a small host of documentary film-makers. The subsequent factual accounts, it is worth noting, whether broadcast on television or made specifically for the video market, tended to repeat the general consensus on what had happened and did not tend to deal with controversial or new questions. This suggests that, if only for a niche set of interested parties, the legend was not being forgotten even as the drama market dried up. For wider consumption there was also the flow of high-profile new books about the battle as well as the creation through the support of a variety of celebrities of the Battle of Britain Historical Society in 1996.[23]

*   *   *

The dawn of the twenty-first century witnessed no change in the status quo as far as British productions were concerned. Films from abroad, however, were another matter.

The often contrasting critical reactions to two foreign films, dealing tangentially with the battle, that appeared within a year of each other on British screens at this point illustrate the way in which, at least for some, how The Few were presented still mattered in Britain. *Pearl Harbor*, from the United States, and *Dark Blue World*, from the Czech Republic, would be received in markedly different ways.

The third most expensive movie ever made by a single studio ($135 million from Disney), *Pearl Harbor* was, as the title implied, an epic in which the Japanese surprise attack on the US Pacific Fleet on 7 December 1941 takes centre stage. The plot revolves around a love triangle that develops between the three main characters as a result of one of them, Captain Rafe McCawley (Ben Affleck), being presumed killed in action after joining an RAF Eagle Squadron to help win the Battle of Britain. Though shot in England with the help of period planes from the Historic Aircraft Collection based at Duxford, the Battle of Britain sequences, lasting about seven minutes in all within a film that ran a total of 183 minutes, contained numerous factual inaccuracies that went beyond the common resort to a late-model Spitfire for the flying scenes. Among other things, as the makers apparently were fully aware, the Eagle Squadrons did not become operational until well after the battle, and were not composed of volunteers arriving in the uniform of the United States Army Air Corps. The Spitfires bear the code letters of 303 (Polish) Squadron rather than those of any of the Eagle squadrons. Someone involved in the production, perhaps impressed by the opening scenes of *Battle of Britain* or the first half of *Piece of Cake*, in which châteaux had featured (albeit in France, not England), placed the Spitfires of 'RAF Oakley' around Badminton House, Gloucestershire. What was more, in the wake of earlier complaints about the way Hollywood seemed intent on showing how America won the war in Europe single handedly in films such as *Saving Private Ryan* and *U-571*, there were also potential problems with the script.[24]

The sequences in England begin with setting-the-scene documentary footage accompanied by a *March of Time*-style American voice-over announcing that 'the *Luftwaffe* relentlessly bombs downtown London [to which a British critic rhetorically asked "Can you show me where that is, exactly?"], while Churchill's Royal Air Force is in a deadly struggle to maintain control of the British skies.' Black-and-white shots of Spitfires – several clearly damaged – lined up outside

Badminton House turn into colour as Rafe arrives, salutes his new CO (Nicholas Farrell), and announces: 'Lieutenant McCawley reporting for duty, sir.' When the CO proposes that he show the new arrival his quarters before introducing him to his aeroplane, McCawley responds that 'housekeeping' should be put aside in order to allow him to get airborne as quickly as possible. The CO looks at him and asks, 'Are all Yanks as anxious to get themselves killed, pilot officer?' to which Rafe earnestly replies 'Not anxious to die, sir; just anxious to matter' (a line which several British reviewers thought too over-the-top for words). Throughout the scene, the impression is given that Britain is on its last legs and will fall without the likes of McCawley coming to the rescue. 'Just a few British pilots are all that stand between Hitler and total victory in Europe,' Major Jimmy Doolittle (Alec Baldwin) announces to the soon-to-be Eagle pilot earlier in the film, 'they're going to need all the help they can get.'[25]

A montage sequence later shows McCawley in dogfights while the audience hears lines from the letters he is writing to his sweetheart. 'It's different than I thought it would be here,' he notes; but it turns out that he is talking about the weather rather than combat: 'It's cold. So cold it goes deep into your bones' (prompting one British reviewer to comment on this reaction to the Dover climate, 'Christ, you should try Glasgow, mate'). Our hero is clearly doing well, however, since we see the CO approach Rafe outside a pub as he is writing yet another letter. 'A lot of people frown on the Yanks for not being in this war yet,' the CO states. 'I'd just like to say, if there are many more back home like you, God help anyone who goes to war with America' (a line which one viewer described as 'putrid'). A few minutes later in the film the airfield receives an air-raid warning ('incoming!') and the ground crew and pilots – ignored by a small terrier pushing a ball – scramble to get their Spitfires airborne. McCawley's fitter tells him that there are oil problems with his engine, to which Rafe, settling into his cockpit, retorts 'Just crank it, Ian!' So impressed is Ian (Tony Curran) by the dauntless courage of this American hero that he in turn replies 'God speed you, sir!' In the subsequent dogfight, in which McCawley leads a section and is eventually shot down into the sea, he repeats 'hammer down!' every time he presses the gun button. Dialogue such as this was unlikely to impress those already worried about an apparently hegemonic American appropriation of World War II.[26]

Reviewers everywhere were not kind to *Pearl Harbor* for a variety of reasons, criticism ranging from the awful script and bad acting to the way in which the Doolittle Raid was tacked on to provide a happy ending. In Britain there was also a certain amount of irritation over the actions of the Yank in the RAF. Barbara Ellen, writing for *The Times* in late May 2001 when the film first opened in London, took aim at the way McCawley arrives in England 'presumably to show the limeys how "flashing" is really done'. Peter Bradshaw, writing for *The Guardian*, had this to say:

> Ben Affleck is Rafe, the square-jawed, cubic-headed US army pilot who is temporarily away in England, winning the Battle of Britain single-handed. If you thought that the War in the Pacific would be one second world war story which didn't patronise the Brits, you were dead wrong. The RAF squadron leader, soaking his stiff upper lip in a pint of limey warm brown beer, is overcome with gratitude for Ben . . .

Doubtless he would have agreed with Nicholas Barker in *The Independent* when he called *Pearl Harbor* 'revoltingly pro-American'. Ian Buruma, also in *The Guardian*, commented on the way in which the RAF officers ('pale, weedy, English') serve as a contrast to the 'jock' from America. The film 'serves as an ignorant riposte to those who ever imagined Britain and the [other] Allies were the true, committed, long-term heroes of the Second World War', argued a disgusted Andrew O'Hagan in the *Daily Telegraph*. It is worth noting, however, that poor reviews did not stop the heavily promoted *Pearl Harbor* from raking in £12 million at the British box-office. Bad history, it seemed, came a poor second to the desire to see a romance with lots of fireball explosions: especially, perhaps, since most of the history had to do with America and Japan rather than Britain.[27]

Dark Blue World was another love triangle film, this time one involving two Czech pilots flying for the RAF and an Englishwoman. Though the chronology is a little unclear, it appears that it is only in September–October 1940 that the Czech fighter squadron shown in *Dark Blue World* goes operational. The story is presented through a series of flashbacks from the perspective of the central character, ex-fighter pilot and playboy Franta Sláma (Ondrej Vetch), who in 1950 is serving an indefinite labour-camp sentence in the wake of the 1948 Communist coup in Czechoslovakia for having fought for the capitalist West rather than for the communist east during the Second World War. *Dark Blue World* chronicles his escape from Czechoslovakia in 1939 accompanied by his young protégé, Karel Vojtíšek (Kryštof Hádek), the difficulties experienced by Czech pilots in adapting to the RAF, various combat operations between 1940 and 1943, and above all, the close comradeship which develops between Franta and Karel that is ultimately shattered by their mutual infatuation for the beautiful Susan (Tara Fitzgerald).[28]

Made on what British co-producer Eric Abraham regarded as a 'shoestring budget' of under £5 million raised with some difficulty from various European sources, *Dark Blue World* was the follow-up project by the father-and-son team Zdeněk and Jan Svěrák to their Oscar-winning film *Kolya*. Both men had long known about the unhappy post-war fate of the Czech patriots who had flown with the RAF and were eager to tell their story in the context of a romantic tale examining issues of conscience. 'It's a "thank you"', director Jan Svěrák explained in an interview. 'And a "sorry". The film immortalises them.'[29]

Despite the financial constraints which, among other things necessitated shooting almost exclusively in the Czech Republic, the film-makers involved in *Dark Blue World* aimed to make the aerial and ground-based scenes set in England look as authentic as possible. Locations were carefully chosen for their resemblance to the real thing, vintage cars and other vehicles were procured, and Spitfires of the Old Flying Machine Company – costing $10,000 an hour in the air as they flew from a suitably redressed old Soviet air base outside Prague – were once again put into play. Shortage of airworthy aeroplanes was, as always, a problem though, in this case, largely ameliorated through the use of both computer-generated imagery and full-scale models (some equipped with lawnmower engines to spin the prop). The combat scenes were created through a blend of aerial photography – a B-25 camera plane again – computer-generated imagery and plenty of computer-enhanced out-takes from *Battle of Britain*.[30]

A huge hit in the Czech Republic, this largely foreign-language film was not distributed in Britain on anywhere near the scale of *Pearl Harbor* but, nonetheless, received a warm welcome from most critics. By and large, they accepted that the foreign squadrons flying for the RAF had not been given much time on screen (barring, of course, the few minutes devoted to the Poles in *Battle of Britain* and, rather more distantly, *Dangerous Moonlight*), and liked the aerial sequences. Interestingly, they also took no exception to a caricature stiff-upper-lip RAF station commander by the name of Bentley played by Charles Dance. After a damaged Spitfire taxies to a halt in the wrong place in the wake of the Czech pilots' first rather disastrous encounter with the *Luftwaffe*, Bentley sternly admonishes a shaken Czech pilot: 'This is England. Keep off the grass.' The *Daily Telegraph* critic, Tim Robey, found *Dark Blue World* to be 'quietly heartbreaking', Robert Fox in the *New Statesman* called it 'a little masterpiece', and Quentin Falk for the *Sunday Mirror* claimed it was 'fascinating', and placed it at number 7 in his top-ten film list for the year. 'Medal of honour goes to Charles Dance as a laconic Wing Commander,' Anthony Quinn argued in *The Independent*, 'addressing his squadron in tones as dry as a gin martini.' As Paula Kennedy of the BBC put it, 'it's good to be reminded that small countries such as Czechoslovakia also made their own heroic contribution to saving the world from fascism, and Czech director Jan Sverak's latest film, *Dark Blue World*, does just that.'[31]

There were, however, some exceptions to the generally positive mood. The various factual inaccuracies present in *Dark Blue World*, such as commissioned and non-commissioned pilots being shown eating in a single mess together and sharing sleeping accommodation, were overlooked (probably because reviewers were unaware of the way in which NCO pilots were treated). The way in which the film appeared to echo those of the past, on the other hand, was subject to some negative scrutiny. In *The Guardian* Peter Bradshaw, while admitting there were 'some very impressive aerial-combat scenes' and that both Charles Dance and Tara Fitzgerald gave 'sterling' supporting-role performances, thought *Dark Blue World* to be the mixture as before. As he saw it, 'all the RAF stuff looks very familiar, right down to the air ace's trusty dog, and short of actually seeing Kenneth More scuttling along on his tin legs, it couldn't be more clichéd'. Christopher Tookey, writing for the *Mail on Sunday*, agreed: 'there's very little in the movie that hasn't been done before, and with more verve and conviction'. The Battle of Britain cast once more in heroic terms, it seemed, was for some at least a nostalgia-laden film subject that had long since passed it sell-by date. In the eyes of Michael Hayden, writing for *Empire* magazine, *Dark Blue World* 'lurches from one contrived scene to the next', the critic adding that the 'recreated battle scenes become very boring very quickly'.[32]

Limited distribution, combined with the fact that *Dark Blue World* was mostly in a foreign language, meant that, whether reviewers liked it or not, the film's box-office prospects in Britain were limited. Despite efforts by the Czech Centre in London to promote *Dark Blue World*, including sponsoring a gallery exhibition staged in association with the Imperial War Museum, by the end of 2002 it had grossed a mere £198,538.[33]

How the Battle of Britain was received as screen drama in the last decade of the twentieth century seemed to reflect a number of different attitudes toward the Finest Hour. *A Perfect Hero* was a calculated attempt to revive the sacrificial heroic status of The Few that, despite critical disdain, successfully tapped into a vein of popular nostalgia. (Albeit perhaps as much because of the popularity of Nigel Havers in period dramas than because, say, of the recent anniversary of the battle.) Some of those reviewers who might dismiss such nostalgia as stale and backward, however, could take a much less cynical line if the screen representation of the Battle of Britain was made overseas rather than at home. To the wider public such things might not matter either because the sequences were tangential to the main plot or because so few people had seen the film in question. But how The Few were treated in *Pearl Harbor* and *Dark Blue World* could generate surprisingly patriotic instincts among at least some of the film critics: as indicated, for most of them the Czechs had understood the Finest Hour in a way that the Yanks certainly had not. The Battle of Britain, in short, still had at least some degree of resonance in the first years of the twenty-first century.

Notes

1. *Northern Echo*, 17 May 1991, p. 17.
2. On the Battle of Britain Memorial near Folkestone see e.g. http://www.jackson harrison.co.uk/BoB2/General/Memorials/capel.htm (accessed 5 January 2005); Jeremy A. Crang, 'Identifying "The Few": The Personalisation of a Heroic Military Elite', *War and Society*, 24 (2005), pp. 21–2. On press coverage of the fiftieth anniversary, which included a fly-past of 168 RAF aircraft over London led by a Spitfire, the biggest aerial spectacle over the capital since the coronation, see e.g. *The Times*, 15 September 1990, p. 4; *Guardian*, 15 September 1990, pp. 2, 11. On worries about the fading of past glories see e.g. Peter Hitchens, *The Abolition of Britain: From Lady Chatterly to Tony Blair* (London: Quartet, 1999), p. 52 et al. On more radical reinterpretations see Alan Clark in *The Times*, 2 January 1993, p. 12; *New Statesman*, 8 September 1989, p. 4; Clive Ponting, *1940: Myth and Reality* (London: Hamilton, 1990), pp. 130–2, 135–6; John Charmley, *Churchill: End of Glory – A Political Biography* (London: Hodder and Stoughton, 1993), pp. 400, 402, 406, et al. Despite its provocative title, Angus Calder's *The Myth of the Blitz* (London: Jonathan Cape, 1991) was a much more subtle and sophisticated effort at understanding the origins and nature of the mythology that developed around the events of 1940. On the Establishment desire to retain control of how World War II was remembered in the 1980s see e.g. Patrick Wright, *On Living in an Old Country: The National Past in Contemporary Britain* (London: Verso, 1985), ch. 11. On Thatcherite appropriation of the Spitfire and other symbols of 1940 see ibid., pp. 45–6; Lucy Noakes, *War and the British: Gender, Memory and National Identity* (London: I. B. Tauris, 1998), pp. 105, 110; Graham Dawson, *Soldier Heroes: British Adventure, Empire and the Imagining of Masculinities* (London: Routledge, 1994), p. 14.

3. Prior, Allan, *Script to Screen: The Story of Five Television Plays* (London: Ver, 1996), pp. 1, 141–45.

4. Author acknowledgements, Christopher Matthew, *The Long-Haired Boy* (London: Hamilton, 1980). The episode in which the protagonist, Hugh Fleming, first looks in the mirror after being burned almost exactly matches the real-life experience of Geoffrey Page. See Geoffrey Page, *Shot Down in Flames: A World War II Pilot's Remarkable Tale of Survival* (London: Grub Street, 1999), pp. 87–8. On Whitehall, Havers, and the book see Prior, *Script to Screen*, p. 142; *TV Times*, 11–17 May 1991, pp. 8–9.

5. *Times Literary Supplement*, 7 March 1980, p. 278; *New Statesman*, 15 February 1980, p. 251; *Observer*, 10 February 1980, p. 39. See also, however, the review by Patricia Craig, in which she concluded: 'On the whole, "workmanlike" is the best that can be said about *The Long-Haired Boy*.' *Books and Bookmen*, March 1980, p. 21.

6. C. Foxley-Norris in *Battle of Britain: The Truth* (DD/Proteus Productions, 1990); C. F. Currant in *Aviation Heroes of World War II: The Battle of Britain* (Greenwich Workshop, 1990); Prior, *Script to Screen*, pp. 142–4.

7. Prior, *Script to Screen*, p. 142.

8. Ibid., p. 144; see Martin W. Bowman, *Low Level From Swanton: The history of Swanton Morley airfield from World War Two to the present day* (Walton-on-Thames: Air Research Publications, 1995), p. 233. On the cost see *Liverpool Echo*, 17 May 1991, p. 17.

9. Prior, *Script to Screen*, pp. 149, 152. The exchange between Hugh and Julian came from the pen of Prior rather than Matthew. It is worth noting that Prior evidently decided to recast Hugh's parachute descent so that he was not, as was the case in the novel, hit in the legs by shotgun pellets fired by an over-zealous Home Guard (something that did in fact happen in the actual battle to James Nicolson). See Christopher Matthew, *A Perfect Hero* (London: Mandarin, 1991), pp. 9, 45; Richard Hough and Denis Richards, *The Battle of Britain: The Jubilee History* (London: Hodder and Stoughton, 1989), p. 195. The 'CK' code letters on the Spitfires of '89 Squadron', which did not exist, were never allocated to an RAF squadron during the war. See Michael J. F. Bowyer and John D. R. Rawlings, *Squadron Codes, 1937–56* (Cambridge: Patrick Stephens, 1979), pp. 26, 146.

10. Prior, *Script to Screen*, pp. 167, 162, et al.

11. The character of Bunty Morell, who plays a central role in *A Perfect Hero*, is a relatively minor figure in *The Long-Haired Boy* while, in the novel, Jean is a volunteer nurse rather than a Land Girl.

12. In *The Long-Haired Boy* Julian is killed quite early on and Bunty does not appear after her first and last visit to Ashford hospital. The love triangle, in short, was something developed by Prior rather than Matthews.

13. *TV Times*, 11–17 May 1991, p. 9. The scenes at the school and the film studio follow the book comparatively closely.

14. In *The Long-Haired Boy* it is Hugh who is ambivalent about flying again and Marg who is in favour of the idea.

15. In *The Long-Haired Boy* 'Dickie' Bird also numbers among Hugh Fleming's former comrades who get killed in action. The scene at Woodfold in which Julian's death is announced is a version of a section in the book set at 'RAF Middleton' in which the death of a major character missing from the television version – Robin Bailey – is announced.

16. In *The Long-Haired Boy* Hugh has to settle, as did Richard Hillary, for a training unit; though to be fair there were burned pilots such as Geoffrey Page who returned to fighter ops.

17. Prior, *Script to Screen*, pp. 142, 145; *TV Times*, 11–17 October 1991, p. 8. For examples of the way in which *A Perfect Hero* was plugged before broadcast see e.g. *The People*, 12 May 1991, magazine, p. 21; *Today*, 15 May 1991, pp. 20–1; *Daily Record*, 17 May 1991, p. 27; *Oxford Mail*, 17 May 1991, p. 17; *Yorkshire Evening Post*, 17 May 1991, p. 12; *Western Morning News*, 11 May 1991, p. 14; *Eastern Daily Press*, 11 May 1991, p. 12; *Birmingham Post*, 17 May 1991, p. 2; *The Scotsman*, 17 May 1991, p. 31.

18. *Northern Echo*, 17 May 1991, p. 17; *Observer*, 12 May 1991, p. 71; *Daily Telegraph*, 24 May 1991, p. 33; *Sunday Times*, 19 May 1991, Section 5, p. 16; *Guardian*, 7 June 1991, p. 38, 14 June 1991, p. 36, 21 June 1991, p. 40.

19. *The Independent*, 14 June 1991, p. 27; *Sun*, 22 May 1991, p. 25; *News of the World*, 19 May 1991, pp. 8–9; *Daily Mirror*, 24 May 1991, p. 23, 31; *Evening Standard*, 17 May 1991, p. 32, 24 May 1991, p. 31; *The Independent*, 24 May 1991, p. 29, 7 June 1991, p. 27; see also *Broadcast*, 31 May 1991, p. 38; *Television Today*, 23 May 1991, p. 19; *Today*, 18 May 1991, p. 23. On the soft-focus problem see also *Financial Times*, 22 May 1991, p. 15; *Sunday Times*, 19 May 1991, Section 5, p. 16.

20. *Broadcast*, 18 October 1991, p. 23; *Broadcast*, 7 June 1991, p. 21; *Broadcast*, 14 June 1991, p. 52; *Broadcast*, 21 June 1991, p. 24; *Broadcast*, 28 June 1991, p. 22; *Broadcast*, 5 July 1991, p. 22; *Broadcast*, 12 July 1991, p. 21; see also *Broadcast*, 16 April 1993, p. 58.

21. *Television Today*, 23 May 1991, p. 19; see Stephen Haseler, *The English Tribe: Identity, Nation and Europe* (Basingstoke: Macmillan, 1996), p. 92; see also Lucy Noakes, 'Making Histories: Experiencing the Blitz in London's Museums in the 1990s', in M. Evans and K. Lunn (eds), *War and Memory in the Twentieth Century* (Oxford: Berg, 1997), pp. 100–1 on 'unifying' nostalgia via a different medium.

22. *A Rather English Marriage*, based on the 1992 novel of the same name by Angela Lambert, employed flashback sequences made up in part of footage from *Battle of Britain* and featured a young Reggie (played by John Light) who bore a notable physical resemblance to Squadron Leader Rex (Tim Woodward) in *Piece of Cake*.

23. On the formation of the Battle of Britain Historical Society see Adrian Gregory, 'The Commemoration of the Battle of Britain', in J. Crang and P. Addison (eds), *The Burning Blue: A New History of the Battle of Britain* (London: Pimlico, 2000), p. 228. On liberal dislike of 'our endless tribal war dance' see e.g. Anne Mcelvoy piece in *The Independent*, 30 March 2000; Richard Cockett piece in *Times Higher Education Supplement*, 25 April 1997; see also the widespread negative reactions to the Germanophobic *Daily Mirror* front page spread on the England-Germany match in the Euro 96 championship in Piers Morgan, *The Insider* (London: Ebury, 2005), pp. 127–28. On video documentaries, which vary greatly in quality, see e.g. *The Official Battle of Britain 50th Anniversary Video* (Roymark Productions, 1990); *The Battle of Britain: The Truth* (DD/Proteus Productions, 1990); *The War Years: Battle of Britain* (Lamancha/Trax Video, 1993); *Battle of Britain* (Classic Pictures, 1995); *True Stories of the Battle of Britain* (Revelation Films, 2000). New books included such highly successful titles as Richard Overy's *The Battle* (London: Penguin, 2000) and Patrick Bishop's *Fighter Boys: Saving Britain 1940* (London: HarperCollins, 2003).

24. On the furore over *Saving Private Ryan* and *U-571* see e.g. http://britsversus yanks.tripod.com (accessed 25 November 2000). On the location shooting in England see 'Pearl Harbor in Britain', http://www.geocities.com/antzero/pearlhar bor.htm?20054 (accessed 4 November 2005); see also http://www.historicaircraft collection.ltd.uk/activities (accessed 1 November 2005). On the code letters RF see Bowyer and Rawlings, *Squadron Codes*, p. 89. On the real Eagle Squadrons see

Philip D. Caine, *Eagles of the RAF: The World War II Eagle Squadrons* (Honolulu: University Press of Hawaii, 2002). On the film-maker's obvious knowledge of the truth about the Eagle Squadrons see Disney Enterprises, *Pearl Harbor* (New York: Hyperion, 2001), pp. 39–41. But then again the screenwriter, Randall Wallace, appears to have been under the impression that the Battle of Britain took place in 1941, to judge by the novel from the screenplay: see Randall Wallace, *Pearl Harbor* (New York: Hyperion, 2001), pp. 33, 108.

25. On reactions to the 'not anxious to die' line see e.g. *The Times*, 31 May 2001, T2, p. 12; *New Statesman*, 11 June 2001, p. 62.

26. Re. 'putrid' lines see http://www.indielondon.co.uk/dvd/pearl_harbour.html (accessed 4 November 2005); re. the comments on 'downtown' London and the weather see http://www.channel4.com/film/reviews/film_indepth.jsp?id = 106985&page = 2 (accessed 4 November 2005). The crash itself required a good deal of willing suspension of disbelief, involving as it did a trapped pilot surviving a vertical plunge into the sea and providentially being picked up by a passing French fishing boat. To be fair, writer Randall Wallace appears to have known very little about the RAF or England in 1940, to judge by the novel from his screenplay in which, for example, there is mention of the 'eternal dusk of the British Isles', the rank of air commodore is miss-spelt as 'air commander', and A and B flights are called 'Alpha group' and 'Beta group': see Wallace, *Pearl Harbor*, pp. 26, 65, 81, 91.

27. *Daily Telegraph*, 1 June 2001, p. 25; *Guardian*, 31 May 2001, G2, pp. 2–3; *The Independent*, 1 June 2001, Friday Review, p. 10; *Guardian*, 1 June 2001, G2, p. 12; see also e.g. *Sunday Times*, 27 May 1991, section 9, p. 4; *New Statesman*, 11 June 2001, pp. 62–3, 18 June 2001, p. 46; *Sight and Sound*, July 2001, p. 48; http://news.bbc.co.uk/1/hi/entertainment/reviews/1351841.stm (accessed 4 November 2005). On British box-office takings see http://news.bbc.co.uk/1/hi/entertainment/film/1526345.stm (accessed 4 November 2005). *Empire*, the British film magazine, went against the critical consensus by giving *Pearl Harbor* a positive write-up on the basis of its action sequences. See *Empire*, July 2001, p. 60. On the more general historical inaccuracies of *Pearl Harbor* see Lawrence H. Suid, *Guts and Glory: The Making of the American Military Image in Film* (Lexington, KY: Kentucky University Press, 2002), pp. 684–8; Jonathan Vankin and John Whalen, *Based on a True Story: Fact and Fiction in 100 Favorite Movies* (Chicago: Chicago Review Press, 2005), pp. 273–7.

28. The evidence suggesting that it is only at the end of the Battle of Britain that the Czech pilots in the film become operational is as follows. The first scenes set in England show the Czechs undergoing continuous language and R/T procedure training, and only 'three months later' are they allowed to go on their first operational sortie. Franta, we learn, flew for the French air force before joining the RAF, which means that he probably would not have got to England before June or July 1940, and 'three months later' indicates September–October 1940 as the start of operations. The identification letters on the Spitfires, AI, do not correspond to any known squadron of the time, including the first Czech squadron, 310. Bowyer and Rawlings, *Squadron Codes*, pp. 16, 77. Though see Jonathan Glancey, *Spitfire: The Biography* (London: Atlantic, 2006), p. 201.

29. *Daily Telegraph*, 3 May 2002, Arts, p.4; E. Abraham on commentary track of Special Edition DVD version of *Dark Blue World* (Sony Pictures, 2002).

30. On the making of the film see 'Making of' documentary attached to Special Edition DVD version of *Dark Blue World* (Sony Pictures, 2002). The film-makers also appear to have borrowed a brief bit of footage from *Memphis Belle* (Warner Brothers, 1990).

31. P. Kennedy in http://news.bbc.co.uk/1/hi/entertainment/reviews/1671202.stm (accessed 1 November 2005); *The Independent*, 10 May 2002, Review Section, p. 11; *Sunday Mirror*, 12 May 2002, p. 44; *New Statesman*, 18 June 2001, p.46; *Daily Telegraph*, 10 May 2002, p. 25; see also e.g. *The Times*, Play section, 11–17 May 2002, p. 4; *Sunday Times*, 12 May 2002, Sec. 9, p. 6. On limited distribution of *Dark Blue World* in Britain see Connelly, *We Can Take It!*, p. 126, note 23.

32. *Empire*, June 2002, p. 128; *Mail on Sunday*, 12 May 2002, p. 69; *Guardian*, 10 May 2002, G2 p. 15; see also e.g. *Sight and Sound*, May 2002, p. 42; http://www.empireonline.co.uk/incinemas/ReviewComplete.asp?FID = 7913 (accessed 5 November 2005).

33. http://www.nft.org.uk/filmtivinfo/stats/boxoffice/ukfeatures-02.html (accessed 6 November 2005). On the gallery and Czech Centre promotion see http://www.czechcentre.org.uk/press_centre/releases/darkblueworld.html (accessed 6 November 2005). Inaccuracies in *Dark Blue World* also include showing a 1940–vintage Spitfire being equipped with an inflatable dinghy (presumably in order to help set the scene for the film's climax, in which Karel crashes into the sea while trying to throw his dinghy out to Franta who is already in the water).

Conclusion

Over the past sixty-odd years the representation on screen of the Battle of Britain as drama has undergone an evolutionary process in which established images and attitudes have developed roughly in tandem with the changing social and cultural landscape of twentieth-century Britain. *The Lion Has Wings* and *First of the Few* helped develop, under wartime censorship conditions, a basic narrative of events in which The Few vanquish the many with the Spitfire. In the following decade, with more factors able to be discussed openly, elements were added to this basic David-and-Goliath story in *Angels One Five* and *Reach for the Sky*, including the importance of teamwork on the one hand and individual initiative on the other. (And in the context of the ebb and flow of collectivist sentiment across the socio-cultural spectrum.) More than ten years on, in the midst of major generational and attitudinal fluctuation, there emerged the most wide-ranging and comprehensive treatment of events to date, *The Battle of Britain*, in which a variety of problems within the RAF were touched on and some of the horrors of war illustrated[1] while, at the same time, the essential elements of the Finest Hour image, not least the heroism of pilots battling against the odds and saving Britain from invasion, were maintained. Twenty years later, cynicism and revisionist sentiment had developed to a point where *Piece of Cake* could emerge as a de facto effort to debunk the myth of The Few and suggest that the battle was, in fact, not the Finest Hour after all. The hitherto established version of events, however, could not be so easily overturned, as its reassertion only a few years later in the storyline and popular – as opposed to the critical – reception of *A Perfect Hero* indicated.

Yet it is important to recognise this last version of the Battle of Britain was no mere retrograde exercise in the recycling of, say, *First of the Few*, any more than was true of earlier big- and small-screen efforts to capture something of the Battle of Britain. In some cases, difference has been a matter of budgets and technology: the cost of various kinds of film and tape, say, or the presence or non-availability of the right aircraft, or what was considered state of the art in terms of special effects at a particular moment. In other respects the passage of time also altered what was and was not considered acceptable screen drama in terms of actions, language, and overt emotionalism. Though critics sometimes seemed to forget this, the swearing, gore, and the self-doubt present in everything from *The Battle of Britain* to *A Perfect Hero* were a far cry from the rather bloodless, stiff-upper-lip restraint on display in *First of the Few* or *Angels One Five*. The former would most assuredly have been considered unacceptably graphic by board of censorship members of the day, while the latter would have appeared too clean and emotionally arid by film-makers and audiences in the context of cultural shifts occurring from the 1960s onward.[2]

Furthermore, though elements might be consciously or unconsciously borrowed – the presence of a squadron mascot, for instance, or a pilot vomiting when the phone rings[3] – from one screen version to another, changes did occur in storyline and interpretative terms. Each attempt at presenting The Few was, indeed, in some respects *sui generis*. *The Lion Has Wings* was singular in that it projected the positive outcome of a battle that had yet to be fought. *The First of the Few* conceptualised what had actually taken place rather uniquely in terms of the career of Reginald Mitchell. *Angels One Five* not only brought the Hurricane into the picture but also radar. *Reach for the Sky* was the only film specifically to chronicle the actions of a real-life fighter pilot and leader. *The Battle of Britain* was in a class by itself insofar as it tried to tell the story from both sides and at all levels. Among other things, *Piece of Cake* was alone in portraying what happened over France prior to the battle. And *A Perfect Hero* was the only full-length screen attempt at showing what happened after the battle to those who had been badly scarred.

Each representation, in short, was in some respects a unique reflection of the wider socio-cultural context in which it was conceived. How each was received when it first appeared on screen, however, did not necessarily conform to film-makers' expectations, and, furthermore, critics and the viewing public in some cases disagreed with each other about the merits and demerits of a particular film or series. In this respect, *Angels One Five* and *A Perfect Hero* were cases in point. In some instances script, acting and production values had something to do with such dissonance between film-makers and the public or between the public and critics but so, too, did disagreement about how 1940 should be remembered. The epic *Battle of Britain*, for instance, had got into difficulty at the box-office in part because, as historian Malcolm Smith observed some years ago, it was 'in many ways out of sorts with the cultural climate of the 1960s'. Nearly twenty years on, *Piece of Cake* was caught between those critics and viewers who thought it too revisionist and those who thought it did not go far enough.[4]

In this context, the level of historical accuracy could be problematic. On the one hand, film-makers could find themselves in trouble if they departed too far from reality. *The Lion Has Wings*, after all, virtually sank without trace once its predictions came up against the real thing while, in relation to post-war representations of the Battle of Britain, those responsible could be criticised by enthusiasts – today sometimes dubbed 'aero-anoraks' – for unintentional and for unavoidable errors in period detail. On the other hand film-makers could find themselves in trouble with the critics for, in essence, having adhered too closely to the period they were covering in word and deed. Charges of cliché dialogue and action might be the result of similar scenes in other films, but could also be the result of shifts over the years in perceptions of how young people were supposed to think and act under physical and emotional stress. Some of the contemporary criticism of *Angels One Five* and *Reach for the Sky*, in particular, was the result of the first factor. But some of the fault-finding with respect to *A Perfect Hero*, for example, also involved a sense that people simply did not really talk and act as called for in the script. The fact that, however archaic these words and actions might appear many years after the events portrayed, they might still be an accurate reflection of The Few, was secondary to contemporary dramatic considerations. Hence, even a revisionist piece, such as *Piece of Cake*, could be attacked for using the kind of odd-sounding nicknames that were, in fact, common currency in 1940.[5]

Indirectly illustrative of this sort of thinking is the reaction of actor Robert Shaw while filming *The Battle of Britain* in 1968 at Duxford after he had met the real-life Battle of Britain hero Douglas Bader for the first time. Shaw was taken completely off guard when Bader – whose opinions and idiom were frozen in time – ended every other sentence with an 'old boy' and spoke with relish of shooting down the Hun. 'I never knew people *talked* like that,' a thunderstruck Shaw remarked.[6]

Neither, it seemed, did many critics; and if any did, then they, in essence, believed that historical accuracy ought to take second place to contemporary culture. And, of course, the gap between the two tended only to widen with the passage of time. It was no accident that the performance of Kenneth More in *Reach for the Sky* was alluded to in derisive terms by those critics who found *Dark Blue World* or *Piece of Cake* unacceptably old-fashioned. Even some of those who still liked the war films of the 1950s now tended to do so for reasons of nostalgia rather than because the pictures were seen as reflections of historical reality. In a sense, by the end of the century, the past really was becoming a foreign country.[7]

*   *   *

As for the future, the evolution of the Battle of Britain as screen drama remains uncertain both in likelihood and form. Depending on how contemporary trends are read, the Finest Hour is either losing its relevance or healthier than ever as a subject of public interest and potential subject matter for the screen.

On the one hand the battle seems likely to diminish in significance within the British popular imagination as new generations emerge and those who personally remember 1940 inevitably fade away. Battle of Britain Day, as Peter Brown, a surviving member of The Few, lamented a few years ago, 'is not now part of our national calendar' and 'is not normally remembered in schools as part of our great heritage of fighting for freedom'. As *The Independent* discovered through a poll conducted in the summer of 2004, a third of the sample questioned did not know that the Battle of Britain occurred in the Second World War, a figure that rose to half among those between the ages of sixteen and thirty-four. The triumph of RAF Fighter Command, in other words, may soon become no more than another historical marker, of no more relevance to the average person than Trafalgar or Naseby. The number of airworthy period aircraft that might be used for filming, moreover, will certainly continue to decline because of accidents as well as normal wear and tear on engines and airframes, while the cost of flyable replicas is likely to be prohibitive even for Hollywood.[8]

On the other hand, casting backward glances to a supposedly better time does not appear to have diminished within society as a whole. A London monument commemorating the battle was unveiled in 2005, while best-selling and sometimes provocative books on the Battle of Britain continue to appear along with further television documentaries. 'Of course we remember "the few" who held back the Nazi hordes in that balmy summer of 1940,' forty-six year-old television personality Jeremy Clarkson could confidently assert in 2005. Before and since then the RAF Museum and other bodies have continued to try to ensure, with respect to the pilots of those far-off days, that 'the memory of their valour is kept alive for future generations' with some success. The Spitfire, in particular, remains an icon in British popular culture. Meanwhile, even among the young, the sense that the Germans are more threatening than other foreigners has shown remarkable resilience.[9]

As for the dwindling number if airworthy planes, improved computer-generated imagery (CGI) may one day make up for the absence of real aircraft from the Second World War. The way in which the Blitz continues to feature in films and on television, in everything from Narnia to Doctor Who, in which CGI planes look a bit more credible when set against a night-sky background, suggests that, if the technical problems can be overcome – that is to say, if CGI images against a daylight-sky background can look more effective than they mostly do at present – then more works featuring the Battle of Britain will appear. New storylines may yet be developed – witness the episode in the wartime crime-solving ITV television series Foyle's War in which a high-scoring Spitfire pilot turns out to be not only guilty of manslaughter but also gay – and new interpretations made. It is, for instance, notable that no plot has of yet centred on the lives and work of the RAF fitters and riggers who kept the Fighter Boys in the air, or indeed – with the partial exception of Susannah York's ensemble role in Battle of Britain – the WAAFs.[10]

If money, technology, and a willingness to try again appear in combination then The Few may even have a future on the big screen. Indeed, as recently as 2003, plans were announced in Variety for a new Hollywood epic in which the Battle of Britain would figure prominently.[11]

The fuss following the initial announcement of what was to be titled The Few, moreover, suggests that how the Battle of Britain is interpreted remains a sensitive subject. The film, based on a proposal from author Alex Kershaw (who had previously written the book on which the movie Saving Private Ryan had been based), was to be about a ,real-life wealthy American playboy-sportsman who had fought and died with 601 Squadron during the Battle of Britain. Given that Billy Fiske – to be played by Tom Cruise – really had been among The Few, this was not a concept that, on the surface at least, could cause offence. Hackles were raised in Britain, however, when the basic plot was unveiled in *Variety*:

> In 1940, expert German fighters had decimated the Royal Air Force to the point that there weren't enough pilots left to fly the Spitfire planes sitting idly in hangers . . . Unable to rouse the US into action, a desperate Winston Churchill hatched a covert effort to recruit civilian American pilots to join the RAF. Risking prison sentences in the then-neutral US, a ragtag bunch of pilots answered the call.

The movie, to be directed by Michael Mann, would also feature 'ferocious dogfights between overmatched American pilots and the German ace fliers'. Owing as it did rather more to the plot lines of *A Yank in the RAF* and *International Squadron* than to the historical record, this description of what *The Few* would consist of provoked outrage among those who thought that Hollywood had already appropriated more than enough British wartime triumphs for America in recent films such as *U-571*.[12]

The real Billy Fiske, as it happened, had flown only a handful of operational sorties in Hurricanes during the Battle of Britain prior to his death, during which he shot down not a single enemy aircraft. Though there had been a shortage of newly trained pilots when set against the rate at which fighters were being produced, Spitfires had not been sitting in hangers waiting for someone to fly them. As for Yanks joining the RAF, this had not been something that Churchill had instigated and did not bear fruit in the form of the first Eagle Squadron until after the battle was over. Veterans and their supporters were therefore not slow to respond once the news was out. 'I'm appalled,' stated Archie Winskill when questioned by the press. 'We were alone and on the brink of disaster but we stopped the German air force and probably the invasion of Britain.' There had been only a handful of American pilots then serving in Fighter Command. 'I've heard it is almost like he won the war all on his own,' commented Ben Clinch, who had been an armourer with 601 Squadron. 'Hollywood can go and take a dip in the drink,' added Gerald Stapleton, an ex-603 Squadron pilot. 'It's going to be a farce if we have the Yanks shooting down everything in sight,' warned the president of the Battle of Britain Historical Society. 'We are concerned,' he added. As Winskill put it, the fear was that 'Young people who haven't read anything about the Battle of Britain might accept this rubbish as the truth.'[13]

At the time of writing (early 2006), the future of The Few appears uncertain. The book by Kershaw is now supposed to appear at the end of the year, but the film release date has been pushed back to 2008. Whether or not it eventually appears on screen, The Few certainly suggests that, for the time being at least, the Battle of Britain has neither entirely lost its hold on the public imagination nor faded completely as a potential screen subject in the minds of film-makers. Hollywood players such as Michael Mann, to be sure, with the support of major studios, will always have more money to invest than any home-grown producer. But, as another foreigner, Jan Svěrák, demonstrated with Dark Blue World, it is still possible to mount a credible big-screen film about the battle on a relatively modest budget.

If, or more likely when, another Battle of Britain drama makes it to the big or small screen it doubtless will be compared to and contrasted with what has come before. What positions are taken next time, and how these are received both by critics and by the public, will inevitably depend on the social and cultural context. On screen, perhaps more than in print, history is influenced by what is and is not considered timely in terms of both form and subject matter. All that can be said with certainty is that future representations will reflect their times in a general sense as much as the state of historical research.

Notes

1. Oddly, in view of such graphic shots as a German air gunner receiving a burst of machine-gun fire in the eyes, censor John Trevelyan considered The Battle of Britain to be unrealistic in its treatment of violence. See John Trevelyan, What the Censor Saw (London: Michael Joseph, 1974), p. 156.
2. On the way in which the censors had to grapple with the higher level of violence present in Sixties films see Trevelyan, What the Censor Saw, ch. 11.
3. Mascot dogs were present in The Battle of Britain, Piece of Cake, and A Perfect Hero. Photographs and newsreel footage from 1940 attest that this cinematic convention had a basis in fact. Pilots are shown throwing up when the phone rings in both The Battle of Britain and A Perfect Hero.
4. Malcolm Smith, Britain and 1940: History, Myth and Popular Memory (London: Routledge, 2000), p. 123.
5. See e.g. The People, 8 October 1988, p. 22. It is noteworthy that the actors improvising dialogue while playing RAF pilots in the Battle of Britain documentary in the Battlefield Britain series (BBC, 2004), used contemporary rather

than historically correct slang and idiom. The producers were criticised for this technique, used in episodes dealing with more distant battles as well, but clearly thought it a good way to draw in contemporary audiences. See Michael Nelson, 'It May Be History, But is it True? The Imperial War Museum Conference', *Historical Journal of Film, Radio and Television*, 25 (2005), p. 141–6.

6. Robert Shaw after talking to Douglas Bader in Leonard Mosley, *The Battle of Britain: The Making of a Film* (London: Weidenfeld and Nicolson, 1969), p. 143.
7. *Reach for the Sky* was marketed on video as a nostalgia piece (see Smith, *Britain and 1940*, p. 121) while *Angels One Five* was featured as a typical 1950s war film in Stephen Poliakoff's nostalgia-laden television play *Perfect Strangers* (BBC, 2001). On *Perfect Strangers* see Sarah Caldwell, 'Television Aesthetics and Close Analysis: Style, Mood and Engagement in *Perfect Strangers*', J. Gibbs and D. Pye (eds), *Style and Meaning: Studies in the Detailed Analysis of Film* (Manchester: Manchester University Press, 2005), pp. 179–94. On Poliakoff see e.g. *The Guardian*, 13 January 2006, p. 18; *The Independent*, 6 January 2006, pp. 1–4. For derisive allusions to *Reach for the Sky* in reference to *Piece of Cake* and *Dark Blue World* see *Daily Telegraph*, 15 October 1988, p. 19; *The Guardian*, 10 May 2002, G2, p. 15.
8. Peter Brown, *Honour Restored* (Staplehurst: Spellmount, 2005), p. 70; see *The Independent*, 5 August 2004. On comparative lack of interest among the young in the Battle of Britain see also Mark Connelly, *We Can Take It!* (London: Longman, 2004), p. 301.
9. *Royal Air Force Museum Hendon: Souvenir Video* (Aviacam Productions, 1997) [the Battle of Britain Historical Society has similar aims: see http://battle ofbritain.net/bobhsoc/index.html (accessed 3 November 2005)]; Jeremy Clarkson, *I Know You Got Soul: Machines with That Certain Something* (London: Penguin, 2006), p. x. On the persistence of Germanophobia see John Ramsden, *Don't Mention the War: The British and the Germans since 1890* (London: Little, Brown, 2006), ch. 10. On the new London Battle of Britain monument see Battle of Britain Historical Society, *Honouring the Few* (London: Battle of Britain Books, 2005). On the Spitfire as icon see Clarkson, *I Know You Got Soul*, pp. 222–33.
10. Ground personnel without rings on their sleeves or wings on their breast doubtless lack the glamour of the Fighter Boys, but it is worth noting that, in print, it has proven possible to create interesting and credible major ground personnel characters (see Elleston Trevor, *Squadron Airborne* [London: Macmillan, 1955]). A story focusing more on the ground than the air might also save on costs.
11. The episode of *Foyle's War* in question was entitled *Among the Few*. For this and other episodes (*Eagle Day*, *Enemy Fire*) in which the aerial exploits of Foyle's son, Andrew, are shown, Greenlit productions relied on a single airworthy Spitfire Vb courtesy of the Historic Aircraft Collection, and various mock-ups (including wooden one-dimensional models for long-shots), and footage taken from *Piece of Cake*. See Martyn Jones' comments in the production notes attached to the DVD version of *Among the Few*, and http://www.foyles war.com (accessed 1 November 2005). Recently published books related to the Battle of Britain include Derek Robinson, *Invasion, 1940* (London: Constable and Robinson, 2005); David E. Fisher, *A Summer Bright and Terrible* (Emeryville, CA: Shoemaker and Howard, 2005). Recent television documentaries – while tending to be conservative in content though somewhat adventurous in presentation – include *Battlefield Britain: The Battle of Britain* (BBC, 2004) and *Fighting the Blue* (ASA Productions (UK) for UKTV, 2005). It seems likely that

the battle will also continue to attract writers of counter-factual history (see. e.g. Kenneth Macksey, *Invasion* [London: Greenhill, 1999], a book first published in 1980 by Macmillan). On this phenomenon see Gavriel D. Rosenfeld, *The World Hitler Never Made* (Cambridge: Cambridge University Press, 2005), ch. 1. There are also video games devoted to the battle: see http://www.amazon.co.uk. On the the Blitz see note 8. On nostalgia in the first years of the twenty-first century in Britain see e.g. Nick Clarke, *The Shadow of a Nation: The Changing Face of Britain* (London: Weidenfeld and Nicolson, 2003), pp. 3–4.

12. *Independent on Sunday*, 11 April 2004; *Daily Variety*, 10 September 2003, pp. 1, 9. British critics and audiences were also upset by the negative stereotyping of British soldiers in *The Patriot* (Columbia, 2000). See Mark Glancy, 'The War of Independence in Feature Films: *The Patriot* (2000) and the "Special Relationship" between Hollywood and Britain', *Historical Journal of Film, Radio and Television* 25 (2005), pp. 536–9.

13. *Independent on Sunday*, 11 April 2004; *Mail on Sunday*, 11 April 2005; see also e.g. *Daily Mirror*, 17 September 2003; and comments at http://xo.typepad.com/ blog/2004/04/the_battle-of_b.html (accessed 25 January 2005); http://forum.rpg. net/archive/index.php/t-116073.html (accessed 25 January 2006); http://www.ix plosive.com/cgi-bin/yaBB.pl?num = 1064147310/10 (accessed 25 January 2006). For the Blitz on screen in recent years see e.g. *The End of the Affair* (Sony, 1999); 'The Empty Child' episode, *Doctor Who* (BBC, 2005); *Colditz* (Granada, 2005); *Narnia: The Lion, the Witch and the Wardrobe* (Disney, 2005); *Mrs. Henderson Presents* (Weinstein, 2006).

Select Filmography

The Lion Has Wings (London Films, 1939) – 76 minutes
Producer: Alexander Korda
Directors: Michael Powell, Adrian Brunel, Brian Desmond Hurst
Writers: Ian Dalrymple, Adrian Brunel, E. V. H. Emmett
Principal Cast: Ralph Richardson (group captain); Merle Oberon (wife);
  Brian Worth (Bobby); June Duprez (June); Robert Douglas (briefing
  officer); Anthony Bushell (bomber pilot); Derrick De Marney (Bell).

The First of the Few (British Aviation Pictures, 1942) – 117 minutes
Producers: Leslie Howard, George King, John Stafford, Adrian Brunel
Director: Leslie Howard
Writers: Anatole de Grunwald, Miles Malleson
Principal Cast: Leslie Howard (Reginald Mitchell); David Niven
  (Geoffrey Crisp); Rosamund John (Diana Mitchell); Roland Culver
  (Commander Bride); David Horne (Sir Robert McLean); Tonie
  Edgar Bruce (Lady Houston); Filippo del Giudice (Bertorelli).

Angels One Five (Templar, 1952) – 98 minutes
Producers: John W. Gossage, Derek Twist
Director: George More O'Ferrall
Writers: Pelham Groom, Derek Twist
Principal Cast: Jack Hawkins ('Tiger' Small); Michael Denison (Peter
  Moon); John Gregson ('Sceptic' Baird); Dulcie Gray (Nadine Clinton);
  Cyril Raymond (Barry Clinton); Humphrey Lestocq ('Batchy' Salter);
  Andrew Osborn (Bill Ponsford); Veronica Hurst (Betty Carfax).

Reach for the Sky (Pinnacle, 1956) – 135 minutes
Producer: Daniel M. Angel
Director: Lewis Gilbert
Writers: Paul Brickhill, Lewis Gilbert, Vernon Harris
Principal Cast: Kenneth More (Douglas Bader); Muriel Pavlov (Thelma Edwards); Lyndon Brook (Johnny Sanderson); Lee Patterson (Stan Turner); Alexander Knox (Mr. Joyce); Dorothy Allison (Nurse Brace); Michael Warre (Harry Day); Ronald Adam (Trafford Leigh-Mallory); Charles Carson (Hugh Dowding).

The Battle of Britain (Spitfire Productions, 1969) – 151 minutes
Producers: Harry Saltzman, S. Bejamin Fisz
Director: Guy Hamilton
Writers: James Kennaway, Wilfred Greatorex
Principal Cast: Laurence Olivier (Hugh Dowding); Trevor Howard (Keith Park); Hein Reiss (Hermann Goering); Peter Hager (Albert Kesselring); Christopher Plummer (Colin Harvey); Robert Shaw (Skipper); Susannah York (Maggie Harvey); Ian McShane (Andy); Robert Flemyng (Willoughby); Ralph Richardson (David Kelley); Curt Jurgens (Von Richter); Manfred Reddemann (Falke); Edward Fox (Archie); Nicholas Pennell (Simon); James Cosmo (Jamie); Nigel Patrick (Hope).

Piece of Cake (Holmes Associates, 1988) – 300 minutes
Producer: Andrew Holmes
Director: Ian Toynton
Writers: Derek Robinson, Leon Griffiths
Principal Cast: Tom Burlinson ('Fanny' Barton); Neil Dudgeon ('Moggie' Cattermole); Tim Woodward (Squadron Leader Rex); David Horovitch ('Uncle' Kellaway); Richard Hope ('Skull' Skelton); Boyd Gaines (Chris Hart); Nathaniel Parker ('Flash' Gordon); Michael Elwyn (Bletchley); George Anton ('Pip' Patterson); Jeremy Northam ('Fitz' Fitzgerald); Gordon Lovitt ('Sticky' Stickwell); Tom Radcliffe ('Dicky' Starr); Stephen McKenna (Flight Lieutenant Marriot); Gerard O'Hare ('Flip' Moran); Julian Cartside ('Amanda' Steele-Stebbing); Helena Mitchell (Mary); Corinne Dacla (Nicole).

A Perfect Hero (Havahall Pictures, 1991) – 300 minutes
Producer: James Cellan Jones
Director: James Cellan Jones
Writers: Allan Prior, Christopher Matthew
Principal Cast: Nigel Havers (Hugh Fleming); James Fox (Angus Meikle); Bernard Hepton (Arthur Fleming); Barbara Leigh-Hunt (Iris Fleming); Fiona Gillies (Bunty Morrell); Amanda Elves (Marg Fisher); Nicholas Pritchard (Julian Masters); Patrick Ryecart (Tim Holland); Thomas Wheatley ('Dickie' Bird); Joanna Lumley (Loretta Stone); Fiona Mollison (Susan Fleming).

Bibliography

The National Archives
ADM 1; AIR 2, 8, 19, 20, 28, 41; AN 157; CAB 21, 102; FCO 9; FO 371;
HO 186; INF 1, 5, 6; MEPO 2; PREM 11, 13; RAIL 1188; TS 27, 66; UGC
7; WO 32

BBC Written Archive
T6/301/1–2; T6/305/1–8; T6/304; T6/295–312; R9/8/2

Mass-Observation Archive
FR 57, 491

Special Collections, British Film Institute (BFI)
London Films Productions, B/021

Unpublished diaries, correspondence, papers, etc.
D. R. S. Bader (RAF Museum); W. S. Churchill (Churchill College,
Cambridge); M. Dean (Liddell Hart Centre, KCL); P. I. Howard-
Williams (Imperial War Museum); J. Kennaway (National Library
of Scotland); K. Park (RAF Museum); R. A. Morton (Imperial War
Museum).

Taped interviews
Douglas Bader (Imperial War Museum Sound Archive); Joseph Cox
(Imperial War Museum Sound Archive); Trevor Howard (BFI Special
Collections: Cinema [Granada TV, 1964–75] Collection); Michael
Powell (BFI Library, NFT interview); Hugh St Clair Stewart (Imperial

War Museum Sound Archive); Harry Watt (BFI Library, NFT interview); John R. C. Young (Imperial War Museum Sound Archive).

Scripts (BFI Library)
Angels One Five (S6042); Battle of Britain (S1127, S9449, S8479); Dangerous Moonlight (S442); Reach for the Sky (S874).

Pressbooks (BFI Library)
Battle of Britain; Dangerous Moonlight; First of the Few; The One That Got Away; Reach for the Sky; Things to Come.

Newspapers and periodicals
Birmingham Post; Books and Bookmen; Broadcast; Cinema; Daily Express; Daily Herald; Daily Mail; Daily Mirror; Daily Record; Daily Sketch; Daily Telegraph; Daily Variety; Daily Worker; Documentary News Letter; Eastern Daily Press; The Economist; Empire; Evening Chronicle (Newcastle); Evening News; Evening Standard; Film and Filming; Financial Times; Flight; Glasgow Herald; Guardian; Kinematograph Weekly; Listener; Liverpool Echo; Manchester Evening News; Monthly Film Bulletin; Morning Star; New Statesman; News Chronicle; News of the World; Northern Echo; The Observer; Oxford Mail; The People; Picture Show; Picturegoer; Photoplay; Reynolds News; The Scotsman; Sight and Sound; The Spectator; Sun; Sunday Express; Sunday Mirror; Sunday Times; Television Today; Time and Tide; Times Education Supplement; Times Literary Supplement; Today; Today's Cinema; The Times; Tribune; TV Mirror; Variety; Western Mail; Western Morning News; Yorkshire Evening Post; Yorkshire Post.

Published primary sources
Baker, Roy Ward The Director's Cut: A Memoir of 60 Years in Film and Television (London: Reynolds and Hearn, 2000).

Boorman, John Adventures of a Suburban Boy (London: Faber and Faber, 2003).

Boorman, John Hope and Glory (London: Faber and Faber, 1987).

Braham, J. R. B. 'Scramble!' (London: Muller, 1961).

Brickhill, Paul Reach for the Sky: The Story of Douglas Bader (London: Collins, 1954).

Brook, Lindsay, et al. (comps) British Social Attitudes Cumulative Sourcebook: The First Six Surveys (Aldershot: Gower, 1992).

Brunel, Adrian Nice Work: The Story of Thirty Years in British Film Production (London: Forbes Robertson, 1949).

Buchan, W. (ed.) *The Royal Air Force at War* (London: John Murray, 1941).

Caine, Michael *What's It All About? An Autobiography* (New York: Turtle Bay Books, 1992).

Canetti, Elias *Party in the Blitz: The English Years*, Michael Hofmann, trans. (New York: New Directions, 2005).

Chappell, Eric *Rising Damp: The Complete Scripts* (London: Granada Media, 2002).

Charlton, L. E. O. *The Royal Air Force: From September 1939 to December 1940* (London: Hutchinson, 1941).

Chisolm, Roderick *Cover of Darkness* (London: Chatto and Windus, 1953).

Christie, Ian (ed.) *Powell, Pressburger and Others* (London: BFI, 1978).

Churchill, Winston S. *Winston S. Churchill, His Complete Speeches, 1897–1963*: Volume VII, *1943–1949*, ed. R. Rhodes James (New York: Chelsea House, 1974).

Churchill, Winston S. *The Second World War*, Volume II: *Their Finest Hour* (Boston: Houghton Mifflin, 1949).

Collier, Richard *The Past is a Foreign Country: Scenes from a Life* (London: Allison and Busby, 1996).

Colville, John *The Fringes of Power: Downing Street Diaries*, Volume One: *1939–October 1941* (London: Sceptre, 1986).

David, Dennis *My Autobiography* (London: Grub Street, 2000).

Denison, Michael *Double Act* (London: Michael Joseph, 1985).

Disney Enterprises, *Pearl Harbor: The Movie and the Moment* (New York: Hyperion, 2001).

Doe, Bob *Fighter Pilot* (Chislehurst: CCB, 2004).

Foreign Office, *Index to the Correspondence of the Foreign Office, 1937* (London: HMSO, 1970).

Foxley-Norris, Christopher *A Lighter Shade of Blue: The Lighthearted Memories of an Air Marshal* (London: Ian Allen, 1978).

Frankland, Noble *History at War: The Campaigns of an Historian* (London: Giles de la Mere, 1998).

Gallup, George H. *The Gallup International Public Opinion Polls: Great Britain, 1937–1975* 2 vols. (New York: Random House, 1976).

Graves, Charles *Londoner's Life* (London: Hutchinson, 1942).

Graves, Charles *Off the Record* (London: Hutchinson, 1942).

Greene, Graham *Mornings in the Dark: The Graham Greene Film Reader*, ed. D. Parkinson (Manchester: Carcanet, 1993).

Hammerton, John *War in the Air: Aerial Wonders of Our Time*, Volume 1 (London: Amalgamated, 1936).

Hawkins, Jack *Anything for a Quiet Life* (London: Elm Tree, 1973).

Hillary, Richard *The Last Enemy* (London: Macmillan, 1942).

Hough, Richard *One Boy's War* (London: Heinemann, 1975).

Isaacs, Jeremy *Look Me in the Eye: A Life In Television* (London: Little, Brown, 2006).

McFarlane, Brian (ed.), *An Autobiography of British Cinema* (London: Methuen, 1997).

Mayer, J. P. *British Cinemas and their Audiences: Sociological Studies* (London: Dennis Dobson, 1948).

More, Kenneth *More or Less* (London: Hodder and Stoughton, 1978).

Morgan, Piers *The Insider* (London: Ebury, 2005).

Mosley, Leonard *The Battle of Britain: The Making of a Film* (London: Weidenfeld and Nicolson, 1969).

Nichols, Beverley *Cry Havock!* (London: Jonathan Cape, 1933).

Orwell, George *The Complete Works of George Orwell*, Volume Twelve: *A Patriot After All, 1940–1941* ed. P. Davidson (London: Secker and Warburg, 1998).

Page, Geoffrey *Shot Down in Flames: A World War II Pilot's Remarkable Tale of Survival* (London: Grub Street, 1999).

Parliamentary Debates, House of Commons, 5th Series.

Peake, Felicity *Pure Chance* (Shrewsbury: Airlife, 1993).

Powell, Michael *A Life in Movies: An Autobiography* (London: Heinemann, 1986).

Prior, Allan *Script to Screen: The Story of Five Television Plays* (London: Ver, 1996).

Rawnsley, C. F. and Robert Wright *Night Fighter* (London: Collins, 1957).

Raymond, R. and D. Langdon (eds), *Slipstream: A Royal Air Force Anthology* (London: Eyre and Spottiswoode, 1946).

Richards, Denis *It Might Have Been Worse: Recollections 1941–1996* (London: Smithson Albright, 1998).

Richards, Jeffrey and Dorothy Sheridan (eds), *Mass-Observation at the Movies* (London: Routledge and Kegan Paul, 1987).

Saunders, Hilary St John *The Battle of Britain, August – October 1940* (London: HMSO, 1941).

Scott, Peter Graham *British Television: An Insider's History* (Jefferson, NC: McFarland, 2000).

Spaight, J. M. *The Battle of Britain 1940* (London: Geoffrey Bles, 1941).

Stanhope Spragg, T. *The Royal Air Force* (London: Collins, 1941).

Towler, Robert *The Public's View 2001* (London: ITC, 2002).

Townsend, Peter *Duel in the Dark* (London: Harrap, 1986).

Townsend, Peter *Time and Chance: An Autobiography* (London: Collins, 1978).

Wartime Social Survey *The Cinema Audience: An Inquiry Made by the Wartime Social Survey for the Ministry of Information*, L. Moss and K. Box, new series no. 37b (London: MOI, 1943).

Watt, Harry *Don't Look at the Camera!* (London: Elek, 1974).

Wells, H. G. *Things to Come* (London: Crescent Press, 1935).

Young, Freddie *Seventy Light Years: An Autobiography* (London: Faber and Faber, 1999).

Published literary sources

Bennett, Alan, Peter Cook, Jonathan Miller, Dudley Moore *Beyond the Fringe* (London: Souvenir, 1963).

Graves, Charles *The Thin Blue Line* (London: Hutchinson, 1941).

Hough, Richard *The Fight of the Few* (London: Cassell, 1979).

Hough, Richard *Angels One Five* (London: Cassell, 1978).

Kennaway, James *Household Ghosts* (London: Longman, 1961).

Lambert, Angela *A Rather English Marriage* (London: Hamish Hamilton, 1992).

Matthew, Christopher *The Long-Haired Boy* (London: Hamish Hamilton, 1980) [republished as *A Perfect Hero* (London: Mandarin, 1991)].

'Miles' [Stephen Southwold] *The Gas War of 1940* (London: Eric Partridge, 1931).

Groom, Pelham *What Are Your Angels Now?* (London: Jarrolds, 1943).

Robinson, Derek *Piece of Cake* (London: Hamish Hamilton, 1983).

Trevor, Elleston *Squadron Airborne* (London: Macmillan, 1955).

Wallace, Randall *Pearl Harbor* (New York: Hyperion, 2001).

Wells, H. G. *The Shape of Things to Come* (London: Macmillan, 1933).

Willock, Colin *The Fighters* (London: Macmillan, 1973).

Unpublished theses

Bohn, T. W. 'An Historical and Descriptive Analysis of the "Why We Fight" series' (PhD, University of Wisconsin, 1968).

Kuykendall, John Edward 'The Unknown War: Popular war fiction for juveniles and the Anglo-German conflict, 1939–1945' (PhD, University of South Carolina, 2002).

Published secondary sources

Addison, Paul and Jeremy Crang (eds) *The Burning Blue: A New History of the Battle of Britain* (London: Pimlico, 2000).

Aldgate, Anthony *Cinema and History: British Newsreels and the Spanish Civil War* (London: Scolar Press, 1979).

Aldgate, Anthony and Jeffrey Richards *Britain Can Take It: The British Cinema in the Second World War*, 2nd edn (Edinburgh: Edinburgh University Press, 1994).

Bailer, Uri *The Shadow of the Bomber: The Fear of Air Attack and British Politics, 1932–1939* (London: Royal Historical Society, 1980).

Baillieu, Bill and John Goodchild *The British Film Business* (Chichester: John Wiley, 2002).

Baker, David *Adolf Galland: The Authorised Biography* (London: Windrow and Greene, 1996).

Barnett, Correlli *The Audit of War: The Illusion and Reality of Britain as a Great Nation* (London: Pan, 1996).

Barr, Charles *Ealing Studios* 3rd edition (Berkeley: University of California Press, 1998).

Barta, Tony *Screening the Past: Film and the Representation of History* (Westport, CT: Praeger, 1998).

Battle of Britain Historical Society, *Honouring the Few: The Remarkable Story of the Battle of Britain Heroes and Our Tribute to Them* (London: Battle of Britain Books, 2005).

Billson, Anne *My Name is Michael Caine* (London: Muller, 1991).

Bishop, Patrick *Fighter Boys: Saving Britain 1940* (London: HarperCollins, 2003).

Black, Jeremy *Rethinking Military History* (London: Routledge, 2004).

Bowman, Martin W. *Low Level from Swanton: The history of Swanton Morley airfield from World War Two to the present day* (Walton-on-Thames: Air Research Publications, 1995).

Bowyer, Michael J. F. and John D. R. Rawlings *Squadron Codes, 1937–56* (Cambridge: Patrick Stephens, 1979).

Bray, Christopher *Michael Caine: A Class Act* (London: Faber and Faber, 2005).

Brickhill, Paul *Reach for the Sky: The Story of Douglas Bader* (London: Collins, 1954).

Bright, Morris and Robert Ross *Mr Carry On: The Life and Work of Peter Rogers* (London: BBC, 2000).

Brown, Peter *Honour Restored: The Battle of Britain, Dowding and the Fight for Freedom* (Staplehurst: Spellmount, 2005).

Caidin, Martin *Me 109: Willy Messerschmitt's Peerless Fighter* (New York: Ballantine, 1968).

Caine, Philip D. *Eagles of the RAF: The World War II Eagle Squadrons* (Honolulu: University Press of the Pacific, 2002).

Calder, Angus *The Myth of the Blitz* (London: Pimlico, 1992).

Calder, Angus *The People's War: Britain 1939–1945* (London: Jonathan Cape, 1969).

Carmean, Karen and Georg Gaston *Robert Shaw: More than a Life* (Lanham, MD: Madison Books, 1994).

Carnes, Mark C. *Past Imperfect: History According to the Movies* (New York: Henry Holt, 1995).

Carpenter, Humphrey *That Was Satire That Was: The Satire Boom of the 1960s* (London: Gollancz, 2000).

Chapman, James *Past and Present: National Identity and the British Historical Film* (London: I. B. Tauris, 2005).

Chapman, James *The British at War: Cinema, State and Propaganda, 1939–1945* (London: I. B. Tauris, 1998).

Charmley, John *Churchill: End of Glory – A Political Biography* (London: Hodder and Stoughton, 1993).

Clarke, I. F. *Voices Prophesying War: Future Wars, 1763–3749*, 2nd edn (Oxford: Oxford University Press, 1992).

Clarke, Nick *The Shadow of a Nation: The Changing Face of Britain* (London: Weidenfeld and Nicolson, 2003).

Clarke, R. W., J. C. Sterne, J. C. E. Smith *The Hundred Days That Shook the World* (Hemel Hempstead: Christopher Marlowe, 1969).

Clarkson, Jeremy *I Know You Got Soul: Machines with That Certain Something* (London: Penguin, 2006).

Collier, Richard *The Sands of Dunkirk* (London: Collins, 1961).

Colls, Robert *Identity of England* (Oxford: Oxford University Press, 2002).

Connelly, Mark *We Can Take It! Britain and the Memory of the Second World War* (Harlow: Longman, 2004).

Coultass, Clive *Images for Battle: British Film and the Second World War, 1939–1945* (London: Associated University Presses, 1989).

Cull, Nicholas *Selling War: The British Propaganda Campaign Against American "Neutrality" in World War II* (New York: Oxford University Press, 1995).

Curran, James and Vincent Porter (eds) *British Cinema History* (London: Weidenfeld and Nicolson, 1983).

Currie, Tony *A Concise History of British Television, 1930–2000* (Tiverton: Kelly, 2000).

Davidson, Martin and James Taylor *Spitfire Ace: Flying the Battle of Britain* (London: Channel 4, 2004).

Dawson, Graham *Soldier Heroes: British Adventure, Empire and the Imagining of Masculinities* (London: Routledge, 1994).

Dixon, Wheeler Winston (ed.) *Re-Reviewing British Cinema, 1900–1992: Essays and Interviews* (Albany, NY: State University Press of New York, 1994).

Drazin, Charles *Korda: Britain's Only Movie Mogul* (London: Sidgwick and Jackson, 2002).

Eagle, Robert *How They Made* Piece of Cake (London: Boxtree, 1998).

Evans, Martin and Ken Lunn (eds) *War and Memory in the Twentieth Century* (Oxford: Berg, 1997).

Flint, Peter *Dowding and Headquarters Fighter Command* (Airlife: Shrewsbury, 1996).

Frayling, Christopher *Things to Come* (London: BFI, 1995).

French, John *Robert Shaw: The Price of Success* (London: Nick Hern Books, 1993).

Gallagher, Elaine *Candidly Caine* (London: Robson Books, 1993).

Geraghty, Christine *British Cinema in the Fifties: Gender, Genre and the 'New Look'* (London: Routledge, 2000).

Gifford, Denis *The British Film Catalogue, Volume 1: Fiction Film, 1895–1994* (London: Fitzroy Dearborn, 2000).

Gifford, Denis *The British Film Catalogue, Volume 2: Non-Fiction Film, 1888–1994* (London: Fitzroy Dearborn, 2000).

Glancey, Jonathan *Spitfire: The Biography* (London: Atlantic, 2006).

Glancy, Mark *When Hollywood Loved Britain: The Hollywood 'British' Film 1939–45* (Manchester: Manchester University Press, 1999).

Hall, Richard *70 Not Out: The Biography of Sir Michael Caine* (London: John Blake, 2003).

Harper, Sue and Vincent Porter *British Cinema of the 1950s: The Decline of Deference* (Oxford: Oxford University Press, 2003).

Haseler, Stephen *The English Tribe: Identity, Nation and Europe* (Basingstoke: Macmillan, 1996).

Held, Werner and Anton Weiler *Adolf Galland: Ein Fliegerleben in Krieg und Freiden* (Freiburg: Podzun Pallas, 1983).

Hibbin, Sally and Nina Hibbin (comps) *What a Carry On: The Official Story of the Carry On Films* (London: Hamlyn, 1988).

Hitchins, Peter *The Abolition of Britain: From Lady Chatterly to Tony Blair* (London: Quartet, 1999).

Hough, Richard and Denis Richards *The Battle of Britain: The Jubilee History* (London: Hodder and Stoughton, 1989).

Howard, James *Michael Powell* (London: Batsford, 1996).

Howard, Ronald *In Search of My Father: A Portrait of Leslie Howard* (London: William Kimber, 1981).

Hurd, Geoff (ed.) *National Fictions: World War Two in British Film and Television* (London: BFI, 1984).

Hynes, Samuel *The Soldiers' Tale: Bearing Witness to Modern War* (New York: Allen Lane, 1987).

Judge, Philip *Michael Caine* (Tunbridge Wells: Spellmount, 1985).

Kennedy, Michael *Portrait of Walton* (Oxford: Oxford University Press, 1989).

Kershaw, Alex *The Few* (New York: Da Capo, 2006).

Klein, Holger, John Flower, Eric Homberger (eds) *The Second World War in Fiction* (London: Macmillan, 1984).

Korda, Michael *Charmed Lives: A Family Romance* (New York: Random House, 1979).

Landy, Marcia (ed.) *The Historical Film: History and Memory in Media* (New Brunswick, NJ: Rutgers University Press, 2001).

Levin, Bernard *The Pendulum Years: Britain in the Sixties* (London: Pan, 1972).

Lord, Graham *Niv: The Authorized Biography of David Niven*, New York: Thomas Dunn, 2003).

Louis, William Roger (ed.) *The Origins of the Second World War: A. J. P. Taylor and his Critics* (New York: Wiley, 1972).

Lucas, Laddie *Flying Colours: The Epic Story of Douglas Bader* (London: Hutchinson, 1981).

McBride, Joseph *Frank Capra: The Catastrophe of Success* (New York: Simon and Schuster, 1993).

Macdonald, Kevin *Emeric Pressburger: The Life and Death of a Screenwriter* (London: Faber and Faber, 1994).

McLaine, Ian *Ministry of Morale: Home Front Propaganda and the Ministry of Information in World War II* (London: George Allen and Unwin, 1979).

March, Peter R. *Confederate Air Force: Celebrating Forty Years* (Midland, TX: Confederate Air Force, 1997).

Marwick, Arthur *The New Nature of History: Knowledge, Evidence, Language* (Chicago: Lyceum, 2001).

Marwick, Arthur *The Sixties: Cultural Revolution in Britain, France, Italy and the United States, c. 1958–c. 1974* (Oxford: Oxford University Press, 1998).

Mayhew, E. R. *The Reconstruction of Warriors: Archibald McIndoe, the Royal Air Force and the Guinea Pig Club* (London: Greenhill, 2004).

Middlemass, Keith and John Barnes *Baldwin: A Biography* (Weidenfeld and Nicolson, 1969).

Middleton, Drew *The Sky Suspended: The Battle of Britain* (London: Secker and Warburg, 1960).

Miller-Oliver, Edward *The Len Deighton Companion* (London: Grafton, 1987).

Mitchell, Gordon R. J. Mitchell: Schooldays to Spitfire (Olney: Nelson and Saunders, 1986).

Morgan, Guy Red Roses Every Night: An Account of London Cinemas under Fire (London: Quality, 1948).

Morley, Margaret Olivier: The Films and Faces of Laurence Olivier (Godalming: LSP, 1978).

Murphy, Robert British Cinema and the Second World War (London: Continuum, 2000).

Nicholas, Siân The Echo of War: Home Front Propaganda and the Wartime BBC (Manchester: Manchester University Press, 1996).

Noakes, Lucy War and the British: Gender, Memory and National Identity (London: I. B. Tauris, 1998).

Oakley, C. A. Where We Came In: Seventy Years of the British Film Industry (London: Allen and Unwin, 1964).

Palmer, Warren James Battle of Britain Memorial Flight: The Inside Story of the Royal Air Force Memorial Flight (Epsom: Ripping, 1996).

Paris, Michael Warrior Nation: Images of War in British Popular Culture (London: Reaktion, 2000).

Paris, Michael From the Wright Brothers to Top Gun: Aviation, Nationalism and Popular Cinema (Manchester: Manchester University Press, 1995).

Paris, Michael The Novels of World War Two: An Annotated Bibliography of World War Two Fiction (London: Library Association, 1990).

Parkin, Frank Middle Class Radicalism: The Social Bases of the British Campaign for Nuclear Disarmament (Manchester: Manchester University Press, 1968).

Pendo, Stephen Aviation in the Cinema (Metuchen, NJ: Scarecrow Press, 1985).

Pettigrew, Terence Trevor Howard: A Personal Biography (London: Peter Owen, 2001).

Ponting, Clive 1940: Myth and Reality (London: Hamilton, 1990).

Pronay, Nicholas and D. W. Spring (eds) Propaganda, Politics and Film, 1918–45 (London: Macmillan, 1982).

Ramsden, John Don't Mention the War: The British and the Germans since 1890 (London: Little, Brown, 2006).

Rattigan, Neil This is England: British Film and the People's War, 1939–1945 (Madison, NJ: Farleigh Dickinson University Press, 2001).

Reynolds, David In Command of History: Churchill Fighting and Writing the Second World War (London: Allen Lane, 2004).

Richards, Jeffrey *The Age of the Dream Palace: Cinema and Society in Britain, 1930–1939* (London: Routledge and Kegan Paul, 1984).

Roberts, Graham and Philip M. Taylor (eds) *The Historian, Television and Television History* (Luton: University of Luton Press, 2001).

Robinson, Derek *Invasion 1940: The Truth About the Battle of Britain and What Stopped Hitler* (London: Constable, 2005).

Rose, Sonya O. *Which People's War? National Identity and Citizenship in Wartime Britain, 1939–1945* (New York: Oxford University Press, 2003).

Rosenfeld, Gavriel D. *The World Hitler Never Made: Alternate History and the Memory of Nazism* (Cambridge: Cambridge University Press, 2005).

Rosenstone, Robert A. *Visions of the Past: The Challenge of Film to Our Idea of History* (Cambridge, MA: Harvard University Press, 1995).

Ross, David *Richard Hillary: The Definitive Biography of a Battle of Britain Fighter Pilot and Author of* The Last Enemy (London: Grub Street, 2000).

Ross, Robert *The Carry On Companion* (London: Batsford, 1996).

Royle, Trevor *James & Jim: A Biography of James Kennaway* (Edinburgh: Mainstream, 1983).

Rudhall, Robert J. *'Battle of Britain': The Movie* (Worcester: Ramrod, 2000).

Sandbrook, Dominic *Never Had It So Good: A History of Britain from Suez to the Beatles* (London: Little, Brown, 2005).

Short, K. R. M. *Screening the Propaganda of British Airpower: From R.A.F. (1935) to* The Lion Has Wings *(1939)* Studies in War and Film 6 (Trowbridge: Flicks, 1997).

Short, K. R. M. (ed.) *Film and Radio Propaganda in World War II* (London: Croom Helm, 1983).

Short, K. R. M. (ed.) *Feature Films as History* (Knoxville, TN: University of Tennessee Press, 1981).

Shrapnel, Norman *The Seventies: Britain's Inward March* (London: Constable, 1980).

Smith, David C. *H. G. Wells, Desperately Mortal: A Biography* (New Haven, CT: Yale University Press, 1986).

Smith, Don G. *H. G. Wells on Film: The Utopian Nightmare* (Jefferson, NC: McFarland, 2002).

Smith, Malcolm *Britain and 1940: History, Myth and Popular Memory* (London: Routledge, 2000).

Smith, Richard C. *Al Deere: Wartime Fighter Pilot, Peacetime Commander: The Authorised Biography* (London: Grub Street, 2003).

Smith, Richard C. *Hornchurch Scramble: The Definitive Account of the RAF Fighter Airfield, its Pilots, Groundcrew, and Staff, Volume One, 1915 to the End of the Battle of Britain* (London: Grub Street, 2000).

Sorlin, Pierre *The Film in History: Restaging the Past* (Oxford: Blackwell, 1980).

Spraos, John *The Decline of the Cinema: An Economist's Report* (London: Allen and Unwin, 1962).

Stokes, Doug *Wings Aflame: The Biography of Group Captain Victor Beamish* (Manchester: Crecy, 1988).

Suid, Lawrence H. *Guts and Glory: The Making of the American Military Image in Film* (Lexington, KY: University Press of Kentucky, 2002).

Sussex, Elizabeth *The Rise and Fall of British Documentary: The Story of the Film Movement Founded by John Grierson* (Berkeley: University of California Press, 1975).

Svennevig, Michael *Television Across the Years: The British Public's View* (Luton: University of Luton Press, 1998).

Swann, Paul *The British Documentary Film Movement, 1926–1946* (Cambridge: Cambridge University Press, 1989).

Tabori, Paul *Alexander Korda* (London: Oldbourne, 1959).

Taylor, A. J. P. *The Origins of the Second World War* (London: Hamish Hamilton, 1961).

Taylor, Philip M. *British Propaganda in the 20th Century: Selling Democracy* (Edinburgh: Edinburgh University Press, 1999).

Terraine, John *The Right of the Line: The Royal Air Force in the European War 1939–1945* (London: Hodder and Stoughton, 1985).

Tierney, Neil *William Walton: His Life and Music* (London: Hale, 1984).

Toplin, Robert Brent *Reel History: In Defense of Hollywood* (Lawrence, KS: University of Kansas Press, 2002).

Turner, John Frayn *Douglas Bader: A Biography of the Legendary World War II Fighter Pilot* (Shrewsbury: Airlife, 2001 edn).

Vankin, Jonathan and John Whelan *Based on a True Story: Fact and Fiction in 100 Favorite Movies* (Chicago: Chicago Review Press, 2005).

Walker, Alexander *Hollywood, England: The British Film Industry in the Sixties* (London: Michael Joseph, 1974).

Walker, John *The Once and Future Film: British Cinema in the Seventies and Eighties* (London: Methuen, 1985).

Wallace, Graham *R.A.F. Biggin Hill* (London: Putnam, 1957).

Wapshott, Nicholas *The Man Between: A Biography of Carol Reed* (London: Chatto and Windus, 1990).

Ware, John (adapt.) *The Lion Has Wings* (London: Collins, 1940).

Webster, Charles and Noble Frankland *The Strategic Air Offensive Against Germany 1939–1945*, Vol. 1 (London: HMSO, 1961).

Weight, Richard *Patriots: National Identity in Britain, 1940–2000* (London: Macmillan, 2002).

West, Anthony *H. G. Wells: Aspects of a Life* (New York: Random House, 1984).

Wood, Derek and Derek Dempster *The Narrow Margin: The Battle of Britain and the Rise of Air Power* (London: Hutchinson, 1961).

Wright, Patrick *On Living in an Old Country: The National Past in Contemporary Britain* (London: Verso, 1985).

Wright, Robert *Dowding and the Battle of Britain* (London: Macdonald, 1969).

Zimmerman, David *Britain's Shield: Radar and the Defeat of the Luftwaffe* (Stroud: Sutton, 2001).

Articles and chapters

Aldgate, Tony, 'The Battle of Britain on Film', in P. Addison and J. Crang (eds), *The Burning Blue* (London: Pimlico, 2000), pp. 207–16.

Anon., 'War Films in the Making: Battle of Britain', *After the Battle*, 1 (1973), pp. 50–4.

Barley, M. P., 'Contributing to its Own Defeat: The *Luftwaffe* and the Battle of Britain', *Defence Studies*, 4 (2005), pp. 387–411.

Browning, H. E. and A. A. Sorrell, 'Cinemas and Cinema-going in Great Britain', *Journal of the Royal Statistical Society*, 117 Pt II (1954), pp. 133–65.

Bruccoli, Matthew J., 'Interview with Derek Robinson', *DLB Yearbook 2002* (Farmington Hills, MI: Gale, 2002), pp. 345–51.

Buckman, Keith, 'The Royal Air Force Film Production Unit', *Historical Journal of Film, Radio and Television*, 17 (1997), pp. 219–44.

Cable, Boyd, 'When War Does Come: Terrifying Effects of Gas Attacks', in John Hammerton (ed.), *War in the Air: Aerial Wonders of Our Time*, Volume One (London: Amalgamated, 1936), pp. 272–4.

Caldwell, Sarah, '"Television Aesthetics" and Close Analysis: Style, Mood and Engagement in *Perfect Strangers*', in J. Gibbs and D. Pye (eds), *Style and Meaning: Studies in the Detailed Analysis of Film* (Manchester: Manchester University Press, 2005), pp. 179–94.

Chapman, James, 'The World at War: Television, Documentary, History', in G. Roberts and P. M. Taylor (eds), *The Historian, Television and Television History* (Luton: University of Luton Press, 2001), pp. 127–44.

Chapman, James, 'Our Finest Hour Revisited: The Second World War in British Feature Films since 1945', *Journal of Popular British Cinema*, 1 (1998), pp. 63–75.

Crang, Jeremy, 'Identifying "The Few": The Personalisation of a Heroic Military Elite', *War and Society*, 24 (2005), pp. 13–34.

Culbert, David, '"Why We Fight": Social Engineering for a Democratic Society at War', in K. R. M. Short (ed.), *Film and Radio Propaganda in World War II* (London: Croom Helm, 1983), pp. 173–91.

Dalrymple, Ian, 'The Crown Film Unit, 1940–43', in N. Pronay and D. W. Spring (eds), *Propaganda, Politics and Film, 1918–45* (London: Macmillan, 1982), pp. 209–20.

Eley, Geoff, 'Finding the People's War: Film, British Collective Memory, and World War II', *American Historical Review*, 106 (2001), pp. 818–38.

Gillett, John, 'Westfront 1957', *Sight and Sound*, 27 (1957/58), pp. 123–27.

Glancy, Mark 'The War of Independence in Feature Films: The Patriot (2000) and the "Special Relationship" between Hollywood and Britain', *Historical Journal of Film, Radio and Television*, 25 (2005), pp. 523–45.

Gregory, Adrian, 'The Commemoration of the Battle of Britain', in P. Addison and J. Crang (eds), *The Burning Blue* (London: Pimlico, 2000), pp. 217–28.

Harper, Sue and Vincent Porter, 'Cinema Tastes in 1950s Britain', *Journal of Popular British Cinema*, 2 (1999), pp. 66–82.

Harper, Sue, 'Popular Film, Popular Memory: The Case of the Second World War', in M. Evans and K. Lunn (eds), *War and Memory in the Twentieth Century* (Oxford: Berg, 1997), pp. 163–76.

Inglis, Fred, 'National Snapshots: Fixing the Past in English War Films', in I. Mackillop and N. Sinyard (eds), *British Cinema of the 1950s: A Celebration* (Manchester: Manchester University Press, 2003), pp. 35–50.

Jackson, Martyn, 'Black and White Army: The British at War', *Classic Television*, vol. 1, no. 2, December 1996/January 1977, pp. 28–35.

Lake, Jeremy and John Schofield, 'Conservation and the Battle of Britain', in P. Addison and J. Crang (eds) *The Burning Blue* (London: Pimlico, 2000), pp. 229–42.

Medhurst, Andy, '1950s War Films', in G. Hurd (ed.), *National Fictions: World War Two in British Films and Television* (London: BFI, 1984), pp. 35–8.

Nelson, Michael, 'It May be History, But is it True? The Imperial War Museum Conference', *Historical Journal of Film, Radio and Television*, 25 (2005), pp. 141–6.

Noakes, Lucy, 'Making Histories: Experiencing the Blitz in London's Museums in the 1990s', in M. Evans and K. Lunn (eds), *War and Memory in the Twentieth Century* (Oxford: Berg, 1997), pp. 89–104.

Poole, Julian, 'British Cinema Attendance in Wartime: audience preference at the Majestic, Macclesfield, 1939–1946', *Historical Journal of Film, Radio and Television*, 7 (1987), pp. 15–34.

Popple, Trevor, 'Reach for the Sky', *After the Battle* 35 (1982), pp. 38–53.

Popple, Trevor, 'Angels One Five', *After the Battle* 30 (1980), pp. 11–18.

Prins, François, 'Battle of Britain', *Fly Past* 98/99 (1989), pp. 14–20, 52–4.

Prins, François, 'Taking the Cake!', *FlyPast* 87/88 (1988), 8–13, 40–3.

Prins, François, 'The One that Got Away', *FlyPast* Special (1990) pp. 51–3.

Pronay, Nicholas, 'The British Post-bellum Cinema: a survey of the films relating to World War II made in Britain between 1945 and 1960', *Historical Journal of Film, Radio and Television*, 8 (1988), pp. 39–53.

Ramsden, John, 'Refocusing "The People's War": British War Films of the 1950s', *Journal of Contemporary History* 33 (1988), pp. 35–63.

Rattigan, Neil, 'The Last Gasp of the Middle Class: British War Films of the 1950s', in W. W. Dixon (ed.), *Re-Viewing British Cinema* (Albany, NY: State University Press of New York, 1994), pp. 143–53.

Richards, Denis, 'Writing RAF History', *Journal of the Royal Air Force Historical Society*, 15 (1995), pp. 76–86.

Richards, Jeffrey, 'Wartime Cinema and the Class System: The Case of *Ships With Wings* (1941)', *Historical Journal of Film, Radio and Television*, 7 (1987), pp. 129–41.

Sarkar, Dilip, 'Just How Accurate Was *Battle of Britain?*', in R. J. Rudhall (ed.), *'Battle of Britain': The Movie* (Worcester: Ramrod, 2000), pp. 173–82.

Scuts, J. C., 'The Battle of Britain Memorial Flight', *After the Battle*, 4 (1974), pp. 43–5.

Summerfield, Penelope, 'Mass Observation: Social Research or Social Movement?', *Journal of Contemporary History*, 20 (1985), pp. 439–51.

Whittaker, Christine 'History on Television: A Conference at the Imperial War Museum', *Historical Journal of Film, Radio and Television*, 25 (2005), pp. 139–40.

Internet sites

http://www.raf.mod.uk/bbmf/history.html (accessed 1 May 2005); http://www.jackson.harrison.co.uk/BoB2/General/Memorials/ca pel.htm (accessed 1 May 2005); http://aeroflt.users.netlink.co.uk/mus/ uk/1–b/b_of_b_memorial.htm (accessed 1 May 2005); http:// www.czechcentre.org.uk (accessed 6 November 2005); http:// www.empireonline.co.uk (accessed 6 November 2005); http://news. bbc.co.uk (accessed 4 November 2005); http://www.amazon.co.uk (accessed 1 November 2005).

Television programmes and documentaries

Aviation Heroes of World War II: The Battle of Britain (Greenwich Workshop, 1990)

Battle of Britain (Classic Pictures, 1995)

Battle of Britain Special Edition DVD features (MGM, 2004)

Battle of Britain: The Truth (DD Video/Proteus Productions, 1990)

Battlefield Britain: The Battle of Britain (BBC, 2004)

Ferry Pilot (Crown Film Unit, 1941, Imperial War Museum/DD Video, 2004)

Fighter Pilot (British Movietone News, 1940) in *Spitfire: Frontline Fighter* (Imperial War Museum/DD Video, 2004)

Fighting the Blue (ASA Productions (TV) for UKTV, 2005)

Filming for Victory: British Cinema, 1939–1945 (BBC, 1989)

First of the Few: The True Story (Dowty Group, 1997)

Making of Dark Blue World attached to Special Edition DVD of *Dark Blue World* (Sony Pictures, 2002).

Making of the World at War attached to *The World at War* 30th anniversary DVD edition (Freemantle Home Entertainment, 2005).

The Making of the Series World at War (1989 talk by Jeremy Isaacs) attached to 2001 DVD region 1 edition of *The World at War* (Thames TV, 1973–74).

The *Official Battle of Britain 50th Anniversary Video* (Roymark
    Productions, 1990).
Royal Air Force Victory (IWM/DD Video, 1995)
Secret Lives: Douglas Bader (Twenty Twenty Productions, 1996)
The South Bank Show: Michael Powell (ITV, 1986)
Spitfire (Classic Pictures, 2004)
Spitfire Ace (RDF Media, 2004)

Index